GOD WILL BE
ALL IN ALL

GOD WILL BE ALL IN ALL

The Eschatology of Jürgen Moltmann

Edited by
RICHARD BAUCKHAM

T&T CLARK
EDINBURGH

T&T CLARK LTD
59 GEORGE STREET
EDINBURGH EH2 2LQ
SCOTLAND

www.tandtclark.co.uk

First published 1999

ISBN 0 567 08663 1

British Library Cataloguing-in-Publication Data
A catalogue record for this book is available from the British Library

Typeset by Waverley Typesetters, Galashiels
Printed and bound in Great Britain by Bell & Bain Ltd, Glasgow

To Margaret Kohl

CONTENTS

❧

CONTRIBUTORS

JÜRGEN MOLTMANN is Emeritus Professor of Systematic Theology in the Protestant Theological Faculty of the University of Tübingen.

RICHARD BAUCKHAM is Professor of New Testament Studies in St Mary's College, University of St Andrews, Scotland.

TIMOTHY GORRINGE was Reader in Contextual Theology in St Mary's College, University of St Andrews, Scotland, until 1998, and is now Professor of Theology in the University of Exeter.

TREVOR HART is Professor of Divinity in St Mary's College, University of St Andrews, Scotland.

MIROSLAV VOLF is Henry B. Wright Professor of Theology at Yale University Divinity School.

ABBREVIATIONS FOR THE WORKS OF JÜRGEN MOLTMANN

The following abbreviations for Moltmann's works are used in this book:

CJF   *Creating a Just Future: The Politics of Peace and the Ethics of Creation in a Threatened World.* Tr. J. Bowden. London: SCM Press/Philadelphia: Trinity Press International, 1989.

CoG   *The Coming of God: Christian Eschatology.* Tr. M. Kohl. London: SCM Press, 1996.

CG   *The Crucified God: The Cross as the Foundation and Criticism of Christian Theology.* Tr. R. A. Wilson and J. Bowden. London: SCM Press, 1974.

CPS   *The Church in the Power of the Spirit: A Contribution to Messianic Ecclesiology.* Tr. M. Kohl. London: SCM Press, 1977.

EG   *Experiences of God.* Tr. M. Kohl. London: SCM Press, 1980.

EH   *The Experiment Hope.* Ed. and tr. M. D. Meeks. London: SCM Press, 1975.

FC   *The Future of Creation.* Tr. M. Kohl. London: SCM Press, 1979.

GOD WILL BE ALL IN ALL

GC	*God in Creation: An Ecological Doctrine of Creation*. Tr. M. Kohl. London: SCM Press, 1985.
GPMW	*Gott im Projekt der modernen Welt: Beiträge zur öffentlichen Relevanz der Theologie*. Gütersloh: Chr. Kaiser/ Gütersloher Verlaghaus, 1997.
HTG	*History and the Triune God: Contributions to Trinitarian Theology*. Tr. J. Bowden. London: SCM Press, 1991.
IK	P. Lapide and J. Moltmann, *Israel und Kirche: ein gemeinsamer Weg? Ein Gespräch*. München: Chr. Kaiser, 1980.
JCTW	*Jesus Christ for Today's World*. Tr. M. Kohl. London: SCM Press, 1994.
KG	*Das Kommen Gottes: Christliche Eschatologie*. Gütersloh: Chr. Kaiser/Gütersloher Verlaghaus, 1995.
RRF	*Religion, Revolution, and the Future*. Tr. M. D. Meeks. New York: Charles Scribner's, 1969.
SL	*The Spirit of Life: A Universal Affirmation*. Tr. M. Kohl. London: SCM Press, 1992.
TH	*Theology of Hope: On the Ground and the Implications of a Christian Eschatology*. Tr. J. W. Leitch. London: SCM Press, 1967.
TKG	*The Trinity and the Kingdom of God: The Doctrine of God*. Tr. M. Kohl. London: SCM Press, 1981.
TT	*Theology Today: Two Contributions towards Making Theology Present*. Tr. J. Bowden. London: SCM Press, 1988.
WJC	*The Way of Jesus Christ: Christology in Messianic Dimensions*. Tr. M. Kohl. London: SCM Press, 1990.
ZS	*Zukunft der Schöpfung: Gesammelte Aufsätze*. München: Chr. Kaiser, 1977.

INTRODUCTION

Jürgen Moltmann's first major work was his *Theology of Hope*, first published in 1964, arguably one of the great theological works of the last few decades and indisputably one of the most influential. It changed the way Christian eschatology was understood over a wide spectrum of contemporary theology, quite apart from its mediated influence far beyond the bounds of academic theology. For many of us it made truly eschatological thought not only possible again, but also powerfully relevant in our contemporary world. Even for those who strongly dissented from Moltmann's approach, *Theology of Hope* shifted the discussion and redefined the issues. So the publication of *The Coming of God: Christian Eschatology* (the German original, *Das Kommen Gottes: Christliche Eschatologie*, appeared in 1995, the English translation in 1996), a major new work on eschatology by the author of *Theology of Hope*, was a significant theological event, the more so since it is a long time since any other major book on eschatology has been published. Since all of Moltmann's considerable corpus of work since *Theology of Hope* has had an eschatological orientation and eschatological themes have often recurred in it, some might wonder whether Moltmann could have had anything left to say about eschatology. In fact in *The Coming of God* he does something he has not done before. *Theology of Hope* was not so much a book about the content of the eschatological expectation, more a book about the eschatological orientation of the whole of theology. It set the eschatological direction for the rest of his theological work. But only in *The Coming of*

God has he finally written a systematic eschatology. While it does contain further development of already familiar themes, there is also much that is largely new. This is Moltmann's mature eschatological vision, the climax which his previous volumes of dogmatics require to complete them, a work as innovative, as fecund and as contextually aware as the best of his previous work.

The present book results from the conviction of its authors that *The Coming of God* is a work which not only repays attentive study but also provokes further thought and discussion. Three of us who were then colleagues in the School of Divinity in the University of St Andrews – Richard Bauckham, Trevor Hart and Timothy Gorringe (who has since moved to Exeter) – met to discuss Moltmann's book, along with two others: Michael Partridge and Darrell Cosden. Both, although they have not written for this volume, contributed to it by taking part in our common exploration of Moltmann's eschatology, while Michael Partridge has also been a demanding critic of some of the chapters. Our series of informal but intensive discussions concluded with a weekend in June 1997 when Jürgen Moltmann joined us in St Andrews to discuss his work at length with us. Most of the chapters in the book have therefore emerged from a process of discussion, as well as from individual work, and the process is continued in the book by Moltmann's own responses to our chapters. Miroslav Volf's chapter is not a product of this St Andrews' process, but coheres so well with it that we were eager to include it in the volume. We have all found the experience of dialogue, discussion, mutual critique and shared reflection extremely valuable, and hope that the book will draw readers into the discussion we have begun and into further thought along the lines we have opened up. Moltmann's own enthusiasm for engaging in dialogue about his work corresponds to the way in which his theology is open to critical interaction and constantly a stimulus to further reflection.

The first chapter of this book contains a comprehensive general account and analysis of Moltmann's eschatology in *The Coming of God*. The following five chapters take up various aspects of Moltmann's eschatology or approach it from different angles. Each of the first six chapters consists of a discussion of Moltmann's work, followed by a response from Moltmann. These substantial responses are invaluable in clarifying Moltmann's thinking and also, in some cases, taking it further than he had done in *The Coming of God* itself. To the first chapter we have also added (I/3) an essay in which Moltmann discusses a significant aspect of his eschatology (universal salvation) not elsewhere given much attention in this book. The final chapter is a previously unpublished essay in which Moltmann develops the ethical dimension of his eschatology, drawing out the implications of his thinking in *The Coming of God* in this respect and writing virtually an additional chapter of that book.

The title of this volume, *God Will Be All In All*, is taken from 1 Corinthians 15:28, which is the eschatological text Moltmann has cited most frequently throughout his writings. It sums up for him the vision of the new creation which God himself will indwell, as he explains in chapter I/2 of this book.

Moltmann's contributions to this book have been translated by Margaret Kohl, who has translated into English all six of Moltmann's major works since *The Church in the Power of the Spirit*, as well as several of his smaller works and collections of essays (*The Future of Creation, Experiences of God, The Power of the Powerless, Jesus Christ for Today's World* and *The Source of Life*). All English-speaking readers of Moltmann are immensely indebted to her skilful and readable translations, which are informed by her own considerable familiarity with his work and undertaken with enthusiasm for it to be widely read and appreciated. As an expression of gratitude we are dedicating this book to her.

RICHARD BAUCKHAM
St Mary's College, St Andrews
May 1998

ESCHATOLOGY IN
THE COMING OF GOD

RICHARD BAUCKHAM

The Coming of God is not difficult to read, but it is a demanding
book, and a difficult book fully to appreciate. It presupposes
the previous four volumes of Moltmann's dogmatics (the series
which began with *The Trinity and the Kingdom of God*). Since all
of Moltmann's theology has a strong eschatological orientation,
this volume is not just one of the five, but the one which draws
the themes of the other four together into a concluding
synthesis. This means that it cannot be read adequately by itself:
it takes as read much that has been said in the other four
volumes. Eschatological themes already treated in some detail
in other volumes sometimes receive only brief, recapitulatory
treatment in this. Moreover, the book is organized as a series of
discrete aspects of eschatology. The main parts of the book,
after the introductory reflection on eschatology today in the
light of its twentieth-century history (chapter I), deal respectively
with personal (II), historical (III), cosmic (IV) and divine
eschatology (V). Even within each chapter the relative lack of
summarizing passages can make the overall line of argument or
the coherence of various topics not entirely obvious on first
reading. But the connexions between the five chapters are even
less explicit. The unity and coherence of Moltmann's eschatological vision will emerge for most readers only on the far side
of strenuous engagement with the detail of each particular
aspect. But unity and coherence there certainly are. Moltmann's

1

eschatology in *The Coming of God* is in fact strongly unified by a number of significant features which characterize it as a whole and determine in many respects the treatments of individual topics. The function of this first chapter of the present book is to bring to light the nature of Moltmann's eschatology by outlining and analysing its broad and unifying characteristics. We shall present seven such general characteristics, by explaining how Moltmann's eschatology is (1) christological, (2) integrative, (3) redemptive, (4) processive, (5) theocentric, (6) contextual, (7) politically and pastorally responsible.

1. Christological Eschatology

According to Moltmann, Christian eschatology speaks of the future promised and entailed by the resurrection of the crucified Christ. It seeks the eschatological future projected by the eschatological history of Jesus. It gives content to hope for his future through remembrance of his history. Its central sources and principal criteria are found in Jesus Christ, his messianic mission, his cross and his resurrection. However, these statements are properly understood only when christology and eschatology are seen to stand in a mutually interpretative relationship. The history of Jesus can only be adequately understood against an eschatological horizon, which makes clear its universal significance for the future of all things. Understood against an eschatological horizon, the history of Jesus, as the paradigmatic and creative beginning of the eschatological future of the world, gives to the eschatological hope its character and content.

It is this christological principle of eschatology which links *The Coming of God* most significantly with Moltmann's earliest eschatological thinking in *Theology of Hope* (1965).[1] He later stated the 'central thesis' of *Theology of Hope* as: 'There can be

---

[1] On Moltmann's early eschatology, see R. Bauckham, *Moltmann: Messianic Theology in the Making* (Basingstoke: Marshall Pickering, 1987) chapters 1–2; idem, *The Theology of Jürgen Moltmann* (Edinburgh: T. & T. Clark, 1995) chapters 1–2; M. D. Meeks, *Origins of the Theology of Hope* (Philadelphia: Fortress Press, 1974); A. J. Conyers, *God, Hope, and History: Jürgen Moltmann and the Christian Concept of History* (Macon, Georgia: Mercer University Press, 1988).

no christology without eschatology and no eschatology without christology' (HTG 95, 193 n. 28; this was written in 1982). In *Theology of Hope* itself he wrote:

> [H]ow, then, can Christian eschatology give expression to the future? Christian eschatology does not speak of the future as such. It sets out from a definite reality in history and announces the future of that reality, its future possibilities and its power over the future. Christian eschatology speaks of Jesus Christ and *his* future. It recognizes the reality of the raising of Jesus and proclaims the future of the risen Lord. Hence the question whether all statements about the future are grounded in the person and history of Jesus Christ provides it with the touchstone by which to distinguish the spirit of eschatology from that of utopia. (TH 17; cf. also WJC 320)

The following paragraph states the corollary: just as all eschatological statements must be grounded in christology, so all christological statements are statements of hope and promise, with eschatological implications.

This basic principle of the mutually entailing relationship of christology and eschatology is carried through in Moltmann's later work in the two books *The Way of Jesus Christ* and *The Coming of God*. The former is written under the slogan: 'no christology without eschatology', the latter under the complementary slogan: 'no eschatology without christology'. In *The Way of Jesus Christ* Moltmann characterized its christology by means of the overarching metaphor 'christology of the way', which referred, among other things but primarily, to an understanding of Jesus Christ as on the way to his eschatological goal. There he put the relationship of christology and eschatology in these terms:

> [C]hristology is no more than the beginning of eschatology; and eschatology, as the Christian faith understands it, is always the consummation of christology. (WJC xiv)

Not surprisingly, therefore, the whole book is permeated with eschatology, not only interpreting the mission, death and resurrection of Jesus in eschatological terms, but also looking forward to the parousia and the new creation of all things as 'the consummation of christology'.

Thus *The Way of Jesus Christ* treats christology as 'the beginning of eschatology', and *The Coming of God* treats eschatology as 'the consummation of christology'. The latter may be less obvious than the former. Eschatology is more prominent in *The Way of Jesus Christ* than christology is in *The Coming of God*. This is largely no more than the result of the way Moltmann has allocated material between the two volumes. It is, of course, only to be expected that his treatment of the mission, cross and resurrection of Jesus should appear in *The Way of Jesus Christ*, and be presupposed in *The Coming of God*, but it is perhaps unfortunate that his treatment of the cosmic Christ as 'the redeemer of evolution' at his parousia (WJC 301–305) and of the parousia itself (WJC VII) appear in the former book and are taken as read in the latter (see 261, 370 n. 201).[2] Most of what is said in the chapter on the parousia in *The Way of Jesus Christ* (VII) in fact reappears in considerably expanded form in *The Coming of God* (especially 23–26, 235–255, 279–295), but its connexion with the parousia of Jesus Christ is far less obvious. There is hence a danger that the eschatology of *The Coming of God* looks christological in the sense of being grounded in the history of Jesus, but not in the sense of being focused on his own eschatological role, as redeemer and judge, at his parousia (but see 250–255). The parousia is mentioned from time to time in *The Coming of God*, but is scarcely a central feature or itself a subject of discussion. Besides the avoidance of repetition, there may be another reason for this. Whereas *The Way of Jesus Christ* does not distinguish the parousia of Jesus Christ from the eschatological coming of God, and so freely speaks of it as ending time and bringing about the eternal kingdom and the new creation of all things (e.g. WJC 317, 319–321, 326–328), in *The Coming of God* the millennial kingdom of Christ enters the eschatological prospect.[3] His coming is to inaugurate this kingdom within history (196–197). There are some passages in *The Coming of God* which still associate the parousia with God's coming to end historical time, to establish his eternal kingdom,

---

[2] WJC 316 explains why it was important to Moltmann to treat the parousia in this book.

[3] Moltmann already refers to the millennium in TKG 235 n. 44 (first published in 1980) and gives it an essential role in eschatology in HTG 96, 108–109 (first published in 1982), but seems to ignore it completely in WJC VII.

and to renew and to indwell all creation (e.g. 13, 24, 25–26, 254), but generally this book speaks of the eschatological coming of God in a non-christological way. This may be due to the association of the parousia primarily with the millennial kingdom of Christ within history, rather than with the arrival of the eternal kingdom and the new creation.

However, if the role of Jesus Christ himself in the eschatological future is less prominent in this book than it might be, it is clear that the history of Jesus – in particular his cross and his resurrection, as in *Theology of Hope*[4] – is foundational for the understanding of eschatology in this book. It functions as the ground and the criterion for eschatological expectations. It does so in relation to personal eschatology (69, 77, 85, 100, 104), in relation to historical eschatology (136–137, 194–196, 227, 233, 234), and in relation to cosmic eschatology (28–29, 93, 233, 261, 274, 279).

The way in which it determines the broad structure of the eschatology can be briefly indicated here. Since, 'with the raising of the crucified Christ from the dead, the future of the new creation of all things has already begun in the midst of this dying and transitory world' (136), Jesus Christ, crucified and risen, is the paradigm for the new creation of all things. His rising from the dead has 'proleptic and representative significance for all the dead' (69) – and not just for all human beings, but for all mortal things (69–70), since he died the death of all the living (92–93; cf. WJC 169–170, 252–259). Moltmann does not limit this notion to creatures with biological life, but extends it to the whole creation, which is subject to transience: 'animals, plants, stones, and all cosmic life systems' (WJC 258).[5] In solidarity with the whole creation which sighs under the burden of transience, Christ has inaugurated eternal life.

As the paradigm of new creation, the resurrection of the crucified Christ reveals his *identity* in death and resurrection. The same Jesus Christ who died was raised, and correspondingly the resurrection of the dead and the new creation of all things

---

[4] The prominent place given to Jesus' messianic mission in WJC is not reflected in CoG.

[5] It is surely a lapse when Moltmann claims that stones, like angels, are immortal (CoG 90).

is not the replacement of this creation by another but the renewal of this creation (29): 'everything is to be brought back again in new form' (265). Yet the resurrection of Jesus is *new creation*, a genuine *novum*, which does not develop out of the dead Christ, but is a new creative act of God. Correspondingly, the *novum ultimum*, the ultimate new thing, the new creation of all things, does not issue from the history of the old creation (68). It is God's creative act, in which he, as the Creator who is faithful to his creation, does not annihilate but renews his creation. The continuity of old and new is not provided by the old, but created by God's act of new creation (69). The structure of thought here (271: 'the unity of innovation and identity') was already well established in *Theology of Hope* (especially 197–202).[6]

The resurrection of Christ was not a resumption of mortal life, but entry into eternal life, beyond transience and death. This is the foundation for the eschatological surplus of new creation over this temporal, transient and mortal creation. The new creation is not a mere restoration of creation to an original perfection. It is 'a transformation in the transcendental conditions of the world itself' (272), a participation of creation in the eternal life of God. Temporal creation will become eternal creation, as the mortal Christ became the eternally living Christ. And, just as the resurrection of Jesus was not an historical but an eschatological event (69), so the eschaton cannot be envisaged in the future of historical time, in which everything that is eventually ceases to be. The eschaton is the transformation of historical time into eternal time, as the resurrection of Christ was the transformation of the mortal into the eternally living Christ. This is the christological basis for Moltmann's extensive reflections on the relation of time to eschatological eternity.

The resurrection of Christ was his entry into eternal life, but it was not the survival of some eternal part of him. It was the transformation of his whole, *bodily* form. Correspondingly, the new creation is the transfiguration precisely of this transient

---

[6] See Bauckham, *Moltmann: Messianic Theology in the Making*, 35–36, 42; idem, *The Theology of Jürgen Moltmann*, 36–39.

and mortal creation in its bodily and material form. In this is seen the solidarity of the crucified and risen Christ, in the bodiliness of his mortal and risen forms, with all living things and with the earth, just as human beings in their bodiliness are integrally related to the rest of the material creation and cannot be understood to rise bodily to new life without the resurrection and new creation of the rest of creation also. Thus the bodily resurrection of the crucified Christ forms the foundation for one aspect of the all-embracing and integral character of the new creation as Moltmann portrays it. Eschatology is emphatically not about the transcendence of immaterial and eternal aspects of creation over the bodily and mortal aspects. It is the new creation of the whole of this transient and bodily creation.

The bodily resurrection of the crucified Christ also forms the foundation for another aspect of the all-embracing and integral character of the new creation as Moltmann portrays it: the gathering up of the whole diachronic extent of lived lives into eternal life and of all times into eternal time. The dead Christ's solidarity with all the dead means that the resurrection of the dead is of all who have ever lived. In a sense the eschatological moment of entry into eternal time must be simultaneous with all their lives, spread across the generations of human history. Moreover, as the marks of the crucifixion on the body of the risen Christ indicate (85), the risen Christ is the transfigured form of all that his temporally lived life had made him. The whole diachronic extent of his lived life is taken up into his eternal life. These two considerations have not usually been thought to imply as much as Moltmann derives from them, but they form the christological basis for his development of the idea that the whole of what has happened, in the lives of all creatures and in the whole of the time of this transient creation, will be gathered up, healed and transfigured, into eternal life and eternal time.

Finally, we should consider the fundamental pattern of cross and resurrection to which Moltmann draws attention in his preface:

> Christian eschatology is the remembered hope of the raising of the crucified Christ, so it talks about beginning afresh in the deadly end. 'The end of Christ – after all that was his true beginning,'

said Ernst Bloch. Christian eschatology follows this christological pattern in all its personal, historical and cosmic dimensions: *in the end is the beginning.* (xi)

In the book the pattern is applied in both directions, as it were. On the one hand, in every end, eschatological hope, christologically based, perceives a new beginning: the eschatological *novum* which is not within the potential of what comes to an end but comes from the God who raises the transient and mortal into eternity. In the winter of this transient creation we await the springtime of eternal life (91–92). On the other hand, a new beginning presupposes an end:

> [T]here is no beginning of a new world without the end of this old one, there is no kingdom of God without judgment on god-lessness, there is no rebirth of the cosmos without 'the birth-pangs of the End-time'. The raising of Christ from the dead presupposes his real and total death. It is from this fact that Christian apocalyptic takes its bearings: his real end was his true beginning. (227)

This should not be misunderstood. It does not mean strictly that the world must be annihilated in order to be re-created. Moltmann clearly denies this (cf. 29, 74–75): 'even the end of the world cannot be total annihilation and new creation. It can only be a transformation out of transience into eternity' (271). The point is rather that in principle there is no necessary continuity from this life and this world to eternal life and the new world. In itself this creation is transient and of itself it comes to nothing. Human life is sinful and must come under judgment. We do not know whether the current 'end-time' situation in which humanity itself threatens the end of human history and of most life on this planet will end in catastrophe, but there are no grounds for facile optimism.

> Eschatology is not a doctrine about history's happy end . . . No one can assure us that the worst will not happen. We can only trust that even the end of the world hides a new beginning if we trust the God who calls into being the things that are not, and out of death creates new life. (234; cf. 229)

The christological principle of Moltmann's eschatology requires us to ask whether it is consistently applied. Is it true, as *Theology of Hope* at least required, in the passage quoted above, that '*all* statements' made in *The Coming of God* 'about the future are grounded in the person and history of Jesus Christ' (TH 17: my emphasis)? Certainly it is not true that no other kinds of consideration are allowed a place in Moltmann's eschatological arguments. All kinds of other considerations frequently enter the arguments. This is in accordance with the general character of Moltmann's theology, which always tends to broaden its base and to integrate perspectives. Both the missionary direction of his early christological eschatology, which potentially encompassed all reality in the eschatological horizon projected by the history of Jesus, and the relational principle of his later trinitarian theology, which encouraged the understanding of subjects – including Jesus Christ himself – in their relationships to others, militate against a restrictive understanding of the christological principle in eschatology. The grounding of all eschatological statements in christology does not prohibit drawing on other knowledge and insights which are consistent with and help to develop the fundamental, christological requirements. We should rather understand the christological principle as requiring a christological basis for the regulative structures of eschatological thought. Such structures leave plenty of room for other considerations – theological or otherwise – to play their part. Indeed, since eschatology concerns the future of God's whole creation, it would be odd if knowledge and experience of the creation could not contribute to understanding it.

The christological principle gives *The Coming of God* a complementary relationship especially with *The Way of Jesus Christ*, but the facts that its topic is eschatology and that all of Moltmann's theology has a strongly eschatological orientation necessarily gives *The Coming of God* a complementary relationship also with the other three of Moltmann's five volumes of dogmatics. This is particularly true of *God in Creation*, since eschatology is the completion of creation, and Moltmann in *The Coming of God* resumes major features of his understanding of creation in order to show how they are fulfilled in the eschaton. The major link with *The Trinity and the Kingdom of God* is found not, as one might expect, in the understanding of the kingdom of God itself, but in the notion of eschatology as a trinitarian process, taking place within the changing relationships of the divine Persons, completed when the Son hands over the kingdom to the Father (TKG 91–96; CoG 334–336). Despite this link, explicitly trinitarian theology is rather surprisingly rare in *The Coming of God*.

2. Integrative Eschatology[7]

Moltmann's eschatology is, as a matter of fundamental principle, all-embracing. Because eschatology is about the faithfulness of the Creator to his creation, it is about a new future for the whole creation:

> [T]rue hope must be universal, because its healing future embraces every individual and the whole universe. If we were to surrender hope for as much as one single creature, for us God would not be God. (132)

But the history of eschatology shows a frequent failure to maintain this universality: eschatological thought has all too often abstracted the soul from the body, the individual from human community, human history from the rest of creation. The result, as Moltmann pointed out in his earliest theology, is the danger of a Gnostic yearning for the escape of the spirit from this world, which leaves this world to its own devices and loses the world-transforming power of eschatological hope. A more recent insight of Moltmann's is that this individualizing and spiritualizing of hope has often gone hand-in-hand with a kind of realized millenarianism. The Constantinian state and the triumphalist church embodied the kingdom of God here and now, and so suppressed any hope that was not individual and otherworldly (xv). Finally, though Moltmann does not make this point explicitly, in the modern period the recovery of a universal eschatology has often been highly anthropocentric,

---

[7] Moltmann's term is *integrierende Eschatologie* (KG 15 = CoG xiv).

subsuming nature into the category of human history, in line with the modern understanding of history as the progressive domination of nature. Moltmann's rejection of this modern paradigm, in favour of the mutual interactions of human history and nature (cf. 132, 160), enables him to give the non-human creation its own place in a non-anthropocentric eschatology.

The structure of *The Coming of God* aims to resist the dis-integrating tendencies of eschatology in the past by integrat-ing the perspectives which have often diverged (xiv). It deals in turn with three aspects of created reality, which together make up the whole: personal eschatology (eternal life), historical eschatology (the kingdom of God), and cosmic eschatology (the new heaven and the new earth). (Perhaps it is a weakness of the book that it divides the human world only into the individual and the political: human community on a smaller scale than political society is treated as the context for individual life and death, but not as an eschatological dimension in its own right.) The logic of the order of these chapters (II–IV) is noetic: eschatological hope begins with personal hope but necessarily expands to encompass the future of human society and the redemption of the whole creation (xvi). (But one wonders whether this noetic order is as obvious as Moltmann supposes: in ancient Israel hope for the future of the nation preceded hope that individuals would be raised to participate in it.) Eschatology, however, has a further perspective: that of God's future, the coming of his kingdom and his glory and his indwelling of his creation. This dimension – the glorifying of God in the world – encompasses the others. Indeed, the key to integrating the others lies in seeing eschatology as theocentric – centred neither in the individual nor in the world, but in the God who comes to indwell his whole creation. This perspective, of course, accounts both for the title of the book and for the presence of a final chapter on divine eschatology (glory), to which all the others lead.

Integrative eschatology recognizes that the new creation must be all-encompassing. As Moltmann says of all the experiences of a human life, of all human beings and of the whole cosmos:

nothing will be lost,[8] all will be restored (70, 251, 265; cf. also WJC 239, 303; JCTW 104). The whole extent of God's creation in space and in time, and every one of God's creatures that has existed in space and time, God will redeem and restore in the eternal creation. There are three angles from which the need for such all-encompassing eschatology can be appreciated. One is God's relationship to his creation (259). If eschatological hope rests on God's faithfulness and grace to his creation, then the eschatological act of new creation in which God completes and redeems his creation, giving it eternal life, must be as comprehensive as the creative act which gives creation its present, transient existence. If God's soteriological (and so eschatological) work were a matter of redeeming some parts or aspects of his creation, while leaving the rest to perish, God would cease to be the Creator (cf. 269–270). Thus the unity and consistency of God's relationship to his creation requires that new creation be all-encompassing. Indeed, if God were to allow any of his creatures to be lost, he would not be true to himself (255). (The argument seems to presuppose – what is certainly not self-evident – that God could not create some creatures for a temporary purpose that, once fulfilled, leaves no reason for their eternal preservation. In other words, it takes transience to be *per se* an imperfection which can be a characteristic of God's good creation only if God redeems all transient creatures from their transience. In assessing Moltmann's eschatology, it needs to be considered whether transience cannot be evaluated in a more discriminating way.)

The second angle from which the need for such all-encompassing eschatology can be appreciated is christological. Since Jesus Christ died the death of all the living and rose as the beginning of the new creation,

> resurrection has become the universal 'law' of creation, not merely for human beings, but for animals, plants, stones and all cosmic life systems as well. The raised body of Christ therefore acts as an embodied promise for the whole creation. (WJC 258)

[8] The theme recalls A. N. Whitehead's image of the nature of God as 'a tender care that nothing be lost' (*Process and Reality* [Cambridge: Cambridge University Press, 1929] 490), but Moltmann's understanding of this is, of course, very different from Whitehead's.

That the death and resurrection of Jesus form the basis for the new creation of all things is stated at length in *The Way of Jesus Christ* and taken for granted in *The Coming of God* (cf. e.g. 338). The one point where it is developed at length and in a particular way in the latter book is in Moltmann's discussion of universal salvation (i.e. the final salvation of all human beings).[9] He argues that Christ in his abandonment by God on the cross suffered hell and damnation for all in order that there might no longer be eternal damnation for any (251–254):

> The true Christian foundation for the hope of universal salvation is the theology of the cross, and the realistic consequence of the theology of the cross can only be the restoration of all things. (251)

The third angle from which the need for such all-encompassing eschatology can be appreciated is that of the interconnectedness of all creatures. This is why, starting from the personal hope for eternal life, one can and should move to hope for human community in the kingdom of God and for the whole cosmos in the new creation (69–70, 131–132, 260). Here the integral nature of the human person as bodily is crucial. Only a quite radical anthropological dualism makes the redemption and eternal life of the human spirit apart from the rest of creation conceivable without serious difficulties. If it is the whole, bodily person that is redeemed, then the individual human who is redeemed cannot be isolated from the connexions that bind human persons in human community and that bind human nature to the rest of nature (69–71, 112, 277; cf. WJC 262):

> Human nature is bodily existence and is linked, with all the senses, to the natural world on which it is dependent. Human life is participation in nature. The world of the living, of the earth, the

[9] Although this section (235–255) is called 'The Restoration of All Things', this term is here used for the doctrine of the salvation of all human beings. The extension of the subject at the end of the section (254–255) to include the devil and the fallen angels (cf. GC 169 for the redemption of these) is something of a *non sequitur*, since Moltmann has not suggested (and seems never to suggest) that Christ suffered and died in solidarity with (fallen) heavenly beings as well as with earthly beings.

solar system, our galaxy and the cosmos is the condition for our human world too, for it is in this world that our human world is embedded. Because there is no such thing as a soul separate from the body, and no humanity detached from nature – from life, the earth and the cosmos – there is no redemption for human beings either without the redemption of nature. The redemption of humanity is aligned towards a humanity whose existence is still conjoined with nature. (260)

The interconnexions which situate human persons inextricably both in community with other humans and in community with other creatures exist not only in space but also in time. Moltmann refers here to the notion of human community across the generations (112), to which he has given some notable attention in his recent work (see WJC 189–192, 269–270; SL 236–239). Modern individualism can be seen not only in the isolation of individuals from sociality with contemporaries but also in their isolation from previous generations (cf. WJC 270), whom other societies remembered 'in recollecting solidarity' (108), but forgetfulness of whom in modern society is part of the cultural suppression of death (51–52, 108). Thus Moltmann's desire for a restoration of the Christian sense of community with the dead in Christ (107–108) is an important implication of his integrative eschatology: 'The community of the living and the dead is the praxis of the resurrection hope' (108).

Integrative eschatology not only recognizes that the new creation must be all-encompassing; it also sees the new creation as unitive or integrative, bringing all creation into harmony and unity, restoring to wholeness what has disintegrated through transience and sin, uniting what has been separated in time and space. Of death and resurrection of people, Moltmann writes:

> Death is the power of separation, both in time as the stream of transience, materially as the disintegration of the person's living Gestalt or configuration, and socially as isolation and loneliness. The raising to eternal life, conversely, is the power to unite – in time, as the gathering of all temporal moments into the eternal present; materially as healing for life's configuration in its wholeness; and socially, as a gathering into new community in the eternal

love. . . . Eternal life is the final healing of this life into the completed wholeness for which it is destined. (71)

Elsewhere Moltmann speaks of the resurrection and the new creation as 'the uniting of what has been separated' in five respects: realizing the unity of body and soul, the diachronic unity of the person in his or her life history, the unity between human persons in community, the diachronic unity of the human race across the generations, and the unity between human civilization and nature (WJC 263–273). (These unities do not, of course, imply the elimination of difference, but the overcoming of isolation and separation, and differentiation in reconciliation and mutuality. They can be further explicated in the categories, characteristic of Moltmann's thought, of community and perichoresis.)

The separations which are overcome in eschatological integration are therefore both ethical (the result of enmity, domination and self-isolation) and also metaphysical. The latter comprises both temporal and spatial aspects. It is in the nature of the present creation that it is extended in both time and space. The transformation of time and space in the new creation is a gathering of all the temporal moments of historical time and all the spaces of this creation's space into a kind of temporal and spatial compresence. In Moltmann's argument this is clearer in the case of time:

> In 'the restoration of all things' all times will return and – transformed and transfigured – will be taken up into the aeon of the new creation. In the eternal creation all the times which in God's creative resolve were fanned out will also be gathered together. The unfurled times of history will be rolled up like a scroll. . . . Only this can then be called 'the fulness of the times'. (294–295)

Moltmann does not say the same so explicitly about space. But he does say that in the eschaton creation will participate in the divine attributes of eternity and omnipresence (307; cf. 280). This means, in the case of time, that just as to God all the times of creation are compresent to him in his eternity, so in the eternal time of the new creation the creation in its whole temporal extension will be compresent to itself and in this way live eternally in God. This is a temporal de-restriction of the temporal creation. The parallel spatial de-restriction of the spatial creation means that, just as all the spaces of creation are compresent to God in his omnipresence, so in the new creation the separation of creatures from each other which space entails will be overcome and all creation will be compresent to itself.[10] (Does this idea of the bringing of all times and spaces into compresence in the new creation imply that the temporal and spatial extensions of this present creation are imperfections? When thought of as limiting and restricting temporal and spatial creatures they seem so. But without the history of this creation in time and space the new creation could not be what it will be.)

Finally, the new creation is the uniting of God and creation through the mutual indwelling of God and creation and the perichoresis of God and creation (278, 295, 307–308). The present creation exists only through the divine self-restriction which gives time, space and freedom for creation to be itself in relative distance from God (281–282). This distance will be superseded in the eschatological divine de-restriction. Creation will then participate in the eternal divine life and in the divine omnipresence. 'The Creator no longer remains over against his creation' (295), but is present in it, filling it with his glory:

> A mutual indwelling of the world in God and God in the world will come into being. For this, it is neither necessary for the world to dissolve into God, as pantheism says, nor for God to be dissolved in the world, as atheism maintains. God remains God, and the world remains creation. Through their mutual indwellings, they remain unmingled and undivided, for God lives in creation in a God-like way, and the world lives in God in a world-like way. (307)

This Moltmann holds to be the implication of his favourite eschatological text: 'God will be all in all' (cf. 335).

---

[10] Cf. CoG 77: 'Death de-restricts the human being's spirit in both time and space. The dead are no longer there as temporally limited and spatially restricted "contact persons", but we sense their presence whenever we become aware that we are living "before God"; and wherever we sense their presence, we feel the divine "wide space" which binds us together.'

3. Redemptive Eschatology

God's coming to his creation at the end is its redemption both from sin and evil and from transience and death. Sin and evil have spoiled God's original creation, but transience and death belong to the created nature of this temporal creation. Moltmann rejects the view that they are the consequence of sin, regarding them rather as intrinsic to the temporal character of this creation (90–91). In time all things pass away and all living things die. Therefore, since the eschatological redemption is from transience and death as well as from sin and evil, it cannot be understood merely as a restoration to an original perfection of creation. The present creation must be understood as imperfect in the sense of incomplete, a world whose creation has only begun and awaits completion (264). Transience and death are signs of this imperfection (91). In fact, even with regard to redemption from sin, a restoration of the original goodness of creation could not be equivalent to the eschatological redemption from sin, since the original creation was open to the possibility of sin and the restored creation would similarly be: an endless sequence of falls and redemptions could be envisaged (263–264; cf. CG 261). Creation can only be secured against sin and evil if the new creation exceeds restoration. The eschatological transformation is therefore 'a fundamental transformation in the transcendental conditions of the world' (272). This occurs when the temporal creation becomes eternal creation, as a result, as we have seen, of God's indwelling his creation, sharing his eternal life with it, glorifying it in his presence. To redemption *from* sin and evil, transience and death, there therefore corresponds creation's transformation and transfiguration *into* the eternal creation in glory.

The difference between the temporality of this creation, only possible because God restricts his own eternity to allow creation its own time, and the eternal time of the new creation, which is a relative participation in God's eternity, seems to be of central significance here. Not only do transience and death belong to temporality and lose their power to bring to nothing in the eternal creation, but also sin can only occur within historical time and in the temporal creation's relative distance from God, so that the new creation, which participates in the eternal divine life, is secure from sin and evil. This is why, even though the process of eschatological redemption is already underway in this temporal and mortal creation, the final redemption of all things can only occur in the transition from the temporal to the eternal creation. We can see why ideas about the relationship of time and eternity feature so prominently in *The Coming of God*.

Temporality (meaning the time of this creation, as distinct from the eternal time of the new creation) is, in Moltmann's view, ambiguous. It is what makes creation subject to change. The temporal creation is therefore open to both constructive possibilities and destructive possibilities. Positively, time is 'the time of promise' (283), the temporal creation's openness to completion: 'Its temporality is itself the true promise of its eternity' (264; cf. 266). Negatively, time is 'the time of transience': future becomes past, all things pass away, all living things die: 'In the end everything that could be, and that was, is past, and at the end of the past stands universal death, the total non-being of all temporal things and happenings' (284). Thus, the eschatological transformation of time into eternal time is not only the fulfilment of time's promise, but also redemption from transience, death and final futility. This ambiguous character of this creation's time is what makes death at the same time 'natural' in the sense of belonging to creation's present condition and yet not to be accepted as inevitable fate: 'It is a fact that evokes grief and longing for the future world and eternal life' (92). Since the temporal creation is not only subject to transience and futility, but also structurally open to its perfection by God, in hope we should not come to terms with death 'but remain inconsolable until redemption comes' (93).

From the perspective so far explored in this section, the idea of completion serves to explicate the idea of redemption: it makes clear that redemption is not a mere restoration to the original state of creation, but the perfecting in glory of the originally imperfect creation. However, when Moltmann considers eschatology in relation to human history, the notions of history's completion and history's redemption stand in tension or opposition. By itself the completion of history suggests the nineteenth-century idea of history as steady advance towards history's goal, a millenarian or utopian view which the catastrophes of twentieth-century history shattered. But as a secularized version of the Christian eschatological tradition, this modern historical eschatology took up only one side of the eschatological expectation: the millenarian hope, neglecting the apocalyptic. It views the eschaton

> as the *telos*, the goal and purpose of historical development and struggle, but not as the *finis*, the rupture of history and its end. The apocalyptic expectations of rupture and end do not 'articulate' the course of history, nor do they fulfil it. They do not lend history any meaning, but withdraw from it any legitimation. (134)

Through the experience of historical catastrophe in the first half of this century, the Jewish messianic theology on which Moltmann draws in chapter I of *The Coming of God*, especially the work of Rosenzweig, Scholem and Benjamin (33–41), rejected the idea of the completion of history in favour of that of the redemption of history: 'The question about redemption pushed out the question about the utopian goals of historical progress' (44). Moltmann sees in this form of the eschatological hope 'the redemption of the future from the power of history' (45). The power of history is exercised by the powerful for whom the future they plan and project is the prolongation of their present. Such a future is the one the modern western project of technological civilization has projected, and increasingly now it threatens the future of humanity and nature (45, 202–218). But in the messianic 'moment' which does not belong to the temporal advance of history but interrupts it, the reality of divine redemption from history is perceived as the world's future:

> At that moment another future becomes perceptible. The laws and forces of the past are no longer 'compulsive'. God's messianic future wins power over the present. New perspectives open up. The deadliness of progress towards the economic, ecological, nuclear and genetic catastrophes is recognized; and the modern world's lack of future is perceived. The way becomes free for alternative developments. I should like to call this the redemption of the future from the power of history in the *kairos* of conversion. (45–46)

In relation to human history, then, the hope of redemption enables the future to be perceived neither in terms of goal without rupture (the one-sided secularization of the millenarian hope) nor in terms of end without fulfilment (the one-sided secularization of the apocalyptic expectation of catastrophe). It promotes neither the 'messianic presumption' of utopian progressivism nor the 'apocalyptic resignation' of fatalistic acceptance of inevitable catastrophe (192), both of which in their opposite ways aid and abet the modern historical project in its deadly and destructive progress. By awakening hope in the power of God's redemptive future, it enables resistance to the power of history, anticipates a different future, alternative to that which the trends of past and present project, and in this way proves redemptive already.

4. Processive Eschatology

Moltmann speaks of an eschatological process which began with the resurrection of Jesus and will reach its goal in the new creation of all things. This is 'the process of resurrection' (TKG 91; WJC 242; CoG 335), 'the new process of creation' (FC 123), 'the great process of giving life to the world, and the new creation of all things' (CoG 198; cf. 77). It is 'an End-time process' (WJC 319), characterizing the whole time from the resurrection of Jesus as the End-time in which the eschatological process is under way. It is also a 'trinitarian process' (CoG 335) or 'inner-trinitarian process' (CG 264; TKG 92; CoG 335), part of what Moltmann earlier referred to as 'the trinitarian history of God' (CPS 50), in which creation is included in the divine life through its involvement in the changing trinitarian relationships within God.

Fundamental for Moltmann's understanding of this eschatological process is 1 Corinthians 15:22–28 (see especially CG 264–266; FC 123–125; TKG 91–93; WJC 319; CoG 110, 196, 335). This portrays a process 'which the resurrection of the crucified One has irrevocably set going' (WJC 319). It is a process of resurrection or of the communication of eternal life to the mortal creation, represented in a series of stages: first the resurrection of Jesus Christ, then at his parousia those who belong to Christ, then the resurrection of the rest of the dead and the annihilation of death itself. Moltmann takes this as a kind of outline of a process that began with the resurrection of Jesus from among the dead, a unique event of eschatologically new creation, which 'means the overcoming of death's power and the appearance of imperishable, eternal life' (CoG 337). Into the Pauline outline he inserts the presence and activity of the Spirit, in which Christian believers experience eternal life already here and now in fellowship with the risen Christ (cf. SL 152–153). 'Resurrection happens every day' (WJC 242), because through the risen Christ and the Spirit the life of the new creation is already present within this temporal and mortal creation. But this present, pneumatological dimension must be understood as a stage in a process, which 'has its foundation in Christ, its dynamic in the Spirit, and its future in the bodily new creation of all things' (WJC 241). (Thus Moltmann's exposition of pneumatology, especially in *The Spirit of Life*, is situated within the eschatological process that leads from the resurrection of Christ to the new creation.) The participation of believers here and now with Christ in his death and resurrection leads to their resurrection at his coming, and this in turn leads to the general resurrection of all the dead, the annihilation of death in the whole creation, and the new creation of all things, with which the subjugation of death is finally complete (110). Into this sequence Moltmann also, following Romans 11, inserts the resurrection and redemption of all Israel at the parousia. This, like the resurrection of Christ and of Christians, is resurrection *from among* the dead, and thus a stage in the process which leads to the resurrection of all the dead (198).

Moltmann describes the process primarily as one of giving life to the mortal creation, but, following 1 Corinthians 15, he also sees it as the way in which 'God acquires through history his eternal kingdom' (335). The kingdom of God does not only come all at once in the final transition from historical time to eternal time, but arrives through a process, which 1 Corinthians 15 portrays as a trinitarian one: the risen Christ is given the rule by his Father, and rules until he has subjected all things to his rule, when he finally hands back the kingdom to the Father.

The rule of Christ from resurrection to new creation is itself, according to Moltmann, to be envisaged in two stages: his messianic rule now, and his millennial reign (TKG 235 n. 44), in which the martyrs who have died with him live with him, and in which Israel, raised and redeemed, forms with Christians the messianic people of this messianic kingdom (CoG 195, 198–199; cf. HTG 96). This is 'a transitional kingdom leading from this transitory world-time to the new world that is God's' (195). It is not yet the kingdom of glory, which comes when Christ hands back the kingdom to the Father. It is a transitional kingdom corresponding, in the process of resurrection, to the transitional period between the resurrection of Christians and Israel from the dead and the resurrection of all the dead in the new creation itself. The idea that the new creation arrives in a process of transition, through various different phases, is part of Moltmann's argument for the necessity of millenarianism in Christian eschatology (201–202). (An important question about Moltmann's millenarianism is whether he makes the character and function of the millennium sufficiently clear for the necessity of this particular transitional phase in the eschatological process to be intelligible.) [11]

Although the millennium represents a kind of eschatological goal of history within history, Moltmann's processive eschatology should not be mistaken for a notion of historical progress. Its foundation in the cross and resurrection of Jesus prohibits this. As Moltmann rather often remarks, Christian eschatology is not 'a theology of universal history' – whether in the form of those kinds of salvation-historical scheme which lay out in advance a divine plan of historical development, or in the secularized form of millenarianisms which espouse the modern faith in inevitable progress (145–146, 200; cf. already TH 71). It is 'a theology of combatants, not onlookers' (146), 'a historical theology of struggle and hope' (200). It is not that the powers of the world for whom universal theories of history function as ideological justifications of their own supremacy (cf. 142) prepare the way for the millennial reign of Christ. Rather the martyrs who, in resistance and hope, share in the struggle and the sufferings of

---

[11] See further chapter IV/1 below.

Christ, will share in his resurrection and his reign in the millennium (194–195).

A kind of parallel to the transitional role of the millennium in historical eschatology is the intermediate state (between death and resurrection) in personal eschatology. (The parallel is not chronological, since, for those who are raised from the dead at the commencement of the millennium, the intermediate state precedes it.) While rejecting the doctrine of purgatory in its traditional Roman Catholic form, Moltmann finds 'a true element' in it (106) in the idea that, in the fellowship of Christ, the dead have time for the rectification, healing, growth and completion of this life, which would otherwise be abruptly broken off, left for all people incomplete, and for some people, dead before birth or in the early years of life, broken off before life had really been lived at all (106, 116–118). Prior to the final raising of our whole lives into eternal life, there needs to be 'an on-going history after death with our lives as we have lived them' (116). Presumably, such a history cannot take place in the new creation itself, not because Moltmann envisages the eternal time of new creation as static, but because he images it as cyclical time, unlike the irreversible time of the present creation (295).

It would seem logical to expect cosmic eschatology to require a phase of transition to the new creation, just as Moltmann considers that personal and historical eschatology do. Moltmann does not explicitly supply such a transitional phase for the natural world. He does not explicitly give the millennium this role, but he does point out that it has often been portrayed as a Sabbath of the earth and a paradise of nature (144). The fact that he has placed his discussion of the millennium within the political context of historical eschatology perhaps prevented him from drawing out its possible cosmic significance.[12]

Finally, 1 Corinthians 15:22–28 gives the eschatological process a theocentric goal: that God should be 'all in all'. It is the process in which God is on the way to and achieves the goal for

---

[12] The discussion of the future of the earth in CoG 278–279 (following J. T. Beck's organological eschatology) is most naturally read as referring to the new creation, but may be intended to refer to the earth in the millennial age.

himself which is also his creation's goal. He achieves his kingdom in creation, he comes to his eschatological rest in creation, he indwells his creation, he becomes 'all in all'.

5. Theocentric Eschatology

The central expectation of Jewish and Christian eschatology has always been the coming of God to his creation and the coming presence of God in his whole creation (cf. 23–24). The title *The Coming of God* itself shows that Moltmann intends to put this expectation at the centre of his eschatology. Not only is it central; it also comprehends the other aspects of eschatology: the personal, the historical and the cosmic. The coming presence of God in his creation is also the redemption, transfiguration and eternal life of all creatures, and the source and focus of their eternal jubilation. It is 'the eschatological goal of creation as a whole and of all individual created beings' (318).

This eschatological presence of God differs from his presence in the present creation: it is 'the indwelling of his unmediated and direct glory' (317). It is the de-restriction of his omnipresence which had been self-restricted in relation to the present creation. But whereas the present creation could not bear the immediate presence of God (306), in the eschaton 'we shall be able to look upon his face without perishing' (317; cf. 295). In another image: the presence of God will interpenetrate all things in a 'perichoresis which does not destroy created beings but full-fills them' (318). Thus creation is transformed and fulfilled by this immediate presence of God, but conversely also God himself reaches the goal he has desired. He comes to his rest in his creation and finds his dwelling-place – 'the home of his identity' (xiii) – in creation (307).

In these two notions – rest and dwelling – Moltmann takes up two Jewish theological and eschatological ideas which have long fascinated him: the Sabbath and the Shekinah. Having treated the Sabbath at length in *God in Creation* (XI), he gives more attention in *The Coming of God* to the Shekinah, but the two ideas are linked and in some respects parallel. The link is God's rest (CoG 265–266). The Sabbath of God's rest after creation points forward to the completion of creation when God will both rest from creation and rest in his creation (GC 277–279; CoG 266). The Shekinah is God's dwelling in the midst of his people, his wandering in exile and suffering with his exiled people, awaiting redemption and the eschatological indwelling of God in the whole creation, which thus becomes his resting-place (CoG 283–284, 304–305). The eschatological Sabbath is also the cosmic Shekinah.

The interconnexions of the two notions make for some complexity in Moltmann's thought (especially 265–267, 283). Both offer possibilities of thinking of God's presence in the time and space of this creation in anticipation of the fullness of his presence in the new creation. In Jewish theological terms, the weekly Sabbath (and the sabbatical years) constitutes a rhythm of God's eternal presence in the time of this transient world (138, 266–267, 283–284). In Christian theological terms, the Shekinah of God in Christ and in the Spirit indwells believers in this godless world (305–306). Just as 'the sabbath in time thrusts forward to God's End-time Shekinah', so through the indwelling of the Spirit Christian believers 'are filled with hope for that new creation which God will universally indwell' (267).

6. Contextual Eschatology

Eschatology, no more than any other theological topic, but perhaps even less than some, can be thought in abstract isolation from its historical context. Consciously or unconsciously – but very often consciously – Christian theologians writing eschatology have always been influenced by and responded to the historical movements and crises, the contemporary hopes and fears, of their own context. But since the Jewish and Christian tradition of eschatology has had an enormous influence – direct and indirect, in religious and secularized forms – on the historical movements and projects, the interpretations of history and the aspirations for the future, of Western society down to the present, the writing of Christian eschatology in the modern period belongs to and relates to a context itself strongly determined by various forms of eschatological thought. Contemporary eschatology needs to be self-aware and self-critical with respect to its relationship to its own tradition and its own context, and must engage in assessment and critique of the eschatologies, religious and secular, which are influential in its context.

It is a merit of Moltmann's eschatology in *The Coming of God* that it incorporates a strong interpretation of its historical and global context. It reads that context in terms of the eschatological goals and expectations which have determined it and the eschatological interpretations of it which are influential. In so doing it offers an eschatological critique of the distorted and destructive eschatologies of the modern period and brings the redemptive vision of an eschatology based on the cross and resurrection of Jesus Christ to bear on the damage that modern eschatologies have done and are doing.

Moltmann sees the nineteenth century as a period pervasively influenced by the millenarian dream of the modern world. The modern faith in progress, the vast historical optimism which blossomed in the nineteenth-century West, was the sense of having entered the final age of history, in which no fundamental changes were any longer to be expected, but steady, evolutionary progress along the lines already established was assured. Human perfection, humanly achieved, and the kingdom of God were virtually identical, and formed a goal towards which progress without impediment now seemed well under way (3). This 'historical millenarianism' (meaning a belief in the present as the beginning of the final age of history and as the period in which the goal of history is being achieved) of the modern age took many forms. Especially in a secularized Enlightenment form, it remains, despite twentieth-century history's assaults on any faith in inevitable progress, an influential interpretation of the modern age. The moral and political idealism of the nineteenth century has dissipated and its enthusiasm for a glorious future on the horizon of history has waned, but belief in scientific-technological progress and economic growth still preserves something of nineteenth-century interpretation of the modern world as a millenarian project.

As the secular faith it predominantly became, Moltmann sees the modern millenarian dream not simply as a secularized form of Christian eschatology, as many, including influentially Karl

Löwith, have argued, but as a kind of selective secularization of the Christian eschatological tradition, taking up the millenarian expectation of a historical goal of developments in history, but not the 'apocalyptic' expectation of the end of history as a discontinuous rupturing of history (134). This one-sided distortion of the older eschatological tradition not only enabled the optimistic faith in unbroken and unambiguous progress to flourish. It also functions as theological or ideological justification for the interests of the powerful, who benefit from the modern Western project, and obscures the interests of the victims of alleged progress. Whereas millenarian optimism, which assures the endless prolongation of the present, is an ideology of the dominant, 'apocalyptic' eschatology, which hopes for the downfall of the present system of power and an alternative future, is the perspective of the dominated (135). Since millenarianism sustains the modern world as a system of domination and destruction, apocalyptic is its reverse side, 'its necessary accompaniment' (136).

Moltmann interprets the history of eschatological thought among Christian and Jewish theologians in this century against the background of the blows dealt to nineteenth-century millenarian optimism by the catastrophes of twentieth-century history, especially the events of the two World Wars (4–5, 13–14, 29–30). These experiences of catastrophe led both Christian and Jewish theologians to reject the progressivist understanding of history as a movement of advance towards history's *completion*, according to which the present acquires meaning only from its context in the advancing movement of time. Instead they sought *redemption* from history in the eschatological meaning of the present as a discontinuous moment. For Barth and Bultmann this meant abstraction from time and history in the experience of the timeless 'eternal present' of God. For the Jewish theologians and philosophers, however, redemption cannot in this way leave the world of time and history unredeemed. Though they differed considerably, the eschatological insight Moltmann draws from their work and especially values is an understanding of the experience of redemption in the discontinuous moment as disclosing the prospect of the *redemption of the future from the power of history* (44–46). This is a perspective from which one can not only reject the millenarian dream of the modern world, but also unmask it as an ideology of domination and destruction and resist its catastrophic effects.

The brilliant novelty of this interpretation of twentieth-century theological eschatology derives from its attention (characteristic of Moltmann) to the Jewish messianic thinkers as well as the Christian theologians. This enables Moltmann to show that turning from the progressivist interpretation of history to the eschatological moment in time held two different possibilities. One is the kind of vertical dialectic of time and eternity which abandons the future as a theological category. The other is equally dialectical, but sees the eschatological future of messianic redemption as a radically alternative future, rupturing the endless prolongation of the present and breaking the power of the perspective of the dominant. The latter possibility, of course, is the one Moltmann himself already developed in his early theology of hope, with its basis in the dialectic of the cross and resurrection of Jesus. The effect of the interpretation of twentieth-century theology he now offers is to situate his own theology of hope not only vis-à-vis his predecessors and contemporaries in the German-speaking Christian theological tradition, as he had already done in *Theology of Hope* (I), but also in a wider context of thought which includes Jewish theologians and philosophers, such as Ernst Bloch, to whom his early theology of hope was deeply indebted. His eschatology can in consequence be seen, not only as opposed to the transcendental eschatology of the dialectical theologians, but also as taking their reaction against the nineteenth century in a different direction. (However, a surprising omission from both chapters I and III of *The Coming of God* is serious attention to the Marxist tradition as a dialectical version of modern millenarianism [cf. 32, 189, 219], though Moltmann's critique of Marx is very briefly evident [32, 189], and it is characteristic of his inter-pretation of Bloch to prefer the Jewish to the Marxist elements in his thinking [30–33]. Marxism is a version of the modern millenarian dream which does not project the future as a prolongation of the present power of the dominant, and which arguably takes up precisely the apocalyptic side of the Jewish and Christian eschatological tradition, with its perspective from the underside of history, that Moltmann faults the modern millenarian dream for leaving aside. Marxism does fall foul of the charge of 'messianic presumption' [192] which Moltmann levels against all forms of 'historical millenarianism'. To some extent this already formed the critical element in his critical sympathy with Marxism in the days of his participation in the Christian-Marxist dialogue in the 1960s and his contribution to the political theology of that period. The development of his critique of 'historical millenarianism' in general seems to have strengthened his critique of Marxism, such that he can now say that 'the tendency towards totalitarianism' was 'inherent' in Marx's thought [189]. But this only makes the inclusion of no more than passing reference to Marx in a theological critique of modern millenarianism the more remarkable. The rapid decline of Marxism as a significant influence in the contemporary world hardly explains this, since that decline is itself a significant feature of the contemporary context which Christian eschatology must interpret and address.)

What has emerged in Moltmann's perception of the context since *Theology of Hope* is a more negative view of modernity in general.[13] The optimism of the 1960s rather than the catastrophes of the two World Wars was the more immediate context of *Theology of Hope*. That book should certainly not be regarded as merely a theological expression of the optimistic mood of its context. Its basing of eschatological hope on the dialectical christological basis of the cross and resurrection gave it a critical power in relation to facile optimism and to the use of optimism as an ideology masking oppression and misery. Its enduring theological value in other contexts has been proved. Moltmann's subsequent development of the theology of the cross was already implicit in it. But Moltmann's primary concern to restore hope for the future of the world to Christian theology and praxis encouraged something rather like a critical appreciation of the spirit of modernity. The role of Christian hope in

---

[13] For Moltmann's present understanding of modernity and its crisis, see also GPMW 15–30.

keeping society on the move in changes inspired by the hope of the coming kingdom of God placed Christians in frequent opposition to the status quo in society, but not so obviously to the whole historical project of modernity which Moltmann now calls the millennial dream of the modern world.

Moltmann now sees modernity as the project of the powerful to control and to create the future for themselves, a project of domination which, so far from offering any real future, has led and is leading to catastrophes which threaten the future of humanity and nature. He is not, of course, unappreciative of the real achievements of modernity, of which the recognition of the right of all human beings to freedom and equality is the least equivocal (190–191). But the modern project as a whole is fatally flawed by its aspiration to domination and its millenarian justification of this as progress:

> Rule over the peoples of the earth, the seizure of power over nature, and the project of a civilization that makes human beings the subjects of history: these things constitute the millenarian dream of 'the modern world'. The reality it takes is the scientific and technological civilization of 'modernity', whose inward and outward dissonances we are today experiencing and suffering in ever stronger forms. (190)

In explaining the way in which 'the deadliness of progress' (45) is apparent to those not blinded by the myth of the modern world, Moltmann describes the three main respects in which the domination and violence characteristic of the modern project have come to threaten the survival of the modern world: the nuclear threat, the ecological crisis, and the impoverishment of the Third World through the economic growth of the First (204–216; cf. also WJC 64–68). These constitute 'a crisis of modern scientific and technological civilization itself', a 'crisis of the paradigm in which people in the Western world put their trust and live' (211). They also, in requiring the modern world to be seen from the perspective of its victims, unmask its true nature (218) as a system of violent domination.

The question arises whether these catastrophic and threatening features of the contemporary world should be given an apocalyptic interpretation? Should the millenarian dream of the modern world, which has produced the current crises, be replaced by an apocalyptic interpretation of the impending doom to which it is leading? The question is inescapable, not only because such an apocalyptic interpretation is now itself a factor in the context Moltmann addresses, but also because there clearly is a sense in which these three forms of 'exterminism', as Moltmann calls them, have put human history in an 'end-time' situation. Of the nuclear threat, for example, he writes that 'our time has become time with a time-limit' (204; WJC 159): since the possibility of making nuclear weapons cannot now be removed, human history will now, as long as it lasts, be 'a permanent fight for survival', under a threat which must be staved off in the struggle to make this 'end-time as end-less as possible' (205). But Moltmann is now more aware than he was when he discussed the matter in *The Way of Jesus Christ* (159) that an apocalyptic interpretation of this realistically 'end-time' situation could be dangerous. To call the extermination now threatened by the modern world the 'apocalypse' could lead to irresponsibility, since it would encourage fatalistic resignation to the threat and also since it amounts to pushing onto God the responsibility for what should instead be recognized as human criminality on a vast scale (203, 218). The apocalyptic mood of the Western world in the face of the crisis of Western civilization Moltmann regards as trivial at best, dangerous at worst (203–204). It is a way of aiding and abetting the very exterminism it sees as apocalyptic.

The danger is that the historical implementation of an eschatological category could be as disastrous in this case as in that of the modern millenarian dream. The latter amounts to a premature attempt to realize the eschatological within history – and in doing so only one side of the eschatological expectation: the hope for a millennial goal of historical development. The apocalyptic interpretation of contemporary catastrophism equally amounts to a premature attempt to realize the eschatological within history – and in doing so only one side of the eschatological expectation: in this case, the apocalyptic expectation of a discontinuous end to history. 'Messianic presumption' and 'apocalyptic resignation' are opposite, but equally dangerous, distortions of the Christian eschatological expectation. However, while Moltmann condemns the irresponsibility of apocalyptic fatalism in the Western world, he takes a different attitude to apocalyptic views of the contemporary world among people in the Third World. The difference is that these recognize and unmask the evil of the exterministic systems of the modern world, and, so far from being fatalistic, encourage resistance and hope (218). In this sense they are apocalyptic in the way that the ancient Jewish and Christian apocalypses were. These spoke of historical and cosmic catastrophes, not in order to encourage collaboration with them or resignation to them, but in order to 'awaken the *resistance of faith* and the *patience of hope*. They spread hope in danger, because in the human and cosmic end they proclaim God's new beginning' (203). This is the perspective of the victims of history who anticipate a different future, redeemed from the power of history.

There is a sense in which Moltmann recognizes the contemporary context as an apocalyptic situation, not in the sense that the end to human history threatened by modern exterminism could in itself be the end that comes from God as God's new beginning for his creation (but cf. 234), but in the sense that it resembles the kind of situation to which apocalyptic eschatology in the Jewish and Christian tradition has often been a response. But this means that what is called for is unmasking of the evil and responsibility for it, and the resistance and hope that come from the kind of eschatological faith that the apocalypses expressed and that has its firmest theological foundation in the death and resurrection of Jesus Christ:

> The *memoria resurrectionis Christi* lets us look ... beyond the horizon of this world's end into God's new world. Life out of this hope then means already acting here and today in accordance with that world of justice and righteousness and peace, contrary to appearances, and contrary to all historical chances of success. It obliges us solemnly to abjure the spirit, logic and practice of the nuclear system of deterrence and all other systems of mass annihilation. It means an unconditional Yes to life in the face of the inescapable death of all the living. (233–234)

7. Politically and Pastorally Responsible Eschatology

The later paragraphs of the preceding section are sufficient to show that, in this book as throughout his dogmatics, Moltmann aims to write a politically (in the broadest sense of the word) responsible kind of theology. Eschatology, as his own analysis of the history and the context highlights, plays a political role (cf. 5–6). The point is not that Christian theology should be harnessed to political goals defined on other grounds, but that Christian theology's own political implications be recognized and its political effect be responsibly understood. This requires informed theological interpretation of the context, so that contextual eschatology (section I/1.6 above) and politically responsible eschatology are really two sides of a coin. Some readers may find *The Coming of God* disappointingly lacking in concrete implications for Christian praxis, but once again we need to be aware that this is a book which avoids unnecessary repetition of topics thoroughly discussed in its predecessors. Thus implications for ecological ethics and praxis of the expectation of the redemption of the whole cosmos received extensive treatment in *The Way of Jesus Christ* (270–273, 306–312), so that in his discussion of cosmic eschatology in *The Coming of God* (IV) Moltmann can take them for granted, merely pointing out that the kind of human solidarity with the earth which his eschatological expectation entails makes for an eschatology which is 'ecologically responsibly maintained' (279). On the other hand, the analysis of contemporary millenarianism and apocalyptic in chapter III is a new contribution to relating Christian eschatology to the current political context, and so, as we have seen in the preceding section, offers, not detailed prescriptions for praxis, but something much more fundamental: the kind of total stance towards the current crisis of modernity which Christian eschatological faith requires. This kind of fundamental stance towards key issues of the contemporary world is the kind of contribution to Christian praxis which Moltmann's major dogmatic works most often tend to offer. It is the most appropriate kind of contribution for dogmatics to make, and, since it provides the necessary context for more detailed and concrete practical implications to be drawn, should not be criticized for failing to provide the latter.

What we could call pastoral responsibility – relating more to the individual's personal experience of life, though for Moltmann this is always also life in community – naturally appears most obviously in the chapter on personal eschatology (II). Moltmann's main concern throughout this chapter is with how the expectation of one's own death and the experience of the death of others are an essential part of life lived to the full, with that love for life that Moltmann sees as the key characteristic of fully lived life (54: 'It is the conflict between love and death which confronts us with the only real problem of life'). How can we live without suppressing awareness of death? How can we expect 'life after death' without detracting from this life or diminishing our wholehearted giving of ourselves to life now? How can we help the bereaved to find consolation through mourning and to experience a rebirth of love for life out of their experience of death? These are the kinds of existential and practical questions Moltmann puts to the theological tradition, relates to the contemporary social context in which such issues are currently experienced, and answers in ways that aim at the sustaining of love and hope in human lives.

THE WORLD IN GOD OR GOD IN THE WORLD?

Response to Richard Bauckham

JÜRGEN MOLTMANN

It is not easy for me to reply to Richard Bauckham's first contribution: he knows too much! He knows my theology, with its strengths and weaknesses, better than I do myself. His books *Moltmann: Messianic Theology in the Making*[1] and *The Theology of Jürgen Moltmann*[2] are far and away the best accounts of my theology. But whereas when I come to the end of one book I have to concentrate on the subject of the next, he has the advantage of being able to survey the whole path I have taken, with its deviations, deflections and detours. So if I want to arrive at an overall view of my theological pilgrimage I have to depend on him. He knows better than I do where I have omitted something, or have repeated myself. He knows not only my conscious intentions (expressed at different times in the prefaces to my books) but my unconscious preferences and suppressions too. So from his accounts of my theological progress I can learn more than I would if I were to look back on it myself. My response to him must therefore begin with an expression of deep gratitude for his help. With his detailed

[1] Basingstoke: Marshall Pickering, 1997.
[2] Edinburgh: T. & T. Clark, 1995.

comments, he has set this last book especially, *The Coming of God*, in the context of a broad theological and ecumenical discussion. The fact that his colleagues Trevor Hart and Tim Gorringe have entered into this discussion with contributions of their own makes this book a joint affair between Tübingen and St Andrews, and this gives me great pleasure.

Richard Bauckham has picked out seven perspectives as the guiding and cohesive characteristics of my eschatology. I am well aware of the first three myself:

1. *Its christological foundation.* That is why I called *The Coming of God* a 'Christian' eschatology, using Christian not just as a general or embellishing epithet.

2. Its *integrative and redemptive intention.* When God, the Creator of all things, arrives at their redemption, all the things that have been separated and isolated, forsaken and lost, will be sought out, gathered up, and rescued from the abyss of nothingness.

3. The *processive and theocentric view of time and eternity.* This is self-evident if time and eternity are perceived and considered in the eschatological perspective.

Less conscious, and therefore perhaps unintentional, are the *contextual attention* and the *pastoral intention.* These two characteristics of my theological thinking no doubt seem to me so much a matter of course that I felt no need to make them a matter of deliberate intent. Once a pastor, always a pastor, and once politically involved, always politically interested. Someone who, ultimately speaking, lives consciously in his own time never does theology in the form of abstractions for all times; he pursues it as a contemporary for contemporaries, specifically, contextually, and in relation to its *kairos.* He makes no attempt to chase after every fashion, or the cloudy and mysterious 'spirit of the age', but merely deliberately accepts that his *locus theologicus* is his own place in his own time.

In this first 'response' to Richard Bauckham, I should like to concentrate a whole number of questions on only one point, because it is here that the fundamental decisions that precede every eschatology are made: and that point is the relationship between Trinity and eschatology. The other focus of Richard Bauckham's questions is eschatology and ethics; and I shall talk about this separately and in detail at the end, in my contribution on 'The Liberation of the Future and its Anticipations in History'.

The great eschatological question is this: *What is the ultimate goal? Is it the world in God, or God in the world?* This is the question of whether the world's redemption and consummation takes place within the divine Trinity, or whether the divine Trinity communicates itself and goes out of itself into history and the consummation of the world's salvation, thereby glorifying itself. Behind this is an old cosmological problem: can heaven and earth as the living spaces of finite creatures ever become the dwelling place of the infinite God? Or do all created beings not have to find their redemption in the inner space of the eternal life of the triune God? 'We do not know whether God is the space of his world or whether the world is his space', maintained an ancient Jewish midrash.[3] If we cling to the concept of the infinite God, then the concomitant is the recognition: *finitum non capax infiniti* – that the finite cannot contain the infinite. That is to say, the finite world finds space in the infinite God, but the infinite God does not find space in a finite world. But if we follow the Jewish teaching about the Shekinah, God's 'indwelling', and the Christian doctrine about the incarnation of the Son of God and the indwelling of God's Holy Spirit, then the infinite God can certainly 'indwell' his finite creation, its salvation history and its consummation, as once he indwelt Solomon's temple, and can interpenetrate everything human as in the God-human being Jesus Christ. The divine miracle is then that the finite is able to contain the infinite: *finitum capax infiniti.*

A present-day proponent of the first idea – the redemption and consummation of the world *in God* – is Hans Urs von Balthasar, to whom I have always felt bound from early on through the great respect which spans the differences

---

[3] Cf. M. Jammer, *Concepts of Space* (Cambridge, Massachusetts: Harvard University Press, 1984) 26ff.; Moltmann, GC 150.

between us. He entered into dispute with me in his article 'On a Christian Theology of Hope'.[4] He condemns every messianic interpretation of hope as 'Jewish', 'Old Testament' and 'pre-Christian', and declares that only the 'vertical' and 'presentative' interpretation of hope is Christian. I replied to him in my essay on 'Christian Hope: Messianic or Transcendental? A theological discussion with Joachim of Fiore and Thomas Aquinas'.[5] He then sent me the exposition of his own eschatology, *The Last Act*, volume 4 of his *Theo-Drama*[6] 'with sincere Easter greetings'. The last part, Part III, is entitled 'The World in God'.

Balthasar discovers in all works of the Trinity *ad extra* – creation, reconciliation and redemption – inner-trinitarian processes as well: creation is not an external work on God's part; it is 'a gift given by the Father to the Son'. Through the Holy Spirit, created beings acquire a share in the divine exchange of life of the inner-trinitarian perichoresis. The redemption of created being from sin and death through Christ must then be understood as 'a gift given by the Son to the Father'. By 'uniting all things in himself' (Eph 1:10), the Son draws all created being into his intimate relationship of Sonship to the Father. Redemption is therefore not just community *with* God; it is participation in the eternal inner-trinitarian life *in* God as well. The inner-trinitarian relations of the Father to the Son, of the Son to the Father, and of the Spirit to the Father and the Son are so 'open' that all created being can find its eternal home in them.

Balthasar finds the biblical basis for this integration of eschatology into the doctrine of the Trinity in the perichoretic forms of speech used in the Johannine writings, for example in Christ's high priestly prayer: 'That they may all be one, even as thou, Father, art *in me*, and I *in thee*, that they also may be

---

[4] 'Zu einer christlichen Theologie der Hoffnung', *Münchner Theologische Zeitschrift* 33 (1982) 241–260.

[5] 'Christliche Hoffnung Messianisch oder transzendental? Ein theologisches Gespräch mit Joachim von Fiore und Thomas von Aquin', *Münchner Theologische Zeitschrift* 33 (1982) 241–260.

[6] Vol. 4 (Einselden, 1983) = ET vol. 5 (tr. G. Harrison; San Francisco: Ignatius Press, 1988).

in us. . .' (John 17:21). So the perichoresis is not just something existing between like and like in the divine Trinity; it exists too between the unlike natures of God and human beings. If this acceptance of the fellowship of discipleship into the trinitarian fellowship of God is expanded to take in all created being, then the result is indeed the picture of a 'world in God'. The all-comprehending divine Trinity then becomes the living space and eternal environment of every creature. But then heaven, as the aeonic environment of the angels, and earth, as the temporal environment of human beings, are eliminated. All created beings are ultimately in God: *infinitum capax finiti* – the infinite contains the finite.

In my book *The Trinity and the Kingdom of God* (ET 5th edn, 1996, 90–96), I stressed this side of redemption: the world in the triune God. But in my eschatology, *The Coming of God,* I did not reiterate this idea, but put the other side of redemption at the centre: the glorification of the triune God *in* the new heaven and the new earth. I was moved to do this by the eschatological theme in the Old and New Testaments, where the glorification of God is related to the redemption of human history and the consummation of creation, and the inner-trinitarian glorification of the Father and the Son through the Holy Spirit is seen in precisely this happening. The key promise for the development of my eschatology is to be found in Isaiah's vision: 'The whole earth is full of his glory' (6:3). From that I concluded that this is the goal of creation from the beginning, and that with the creation of a world differentiated from himself and non-divine, God undertook a first kenosis: God involved himself in this endangered creation, and entered into it through his ˙Word and his Wisdom. That is why I chose for the doctrine of creation the title *God in Creation* (ET 1985). Even the creation of human beings to be 'the image of God' means a condescension, a descent on God's part, since he links his glory with this 'image'. How much more is God's transcendence over the world coupled with his immanence in the world in his covenant with Israel: 'I will be your God, you shall be my people.' God dwells in the midst of the Israelites. This promise of presence can be clearly discerned in the history of the Ark of the Covenant, of the Holy of Holies in the temple in Jerusalem, and the companionship on the way and comradeship in suffering of this 'indwelling' of God's in Israel's exiles. Every suffering on Israel's part for his Name's sake is a suffering on God's part too. Israel participates in God's sufferings in this world and will therefore one day be redeemed for participation in God's joy in this world.

In the framework of this Israelite Shekinah theology, the statements of Christian incarnation theology, and utterances about the outpouring and indwelling of God's Holy Spirit on all flesh become comprehensible. The eschatology which follows from both is the vision of the cosmic Shekinah, the cosmic incarnation, and the cosmic temple for the indwelling of the glory of the triune God. The eschatological vision of the new heaven and the new earth in Revelation 21 picks up the promises of Isaiah and Ezekiel, and sees itself as the fulfilment of the Jewish and Christian hope for 'the new Jerusalem'. But if in the end 'the whole earth is full of his glory' – if ultimately God is 'all *in* all' – then the new creation must be fashioned in such a way that it can endure God's glory without perishing from it, just as redeemed human beings must be in a position 'to look on God' without dying. That has to be a *finitum capax infiniti* – a finitude that embraces infinity. The Gospel of John itself sees no problem here about also reversing the indwelling: the Father and the Son will 'make their home' with the person who loves Jesus (14:23). For Paul too the consummation of Christ's rule over everything, and finally over death, is followed by the 'handing over' of the kingdom, so that God may be all *in* all (1 Cor 15:28). So everything will not be in God, but God will be in everything.

Where are the differences? If eschatology is integrated in the divine Trinity, the result is a 'presentative' eschatology of eternity, in which the horizontal dimensions of time no longer play any part. The eschatological history of redemption is played out only *vertically*. This 'presentative', 'vertical' hope of eternity loses the remembrance of the biblical history: the Old Testament and Israel are forgotten. Nor does it now require the hope for a still open, hidden, and real future of God's that is still to come. But the bond with the Old Testament and the Israelite history of promise is constitutive for every Christian eschatology.

Without it the Christian hope of redemption becomes gnostic
– a reproach that is indeed often levelled against Hans Urs von
Balthasar.

Nevertheless, I see no entirely unbridgeable contradiction
between his view, according to which the world's eschatology –
'the last act' – takes place in the eternal Trinity, and my own
view, according to which the eternal Trinity glorifies itself in
the redemption of history and the consummation of the world.
The two can be related to one another like mirror images, as it
were. So I would answer the question in the Jewish midrash by
saying the following: the world will find space in God in a worldly
way when God indwells the world in a divine way. That is a
reciprocal perichoresis of the kind already experienced here
in *love*: the person who abides in love abides *in God*, and *God in
him* (1 John 4:16). According to Paul, this presence of mutual
indwellings is here called love, but then it will be called glory.

THE LOGIC OF HELL

JÜRGEN MOLTMANN

1. Is There Fire in Hell?

A short time ago, in their book *The Mystery of Salvation: The Story of God's Gift*,[1] the Doctrine Commission of the Church of England did away with hell fire, replacing it by 'total non-being': 'Hell is not eternal torment, but it is the final and irrevocable choosing of that which is opposed to God so completely and so absolutely that the only end is total non-being' (199). Although this statement is only made in passing, in a brief paragraph on 'the final judgment', it made something of a sensation in the press. 'Infernal Salvation', wrote the *Guardian* on 12 January 1996. As early as 1962, the somewhat bizarre question, 'Is there fire in hell?' had sparked off fierce discussions in the Norwegian church and led to divisions within it. The fascination of evil has become particularly strong again in the 'post-modern' world. But even in the Middle Ages it awakened atrocious and terrifying visions which painters delighted to paint in elaborate detail in the churches. 'Fire' was a religious method for destroying heretics. The end of the world was imagined as the day when the world will go down to destruction in a great conflagration.

This belief held its ground right down to the day when the bomb fell on Hiroshima in August 1945. But since Hiroshima, the imagination of modern men and women has been fascinated

---

[1] London: Church House Publishing, 1995.

no longer by burning but by annihilation. So it is nothing out
of the way that the Church of England's Doctrine Commission should replace the hell fire of old by the annihilation of
modern times. 'Fire' and 'annihilation' are merely metaphors
for an inescapable remoteness from God, or for a God-
forsakenness from which there is no way out. Hell is not
supposed to be an eternal concentration camp from which
there is no release, even by death. On the contrary, it is supposed
to be 'the ultimate affirmation of the reality of human freedom',
according to the Doctrine Commission: 'It is our conviction
that the reality of hell (and indeed of heaven) is the ultimate
affirmation of the reality of human freedom.' And it is here
that the real theological problem about this modern explanation
of hell lies.

2. The Logic of Hell

The logic of hell is nothing other than the logic of human free
will, in so far as this is identical with freedom of choice. The
theological argument runs as follows: 'God whose being is love
preserves our human freedom, for freedom is the condition of
love. Although God's love goes, and has gone, to the uttermost,
plumbing the depth of hell, the possibility remains for each
human being of a final rejection of God, and so of eternal life'
(198). Does God's love preserve our free will, or does it free
our enslaved will, which has become un-free though the power
of sin? Does God love free men and women, or does he seek
the men and women who have become lost? It is apparently
not Augustine who is the Father of Anglo-Saxon Christianity;
the Church Father who secretly presides over it is his opponent
Pelagius. And it is Erasmus who is the saint of modern times,
not Luther or Calvin. Let us gather together some arguments
against this logic of hell.

The first conclusion, it seems to me, is that it is inhumane,
for there are not many people who can enjoy free will where
their eternal fate in heaven or hell is concerned. What happens
to the people who never had the choice, or never had the power
to decide? The children who died early, the severely handi-
capped, the people suffering from geriatric diseases? Are they

in heaven, in total non-being, or somewhere between, in a limbo? What happens to the billions of people whom the gospel has never reached and who were never faced with the choice? What happens to God's chosen people Israel, the Jews, who are unable to believe in Christ? Are all the adherents of other religions destined for annihilation? And not least: how firm must our own decision of faith be if it is to preserve us from total non-being? Anyone who faces men and women with the choice of heaven or hell, does not merely expect too much of them. It leaves them in a state of uncertainty, because we cannot base the assurance of our salvation on the shaky ground of our own decisions. If we think about these questions, we have to come to the conclusion that in the end not many are going to be with God in heaven; most people are going to be in total non-being. Or is the presupposition of this logic of hell perhaps an illusion – the presupposition that it all depends on the human being's free will?

If ultimately, after God's final judgment on human decisions of will, all that is left is 'heaven' and 'hell', we still have to ask ourselves: what is going to happen to the earth, and all the earthly creatures, which the Creator after all found to be 'very good'? If they too are to disappear into 'total non-being', because they are no longer required, how can there then be 'a new earth'?

The logic of hell seems to me not merely inhumane but also extremely atheistic: here the human being in his freedom of choice is his own lord and god. His own will is his heaven – or his hell. God is merely the accessory who puts that will into effect. If I decide for heaven, God must put me there; if I decide for hell, he has to leave me there. If God has to abide by our free decision, then we can do with him what we like. Is that 'the love of God'? Free human beings forge their own happiness and are their own executioners. They do not just dispose over their lives here; they decide on their eternal destinies as well. So they have no need of any God at all. After a God has perhaps created us free as we are, he leaves us to our fate. Carried to this ultimate conclusion, the logic of hell is secular humanism, as Feuerbach, Marx and Nietzsche already perceived a long time ago.

3. The Gospel of Christ's Descent into Hell

The Christian doctrine of hell is to be found in the gospel of
Christ's descent into hell, not in a modernization of hell into
total non-being. Our century has produced more infernos than
all the centuries before us: The gas ovens of Auschwitz and the
atomizing of Hiroshima heralded an age of potential mass
annihilation through ABC weapons. So many people have
experienced hells! It is pointless to deny hell. It is a possibility
that is constantly round about us and within us. In this situation,
the gospel about Christ's descent into hell is particularly
relevant: Christ suffered the 'inescapable remoteness from God'
and the 'God-forsakenness' that knows no way out, so that he
could bring God to the God-forsaken. He comes 'to seek that
which is lost'. He suffered the torments of hell so that for
us they are not hopeless and without escape. Christ brought
hope to the place where according to Dante all who enter
must 'abandon hope'. 'If I make my bed in hell thou art there'
(Ps 139:8). Through his sufferings Christ has destroyed hell.
Hell is open: 'Hell where is thy victory?' (1 Cor 15:55).

> Thou must look upon hell and the eternity of torment not in
> thyself, not in themselves, not in those who are damned . . . Look
> upon the heavenly picture of Christ who for thy sake descended
> into hell and was forsaken by God as one eternally damned, as he
> said on the cross: My God, why hast thou forsaken me? See, in that
> picture thy hell is conquered and thy uncertain election made sure.
> Seek thyself only in Christ and not in thyself, so wilt thou eternally
> find thyself in him.

So wrote Luther in 1519, in his moving 'Sermon on preparing
for death'. For Luther, hell is not a place in the next world,
the underworld; it is an experience of God. For him, Christ's
descent into hell was his experience of God-forsakenness
from Gethsemane to Golgotha. In the crucified Christ we see
what hell is, because through him it has been overcome.

The true universality of God's grace is not grounded in
'secular humanism'. It is on that humanism, rather – as the
logic of free will shows – that the double end is based: heaven –
hell, being – non-being. But the universality of God's grace is

grounded on the theology of the cross. This is the way it was presented by all the Christian theologians who were criticized for preaching 'universal reconciliation', most recently Karl Barth. In his 'confession of hope' the Swabian revivalist preacher Christoph Blumhardt (who profoundly influenced modern Protestant theology in Germany) put it this way:

> There can be no question of God's giving up anything or anyone in the whole world, either today or in all eternity. The end has to be: Behold, everything is God's! Jesus comes as the one who has borne the sins of the world. Jesus can judge but not condemn. My desire is to have preached this as far as the deepest depths of hell, and I shall never be confounded.

Judgment is not God's last word. Judgment establishes in the world the divine righteousness on which the new creation is to be built. But God's last word is 'Behold, I make *all things* new' (Rev 21:5). From this no one is excepted. Love is God's compassion with the lost. Transforming grace is God's punishment for sinners. It is not the right to choose that defines the reality of human freedom. It is the doing of the good.

IMAGINATION FOR THE KINGDOM OF GOD?

Hope, Promise, and the Transformative Power of an Imagined Future

TREVOR HART

> *Theology . . . is imagination for the kingdom of God in the world, and for the world in God's kingdom* (CoG xiv).

What I propose to do in this chapter is to explore some themes relating to the transformative impact of eschatological hope upon the shape of the Christian present. I begin with some select examples of this which themselves serve to raise a question about an apparent incommensurability between the experienced present and the hoped for future of God. This theme will concern us again later in the chapter. Next I turn to two secular analyses of the transformative impact of the human capacity to imagine future, those of George Steiner and Ernst Bloch. Finally, turning at last to Jürgen Moltmann's work, I shall explore some of the ways in which it forces us to differentiate a distinctively Christian imagining of the future from these extra-Christian versions.

Seeing Beyond the Silence

Shusako Endo's novel *Silence*[1] tells the story of a seventeenth-century Jesuit missionary. Sebastian Rodrigues is sent to Japan

[1] S. Endo, *Silence* (London: Penguin, 1988).

in 1643 at the tail end of the so-called 'Christian century' in that country's history. It is a time of enormous hostility to the Christian faith and all that is associated with it, a backlash of indigenous culture against the rapid growth and flourishing of the church there. Upon his arrival (secretly) Rodrigues is met by some of the many thousands of native believers clinging tenaciously to a way of life outlawed by the authorities and punishable by savage torture and execution. The novel recounts his brief existence as a guerrilla priest, emerging from the forest to baptize, hear confessions and celebrate the eucharist for communities of the faithful who have for several decades been forced to keep their faith well hidden from public gaze, and deprived of priestly ministry. It tells of his capture and torture, and of the awful struggle he has in coming to terms with his own eventual forced apostasy, trampling on an image of the face of Christ in order to save, not himself, but Japanese Christians held in adjacent prison cells, from the cruelty of judicial execution.

At one key juncture in the story the Samurai come and arrest two elders of a village where Rodrigues is being hidden. Accused of practising an outlawed religion, and refusing to spit on a crucifix, the two men are duly sentenced to death. Yet neither they nor anyone else in the community will do that which will secure their immediate release: betray the priest. The men are executed, bound to two stakes on the sea shore, stakes positioned carefully and cleverly so that the incoming tide will not quite cover their heads, but will come and go, gradually sapping their strength and bearing their life away with it. Endo narrates this part of his tale from Rodrigues' own perspective:

> Night came. The red light of the guards' blazing fire could be seen faintly even from our mountain hut, while the people of Tomogi gathered on the shore and gazed at the dark sea. So black were the sea and the sky that no one knew where Mokichi and Ichizo were. Whether they were alive or dead no one knew. All with tears were praying in their hearts. And then, mingled with the sound of the waves, they heard what seemed to be the voice of Mokichi. Whether to tell the people that his life had not yet ebbed away or to strengthen his own resolution, the young man gaspingly sang a Christian hymn:

We're on our way, we're on our way
We're on our way to the temple of Paradise,
To the temple of Paradise . . .
To the great temple . . .

All listened in silence to the voice of Mokichi; the guards also listened; and again and again, amid the sound of the rain and the waves, it broke upon their ears.[2]

The silence of which the novel's title speaks is God's seeming silence in the face of his people's enormous suffering. This, above all, is the issue with which Rodrigues is driven to wrestle as he comes to terms with the vulnerability of his own faith. Yet what stands out in passages such as this one, and what Rodrigues himself eventually discovers through his journey to self-knowledge through suffering, is the striking and ironic juxtaposition of darkness and light, terror and fearlessness, humiliation and great dignity, the inevitability of death and the expectancy of new life. The Japanese Christians go to their deaths singing this hymn not (as Rodrigues himself at first avers) as a form of 'whistling in the dark to keep their spirits up', but because they are possessed by a vision of God's faithfulness and his promised future which subverts the darkness of their experienced present. They are afraid, yet not bowed. In death, as in life, they bear the apparent silence and absence of God because they share a hope which transcends this present, and which bathes it in a quite different light.

It would seem that it is often thus in the experience of God's people. The times of great struggle or suffering, when to all appearances God's face is hidden, have often been precisely those times which have given birth to the most colourful and convicted visions of God's promised salvation, when the sense of promise has, as it were, been renewed and developed. Refusing to buckle under the painful weight of actuality (whether that be persecution, exile or whatever) the faith which holds fast to such hope resists and contradicts it, insisting upon living as if it were not thus, living in the light not of the way things are, but of the way things will be in God's future. Two brief examples from Scripture will suffice to illustrate this further.

[2] Endo, *Silence*, 102.

First, chapters 40–55 of Isaiah, written from the estrangement of exile in Babylon at a time when the nation of Judah was effectively a nation no more, removed from the now ruined sanctuary of Zion around which her faith was focused, frog-marched in fetters some seven hundred miles east across the desert plains, broken on the wheel of events which were also the instrument of God's judgment. The land of promise, the land flowing with milk and honey, was now preserved and cherished only in her corporate memory, the theme of so many folk songs and tales designed to preserve a sense of national identity. The familiar words of the psalmist from this same era capture in a sentence or two what the hearts of the people must have felt: 'By the rivers of Babylon we sat and we wept when we remembered Zion. . . . How can we sing the songs of Yahweh in a strange land?' (Ps 137:1–4).

Yet, curiously juxtaposed with such understandable lament, we find the green and vigorous shoots of new hope bursting through the arid and seemingly inhospitable soil of exile.

> Comfort my people, says your God . . . In the wilderness prepare the way of Yahweh, make straight in the desert a highway for our God . . . For a long time I have held my peace, I have kept still and restrained myself; now I will cry out like a woman in labour, I will gasp and pant . . . Now thus says Yahweh, he who created you, O Jacob, he who formed you, O Israel: Do not fear, for I have redeemed you; I have called you by name, you are mine . . . Do not remember the former things, or consider the things of old. I am about to do a new thing.

And so it continues. As shrewd estimates of political reality go this can hardly number high on anyone's list. Yet Deutero-Isaiah weaves a hopeful vision which contradicts the apparent realities of his people's circumstance, promising what seems beyond the bounds of current possibility, convinced that the redemptive capacities of the God who created all things cannot be circum-scribed or measured by expectations rooted in the actual. In his imagination the prophet sees beyond the given to an un-expected and surprising future, a future in which his fellow Jews are able to find hope even in the midst of despair, renewed purpose in the face of servitude and an identity as the people of God which exile had threatened to obliterate. Holding firm to such a vision, the present suffering loses its ultimacy and hence its capacity to crush the spirit.

Something similar may be observed in the New Testament book of Revelation. Now it is the Christian church rather than the Jewish nation which finds itself in a form of exile in a world dominated by the forces of Roman empire. Writing to those for whom resistance to this regime and faithfulness to Christ may mean persecution, arrest and even death, John unfolds what Richard Bauckham has classified as a 'prophetic apocalypse' which discloses through its imaginative form a transcendent perspective on this world and the events of contemporary history, setting them in the wider and fuller context of God's ultimate purposes for the coming of his kingdom. Bauckham writes as follows:

> John (and thereby his readers with him) is taken up into heaven in order to see the world from the heavenly perspective. He is given a glimpse behind the scenes of history so that he can see what is really going on in the events of his time and place. He is also transported in vision into the final future of the world, so that he can see the present from the perspective of what its final outcome must be, in God's ultimate purpose for human history. The effect of John's visions, one might say, is to expand his readers' world, both spatially (into heaven) and temporally (into the eschatological future), or, to put it another way, to open their world to divine transcendence. The bounds which Roman power and ideology set to the readers' world are broken open and that world is seen as open to the greater purpose of its transcendent Creator and Lord. It is not that the here-and-now are left behind in an escape into heaven or the eschatological future, but that the here-and-now look quite different when they are opened to transcendence.
>
> The world seen from this transcendent perspective . . . is a kind of new symbolic world into which John's readers are taken as his artistry creates it for them. But really it is not another world. It is John's readers' concrete, day-to-day world seen in heavenly and eschatological perspective. As such its function . . . is to counter the Roman imperial view of the world, which was the dominant ideological perception of their situation which John's readers naturally tended to share.[3]

[3] R. Bauckham, *The Theology of the Book of Revelation* (Cambridge: Cambridge University Press, 1993) 7–8.

What we have here, then, is an imaginative vision in which the dominant way of seeing things (both present and future) is fundamentally challenged and an alternative picture painted of the potentialities and possibilities inherent in God's future. Rome is not the ultimate authority, and will not have the final victory. God is not absent, and his kingdom is coming. Whatever experience may suggest, and whatever the voices of power may insist, these are the realities of the readers' situation. The challenge to the Christian church in the midst of the all-too-real discomfort and danger of actuality is, as always, to live in the light of this alternative vision rather than submitting to the dominant ideology, even when the latter is backed up with military and political force. Revelation, like Deutero-Isaiah, offers God's people a subversive vision, furnishing the resources to wage what Amos Wilder calls a campaign of 'guerrilla theatre', a battle for people's hearts and wills, and rooted firmly in a bid to capture their imaginations.[4]

Imagination is a key category for making sense of this hopeful living towards God's future. One of the key functions of imagination is the presentation of the otherwise absent. In other words, we have the capacity through imagination to call to mind objects, persons or states of affairs which are other than those which appear to confront us in what, for want of a better designation, we might call our 'present actuality' (i.e. that which we are currently experiencing). I do not say 'reality' precisely because the real itself may well prove to be other than what appears to be actual. Another key role of imagination in human life is as the source of the capacity to interpret, to locate things within wider patterns or networks of relationships which are not given, but which we appeal to tacitly in making sense of things.[5] We see things as particular sorts of things, and this is, in substantial part, an imaginative activity. And, since more than one way of seeing or taking things is often possible, what appears to be the case may actually change with an imaginative shift of perspective, rendering a quite distinct picture of the

---

[4] A. Wilder, *Theopoetic: Theology and the Religious Imagination* (Philadelphia: Fortress Press, 1976).

[5] On this see, e.g. M. Warnock, *Imagination* (London: Faber, 1976).

real. As numerous accounts of *Gestalt* and paradigm shifts have observed, a useful model for this is the religious 'conversion' in which the selfsame set of particulars is observed or experienced by the subject now quite differently because viewed in a wholly new light, located within a different pattern. In the examples we have just considered, the difference between what the eye of faith 'sees' and what is seen by the faithless eye is precisely a difference of interpretation or, we might say, a different imagining of reality. The prophet in each case feeds the imagination of God's people to enable them to see the world in ways other than those engendered by the dominant ideology.

Imagination, then, enables us to call to mind sets of circumstances other than the actual. These may be things which we (or others) have known in the past but which we are not perceiving or otherwise experiencing in the present (in which case we are dealing either with some form of memory or historical reconstruction). Or, drawing again inevitably on our knowledge and experience of what has been and what is, we may think about the future, about what is yet to be. In this case our expectations will be shaped more precisely by the 'laws' of association/nature which seem to govern the world of our experience. Thus, while we may well imagine any number of futures which could but will not in fact arise (some perhaps highly *unlikely* to do so) we will, in this mode, not be prone to imagine things which are, so far as we are able to judge from a shared human experience of the world, not *possible* futures. States of affairs which trespass beyond the bounds of the unlikely or improbable into the realm of that which is in some obvious way incommensurable with the world as we know it we might ordinarily choose to classify as fantasy rather than expectation, and as such a distinct sort of imaginative activity. In fantasy, for example, while we must always root our imagining in some identifiable way in the regularities and continuities of what we have known (we cannot imagine *ab initio*), we none the less modify the known to such an extent that what results is well removed from either memory or expectation. I labour this point slightly because it is relevant to issues raised later in the chapter.

Imagination and the Grammar of Hope

I want now to focus on the human capacity for hope: the capacity, that is to say, to imagine a future which, in broad terms, furnishes an object of hope for us in the present, a vision of how things may be to which, as we say, we look forward. What I am specifically interested in, again, is the way in which certain aspects of that capacity exercise a necessary and transformative reflexive impact upon our ways of being in the present. As already indicated we shall proceed by drawing on the thought of two Jewish thinkers who have engaged carefully with these issues.

George Steiner in his classic work on the nature of language and translation, *After Babel*,[6] notes that our ability as human beings to think about (we might reasonably substitute the word 'imagine') temporality, to construe past and future as distinct from the present, is in large measure bound up with our use of language. Our possession of a grammar complete with tenses is what makes such imaginative projection possible. 'Language', Steiner writes, 'happens in time but also, very largely, creates the time in which it happens.'[7] Language, that is to say, shapes our perception of the moment of speech or thought as present, and of other times as either past or future. Especially in the case of the future this capacity to transcend the present, to speak of or imagine a state of affairs other than the present, is vital to the direction of our ways of being in the world. 'The status of the future of the verb,' he observes, 'is at the core of existence. It shapes the image we carry of the meaning of life, and of our personal place in that meaning.'[8]

The potential shaping impact of such linguistic or imaginative projection was already clearly grasped by Karl Marx who, in reference to what he deemed illusory hopes of a religious nature, construed that impact in negative terms, as debilitating the urge for political reform in the real world. The substance of religious belief (the opiate of the people) is a deliberately engineered

---

[6] G. Steiner, *After Babel* (2nd edn, Oxford: Oxford University Press, 1992). See especially chapter 3, 'Word Against Object'.

[7] Steiner, *After Babel*, 144.

[8] Steiner, *After Babel*, 145.

illusion designed to generate and sustain fantasies and dreams which will divert the attention of the oppressed masses from the actual awfulness of their circumstance long enough for their labour to be thoroughly exploited. What is required, on Marx's analysis, is a regime of cold turkey sufficient to kick the habit, allowing reality to break through the illusion, and provoking in due course a thoroughly justifiable reaction against those pushing the drug. But Steiner turns this around, and reminds us of the deliberate suppression in former communist regimes not this time of hope, but of memory. The outlawing of the past, the careful editing of national memory was designed precisely to mould and shape present consciousness, and thereby to control it and direct it in particular ways. 'One can imagine a comparable prohibition of the future', he ruminates. 'What would existence be like in a total (totalitarian) present, in an idiom which limited projective utterances to the horizon of Monday next?'⁹ His point is clear. The suppression of imaginative projection into the future, the enforced removal of the future tense from the language, would just as surely be debilitating with respect to present activism and energy, because future tenses necessarily entail the possibility of change of one sort or another. Without them, hope for a better future is simply not possible. Such hope, far from dulling the senses to the pain of the present, is precisely the thing which makes a deprived present unbearable.

Steiner proceeds to suggest that human life as such is characterized (and distinguished from other forms of life) by its essential directedness towards the future, and its fundamental capacity for hope. And the capacity to imagine and to speak of what lies beyond the given here and now is vital to this direction. 'We move forward', he writes in characteristically graphic vein, 'in the slipstream of the statements we make about tomorrow morning, about the millenium.'¹⁰ Through imaginative construction we posit what he calls, paradoxically, 'axiomatic fictions' which, as it were, drag us forward in their wake and energize our living towards tomorrow rather than merely in

⁹ Steiner, *After Babel*, 146.
¹⁰ Steiner, *After Babel*, 168.

today. We live in hope. Apart from it we are inert and, like sharks in water, would quickly drown in our own despair, trapped in an eternal and 'total' present. Change, progress, intention, excitement, anticipation, all the things which enable us to cope with and to overcome the undoubted pains, trials and disasters which we experience, these are bound up with our movement towards the future. 'The conventions of forwardness so deeply entrenched in our syntax make for a constant, sometimes involuntary, resilience. Drown as we may, the idiom of hope, so immediate to the mind, thrusts us to the surface.'[11] This ability to imagine ahead, to see beyond the given to a better and brighter future, Steiner avers, furnishes distinct advantages in the evolutionary process, and has doubtless contributed to the survival and superiority of humankind. 'Natural selection', he suggests, 'has favoured the subjunctive.'[12]

We might, I suppose, prefer a more specifically theological construal of that claim, but its essential point is well made. The capacity to construct futurity, we might rather say, which is a central function of the imagination, is essential to our humanity and to its movement forward in the creative purposes of God.

Steiner identifies another closely related imaginative function as equally important in this regard which we must mention briefly; namely, our capacity for counter-factuality, for the deliberate construction of falsehoods or alternities. The generation of 'counter-worlds' is, of course, the source of fantasy, illusion and lies. But it is also the source of our ability to see how things might be different (i.e. how they might change in the future, or how the present can already be seen or taken differently), to refuse to accept the world as it is given to us. In so far as the language which we habitually use to describe the world, the ways in which we image and construe it, are a vital component in the shaping of our experience of it, to the extent, that is to say, that reality is a social and linguistic construct (and there is no need to capitulate altogether to radical accounts of this in order to recognize some truth in the claim), the capacity to picture and to speak of the world otherwise than in accordance

[11] Steiner, *After Babel*, 167.
[12] Steiner, *After Babel*, 228.

with the currently favoured social construct, is itself a capacity to change reality, to deconstruct and then reconstruct it for ourselves. As Christians, for example, we shall probably want to construe the world in which we live as one in which Christ is Lord, rather than as a meaningless complex bio-chemical accident on a cooling cinder; and this insistence on describing the world differently will generate quite distinct ways of being in the world.

Turning now from Steiner to Ernst Bloch, we find a strikingly similar recognition of the essential directedness of human life towards the future, and of the vital contribution of imaginative hope in the realization of this futured existence. In his massive magnum opus, *The Principle of Hope*,[13] Bloch traces the patterns and manifestations of this constant 'venturing beyond', as he calls it, in the forms of human life.

Human existence, Bloch observes, is driven by cravings, urgings, desires and strivings, all of which are essentially forms of discontent with the way things are. Some of our cravings are duly clothed by imagination with particular form, and transformed into wishes. But the nature of wishes is to be somewhat detached from moral commitment. We may entertain two or more mutually exclusive wishes at once. 'I wish I were playing golf rather than sitting at my word processor' and 'I wish I were sitting in the garden at home with a good book instead of . . .' are wishes which, as such, may both be entertained at once. Only when we choose between them and begin to invest them with moral intent, acting towards their eventual fulfilment, do they become what Bloch calls 'wants'. The central category with which Bloch deals in expounding all this is that of dreams, and especially daydreams. In daydreams, he notes, we are more in conscious control of our imaginings than in dreams, and we are able to bring our wishes and wants to ficititious fulfilment. But daydreams are certainly not just the stuff of self-gratifying entertainment or armchair aspiration. They are not contemplative or analgesic, but invigorating and empowering. All freedom movements, Bloch insists, are inspired and guided by daydreams, by utopian aspirations which posit a disjunction

[13] E. Bloch, *The Principle of Hope* (3 vols, Oxford: Blackwell, 1986).

between knowledge of how bad the world is and 'recognition of how good it could be if it were otherwise'.[14] 'The pull towards what is lacking', he writes, 'never ends . . . The lack of what we dream about hurts not less, but more. It thus prevents us from getting used to deprivation.'[15] Daydreams, then, are the imaginative form in which hope is cast.

Bloch does, however, draw a careful distinction between imagination's construction of daydreams on the one hand and what he calls 'mere fantasizing' on the other. Genuine hope is possessed of both subjective and objective aspects. As a component of human consciousness it is, nevertheless, soundly rooted in real ontological possibilities in the world. Hope, that is to say, as manifest in daydreams, intuits what Bloch calls 'a Not-Yet-Being of an expectable kind'. It 'does not play around and get lost in an Empty-Possible, but psychologically anticipates a Real-Possible'.[16]

Here we must identify Bloch's framework as a metaphysic of the world and its history as an incomplete process which moves forward, above all, through the capacity of human hope to lay hold of the 'Not-Yet-Existent' and the 'Not-Yet-Conscious' and, precisely in anticipating them, to transform the present, energizing us in the here and now to transcend the here-and-now with its apparent limitations and actual deprivations. Hope empowers our striving towards its own realization. But it must be genuine hope, and not mere fantasy. Only a Real-Possible has the resources to draw us forward into the future in this way. The *Novum* (genuinely new thing) to which hope attaches itself and looks forward is, paradoxically, in one sense not new at all. It is wholly new inasmuch as it has never previously existed, and inasmuch as the conditions for the possibility of its existence may not yet themselves even exist. But it is, none the less (and in retrospect will be able to be seen to have been) a real possibility, because the conditions for that possibility are already latent within the conditions and possibilities of the present.

---

[14] Bloch, *The Principle of Hope*, 95.
[15] Bloch, *The Principle of Hope*, 451.
[16] Bloch, *The Principle of Hope*, 144.

An illustration may serve to make the point here. In climbing a mountain, while one may glimpse the summit through the clouds from the car park at the bottom, experience on the climb is often characterized by being able to see only the next ridge, not knowing precisely what lies beyond it, or whether and how the route transcends it and subsequent visual blockages to reach the top. Having glimpsed the top, however, knowing it to be there to be reached, one carries on and overcomes these numerous limited horizons, committed to the task and determined to attain the peak. The apparent disjunctions and discontinuities presented to sight do not make life easy, but they are not insurmountable. We press on, even though we cannot see exactly where we are going or how the top is to be reached. On having reached the top, however, and turning to consider the distance we have climbed, it is sometimes possible for the whole route from the car park to be more or less visible at least in its broad outlines, so that the possibilities and continuities of each stage along the way are manifest in a manner that they were not previously.

What the imagination does in hope, its 'utopian function' as Bloch calls it, is thus twofold. First it leaps over the limits and perceived discontinuities which lie between present reality and the utopian future, even though it cannot yet see clearly the route from here to there – it intuits it as a Real-Possible. Second, through setting this vision before us and enabling us to 'look forward' to it, hope drives us forward, empowering and guiding ways of being in the world in the present which themselves serve to create the conditions in which the object of hope becomes possible. There is no hint of a rationalistic prediction or plotting of the future here, therefore. We cannot, for Bloch, *know* the future, or precisely how it will arise. (In passing, it is perhaps worth asking whether, if we could, there would always be aspects of what lies in front of us which would so cripple us with fear as to render us incapable of action?) Hope, as Bloch sees it, is that activity of the imagination which lays hold intuitively of something which may or may not actually come to pass, but the potential for which lies genuinely within the latent capacities of the system or process of human history. 'The historical content of hope', he writes, 'is human culture referred to its concrete-utopian horizon.'[17]

The Imagination of Glory

In the remainder of this chapter I shall consider some of the key elements in Moltmann's eschatology which, I shall suggest, compels us at certain points to differentiate a distinctively Christian understanding of hope from general analyses such as those offered by Steiner and Bloch, valuable and compatible though these remain in many respects. My overview of Moltmann will draw particular attention to questions pertaining to the nature of the relationship between present and future, old and new creations, and the transition between them, and to the roles of imagination as a locus of God's transforming activity in human life.

The goad of the promised future

Like Steiner and Bloch, Moltmann insists that the capacity to envisage a hoped for future, far from dulling our sensibilities to the pain of the present, actually serves to heighten those sensibilities and is a powerful stimulus to resistance and reaction which itself drives us to break away from the present towards the future (TH 100). Hence:

> Faith, wherever it develops into hope, causes not rest but unrest, not patience but impatience. It does not calm the unquiet heart, but is itself this unquiet heart in man. Those who hope in Christ can no longer put up with reality as it is, but begin to suffer under it, to contradict it. Peace with God means conflict with the world, for the goad of the promised future stabs inexorably into the flesh of every unfulfilled present. (TH 21)

While on the one hand, therefore, this hope certainly strengthens our resolve in bearing 'the cross of the present', granting us a perspective which robs that cross of its finality (TH 31), on the other hand it 'sets loose powers that are critical

---

[17] Bloch, *The Principle of Hope*, 146.

of being' and seek to subvert what is in the name of the One who is to come (TH 119). It is anything but an encouragement towards a resigned or passive submission in the face of injustice, suffering and other characteristic features of the present regime therefore. On the contrary, its transformative impact upon the present lies precisely in its furnishing of 'inexhaustible resources for the creative, inventive imagination of love'.

> It constantly provokes and produces thinking of an anticipatory kind in love to man and the world, in order to give shape to the newly dawning possibilities in the light of the promised future, in order as far as possible to create here the best that is possible, because what is promised is within the bounds of possibility. (TH 34–35)

The possibilities of God's open future are, then, genuinely anticipated in the midst of this present age, with a resultant transformation of present ways of being and doing and thinking in the world on the part of God's people. This takes place, we might aver, primarily through the stretching of their imaginations, and thereby the reshaping of their expectations, desires and values, fashioning an alternative vision of 'the bounds of possibility' and liberating people from the despairing horizons of a history rooted in the past rather than open to the future.

Imagining future and reimaging present

Picking up on the previous point, Moltmann indicates that the nature of hope is to force a radical reinterpretation (reimagining or reimaging) of the real, seeking a meaning for the present which is historical in the sense that it is teleologically determined. The present, in other words, does not contain its full meaning within itself, but only in its relatedness to what is yet to come. To reimagine the future differently in the light of God's promise is thereby also at once to force a reevaluation of the present and its significance. The *Gestalt* shift has to do not with the future alone, but with the present which that future informs and shapes. Our view of what *is* the case as well as what *will be* is transfigured. Here again there would seem to be a positive relationship between the future and the present whereby God's future reaches back into the present and effectively refashions it by altering its meaning, an altered meaning which faith subsequently discerns and seeks to acknowledge in appropriate forms of life and thought.

Since, however, it is in the nature of our 'knowledge' of the future to be at best partial and provisional, a further implication of this would seem to be that questions of meaning and truth may in the interim only be answered in partial and provisional ways. The final answer to the question of the real and the true must wait for that eschatological moment when, as the apostle suggests, we shall know fully as we in turn are fully known. For now we must make do with seeing through a glass darkly, and must not allow our Western eschatological impatience to get the better of us. This ought to drive us to reassess the status not only of eschatological and theological statements, but all the statements we make about the real, and perhaps to moderate the claims which we make for those statements.

The power of the future made present

For Moltmann, the relationship between the here-and-now and the hoped for future which transforms that here-and-now is, we have seen, in certain respects understood to be a positive one, at least in the sense that the power of the future is capable of *being present within and exercising a transforming influence over* the present. At this level, therefore, we must suppose that there is some degree of commensurability and continuity between the two realms.

This is especially clear (as one might reasonably expect) in Moltmann's pneumatology. Here, in discussing the Christian doctrine of regeneration, he insists that while the *palingennesia* of our humanity is decisively rooted in that objective rebirth which occurred on Golgotha and will be fulfilled only in 'that life which is eternal', regeneration is none the less something which spans the period between these two points in the lives of particular Christian people. 'We are still involved in the experience of renewal, and the becoming-new travels with us' (SL 155). The God who is yet to come in glory has already come both in the economy of the incarnate Son and as the Spirit poured out upon the church at Pentecost. In our experiences of this same Spirit 'God himself is present in us', and 'we are possessed by a hope which sees unlimited potentialities ahead'. 'The goals of hope in our own lives, and what we ourselves expect of life, fuse with God's promises for a new creation of all things' (SL 155).

Human experiences of joy, of peace, of sanctification and the affirmation of life, all these things are anticipations of this same promise within that sphere where we would most naturally be *Trauergeister* – sad or grieving spirits. They issue from an experience of the Spirit of the resurrection, the one in whose power Jesus himself was raised from death in that most decisive and paradigmatic anticipation of the new creation within the old. They are 'the presence of eternity' in the midst of history (SL 153). Eternity, indeed, is not some abstract and timeless simultaneity but 'the power of the future over every historical time' (CoG 23). The Christian disciple, therefore, is not limited to hoping for the power of the future, but also experiences that same power in his or her present life; not in its fullness, to be sure, but genuinely none the less. 'Expectations hurry ahead. Experiences follow. They follow like *a divine trail* laid in the life of the individual. Every exodus is accompanied by trials and perils, but also by "signs and wonders", which are perceived by the men and women who are travelling the same road' (SL 152).

The same insistence upon a certain continuous relationship between God's promised future and our experienced present is identifiable in Moltmann's metaphorical extension of the model of conversion to describe what happens to the old in its transition to the new.

> Conversion and the rebirth to a new life change time and the experience of time, for they make-present the ultimate in the penultimate, and the future of time in the midst of time. . . . The future-made-present creates new conditions for possibilities in history. Mere interruption just disturbs; conversion creates new life. (CoG 22)

That which God fashions in the 'new creation', Moltmann insists, is not something novel. God does not set aside his original creation and replace it with one which is 'new' in that sense.

Rather, God is faithful to his original creation and *renews* it through the exercise of that same power which raised up Christ to life from the emptiness of death, and which, in the beginning, called the universe itself into being out of nothing. God's promised future, then, is anticipated in the midst of the old order of things not only through an imaginative looking forward to it, but through actual irruptions of the power of the Spirit who raised Jesus from death.

The contradiction of corruption

Here, though, we reach a point where a rather different emphasis must be taken equally into account. If there is indeed a positive relationship, a measure of commensurability and continuity between the old and the new creations, for Moltmann it is vital that we do not mistake the nature of this positive relation.

The point may be made quite clearly by contrasting Moltmann's account with that offered by Bloch. For the latter, as we have seen, hope is essentially that which intuits a 'Real-Possible' the conditions for which are already latent within the process or system of human history. In Leibniz's phrase (cited by Moltmann in CoG 25) the present is 'pregnant with future'. What remains is for us to grasp the potential inherent in the present, and then work towards its realization, spurred on by the energy of our hopeful imaginative vision. But this will not do as an account of the Christian hope. Here what is presented to us is precisely 'the thing we cannot already think out and picture for ourselves on the basis of the given world and of the experiences we already have of that world' (TH 16). Again, 'Christian eschatology does not examine the general future possibilities of history. Nor does it unfold the general possibilities of human nature in its dependence on the future' (TH 192). This is where Moltmann finds it necessary to part company with Bloch.

For Moltmann the Christian gospel is precisely about something *surprisingly* new, something which is not rooted in and does not rest upon the inherent potentialities and possibilities of the actual present, but upon the capacities of the God of creation and resurrection who has promised to make all things new. Indeed, that upon which Christian hope rests is precisely the action of this same God in summoning life forth out of death in the resurrection of Jesus, an action in which faith discerns both an anticipation and a pledge of the ultimate resurrection and renewal of all things. Just because it is this promise made by this same God which establishes and undergirds Christian hope,

> the expected future does not have to develop within the framework of the possibilities inherent in the present, but arises from that which is possible to the God of the promise. This can also be something which by the standard of present experience appears impossible. (TH 103)

The hope which is rooted in an event discontinuous with the general capacities of the old creation is also a hope which looks beyond those capacities for its eventual fulfilment.

What all this amounts to is an insistence that whatever level of continuity and commensurability between the old and the new may have to be discerned and acknowledged, it is radically offset by a level of stark discontinuity and incommensurability. At its starkest Moltmann puts the matter thus: 'this world "cannot bear" the resurrection and the new world created by resurrection' (TH 226). It can begin to sound as if the here-and-now is not at all the sphere of God's presence and activity, although Moltmann clearly cannot mean this. Yet: 'the kingdom of God is present here as promise and hope for the future horizon of all things, which are then seen in their historic character because they do not yet contain their truth in themselves. If it is present as promise and hope, then this its presence is determined by the contradiction in which the future, the possible and the promised stands to a corrupt reality' (TH 223). Moltmann indicates that the promise of God generates an interim period prior to the fulfilment of promise in which (as hinted above) the kingdom is present in the here-and-now *tectum sub cruce et sub contrario*, rather than in any explicit or apparent manner:

> Yet this its hiddenness is not an eternal paradox, but a latency within the tendency that presses forwards and outwards into that open realm of possibilities that lies ahead and is so full of promise.

Such statements stand in clear tension (although not contradiction) with those which appeal to a genuine suffusing of the present with the transformative power of the future in such a way that that power is manifest in people's lives and actually changes things. That Moltmann wishes to affirm both things is clear; but it provokes questions about the precise extent and nature of the presence of this contradictory and incommensurable future in our midst, questions to which we must return duly.

There is, then, a contradiction between that which characterizes the new creation and that which marks the old, between the promise and our experience of the present. This, we might note, is essentially the point which Barth was making in his notorious dispute with Emil Brunner over natural theology, albeit cast now in terms of an eschatological framework. The old creation is not capable of ('cannot bear', i.e. give birth to) the new creation. The present is not 'pregnant with future', we might say, except in so far as the God of the virgin conception is present and active in its midst, working ever afresh the miracle of life where there is only the potential for not-life. The new creation does not come simply to perfect the old creation, but to do something radically new which transcends any capacities latent within it. There is no natural capacity for the new within the old.

What is especially interesting is the fact that Moltmann and Barth deploy the very same theological examples to drive home their point: in nature *ex nihilo nihil fit*, yet the God who is the author of life is able to call life even *ex nihilo*. The crushed and lifeless form of the crucified has no latent capacity for new life, yet the God who is the author of life is able to raise him out of death as the first fruits of a new humanity. The point which both theologians wish to make is that the proper question is not, and must never be, about the latent capacities of the created, but rather about the capacities of the God of the future to do with his creation that which he has promised.

For Moltmann this relationship of incommensurability or contradiction between the present and the promised future makes the crucifixion-resurrection of Jesus, the 'enigmatic, dialectical identity of the risen Lord with the crucified Christ'

(TH 220) much more than the occasion upon which Christian hope is founded; it is itself *a paradigm for thinking about* the relationship of old to new creation. Again, this is a point to which we must return.

Hope, promise and the logic of grace

One key difference between Moltmann's theology of hope, rooted as it is in the category of the promise of God, and Bloch's principle of hope is that it is an *assured* hope. This certainly does not mean that we know precisely what will happen in the future. On the contrary

> the knowledge of the future which is kindled by promise is . . . prospective and anticipatory, . . . provisional, fragmentary, open, straining beyond itself. It knows the future in striving to bring out the tendencies and latencies of the Christ event of the crucifixion and resurrection, and in seeking to estimate the possibilities opened up by this event. (TH 203)

Yet the Christian hope is assured in the sense that it is invested in the capacities of the one who has raised Christ from the dead (see TH 145). Bloch, on the other hand, while he does not seem seriously to entertain the option of failure, none the less unfolds a model in which hope intuits a future which in principle may or may not ultimately come to pass.

It might be asked whether such a level of assurance ('because he has raised Christ from the dead, therefore the fulfilment of his promise is certain': CoG 145), rooted as it is in an insistence that the hoped for future is not contingent upon preconditions in the here-and-now, is not likely to reduce (if not remove altogether) the transformative impact of such hope? One might suppose so. After all, if the eventual outcome is secure regardless of our striving or lack of it towards the goal of our hope, if redemption does not rest on our fashioning of the conditions for the coming of the kingdom, then surely the more economic and comfortable option is to sit back and wait for it all to happen. Is not Bloch's model with its element of risk and genuine responsibility on the part of those who strive for the utopian future more likely to generate the sort of enthusiasm and effort necessary to see the kingdom at least approximated to in this world?

It would not be surprising if such a question were asked or answered in the affirmative. But the Christian answer to it must be an emphatic negative, for it misunderstands the logic both of the gospel and of Bloch's alternative to it. To begin with, we should observe that if this were so then it would not be the principle of hope about which Bloch was writing at such length, but rather a principle of fear or anxiety (generated by the risk of failure) which drives humans forwards in a frenzied bid to do their best, for fear of the consequences of inaction. To suppose this would in fact be to have missed the entire thrust of Bloch's case. For him it is actually hope, and not fear, which energizes and transforms our present activity. Fear inhibits and cripples. Yet the question is worth asking precisely because it provokes a reasonable counter-question: namely, whether, without the introduction of some transcendent guarantor of the outcomes of hope, without the receipt of something akin to the promise of the God of the resurrection, hope can really be the genuine source of a transformed present at all. If, in the final analysis our hope is rooted in the latent potential of the present, including our own potential to act and thereby generate the conditions for its eventual realization, then it is difficult to see just how we can escape the despair which accompanies the juxtaposition of our self-knowledge and the demands which the road to self-redemption makes. Thus Moltmann writes of Bloch:

> His ontology of 'not-yet-Being' fails to provide a foundation for hope because it inescapably has to become the ontology of 'Being-that-is-no-longer'. If future arises from the tendencies and latencies of the historical process, the future cannot bring anything surprisingly new, and never a *novum ultimum*. Eschatology is then only possible as teleology. But, as Bloch knew, teleology runs aground on death. (CoG 344 n. 58)

Within the logic of the Christian gospel of grace, with its explicit rejection of every attempt at self-justification, the priority of indicatives over imperatives is everywhere apparent. Redemption comes to us as a free gift of God created *ex nihilo*,

rather than a staged initiative which demands the prior fulfilment of conditions on our part before final bestowal of the
'promised' blessing. Yet this utter freeness does not create a
context for antinomian lethargy. Nor, indeed, is it lacking in its
demands. But the evangelical ordering of promise and demand
is all important. Because the gift is offered freely and does not
rest on the adequacy of our response, it actually liberates us
from the culture of fear and anxiety, and thereby sets us free to
act with radical confidence, confidence which is free to make
mistakes because it knows they will not result in rejection. Failure
itself is forgivable and redeemable. When, therefore, God's
promise comes to us and fashions our hope, in the very same
moment it demands what it offers and offers what it demands.
What it demands is that we should become the children of God,
citizens of his kingdom. What it offers is the opportunity to
become children of God, citizens of his kingdom. The demand
is to embrace the freely given gift, that which is promised to us,
and to live it out in the here and now. Hence the promise
certainly calls for obedience: 'It is necessary to arise and go to
the place to which the promise points, if one would have part
in its fulfilment. Promise and command, the pointing of the
goal and the pointing of the way, therefore belong immediately
together' (TH 120). But here the logic of gospel sets us utterly
free from the burden of having to become the condition for
the realization of the kingdom. And it is this liberation, rooted
in the imaginative vision which lays hold of God's promised
future, which transforms our way of being in the present and
generates patterns of obedience and response. Here again the
acknowledgement that this world 'cannot bear' the new creation
lifts from our shoulders the responsibility of having to establish
it by our own labours. Yet it must be held in tension with the
constant call of God to live in the here-and-now as those whose
lives are shaped by the power of his future at work as the
contradiction of corruption.

Modulation, Messiah, and the moment

We have seen that this essential tension between recog-
nising the radical newness of the new creation and its

incommensurability with the present order of things on the one hand, and on the other hand the genuine presence of the *Novum* in the midst of the present order, drawing us forward transformatively into God's future, is maintained in Moltmann's theology. Thus of the resurrection he writes:

> The new thing, the kainos, the novum ultimum, is the quintessence of the wholly other, marvellous thing that the eschatological future brings. With the raising of Christ from the dead, the future of the new creation sheds its lustre into the present of the old world, and in 'the sufferings of this present time' kindles hope for the new life. (CoG 28)

Yet this event 'has no analogies in experienced history' (CoG 28). This, on Moltmann's own account of the matter, is both true and untrue. There are no historical preconditions for the resurrection of Jesus to be sure; yet Christian experience is now filled with happenings which are analogous to it in the sense that they too introduce the lustre of the new into the old order, that they too derive not from potentialities latent within nature, but from the creative power of God calling forth life out of death. There is, in this present order, a repeated and identifiable 'eschatologically new intervention of God's creative activity' (CoG 28). Like Barth's *analogia fidei*, however, the analogy to be discerned here is always in one direction, *from* the paradigm event of the resurrection *to* those subsequent partial and dependent anticipations of the new creation which arise out of its power at work in the world. The relationship is not reversible. The resurrection has no *natural* analogies in this world.

Yet the insistence that there are *unnatural* analogies, arising directly and only out of the power of the future-made-present, forces us to qualify the sense in which we construe the incommensurability between the two orders. It cannot be such that the old 'cannot bear' the new in the sense of 'cannot endure' it or accommodate it in its midst at all, but only in the sense that it cannot give birth to it in and of itself.

Through what figure, then, should we picture the transition from the old to the new creation? Moltmann, we have seen, typically takes the crucifixion and resurrection of Jesus as paradigmatic. This accommodates both a vital degree of continuity (the identity of the historical Jesus with the risen Lord) and the all important discontinuity since, as has often been observed, 'dead men don't rise'! The problem with this figure, though, important and necessary though it may be, is the fact that it emphasizes the discontinuity and incommensurability to such an extent that it becomes hard to make much sense of the genuine presence of the new order in the old, the suffusing and transforming of the old with the power of the new. It tends rather to indicate a model in which the old will be transformed 'in the blink of an eye' into something only faintly (yet none the less genuinely) recognizable as continuous with the old, just as the transfigured and the risen Jesus were. Again, while this may in itself be appropriate and necessary enough as a pointer to what may ultimately occur in God's eschatological future, we also need a model to set alongside it which allows us to say in unequivocal terms that the shift from the old to the new has already begun, that there is an overlap between the two orders *not* in the sense that there is some prior basis or precondition for the new already latent in the old, but in the sense that the new has already begun to create its own presence in the midst of the old by assuming it and drawing it into new self-transcendent anticipations of what it will ultimately be.

> The messianic interpretation sees 'the moment' that interrupts time, and lets us pause in the midst of progress, as the power for conversion. At that moment another future becomes perceptible. The laws and forces of the past are no longer compulsive . . . New perspectives open up . . . The way becomes free for alternative developments. (CoG 45)

The paradigm offered by the compound event of crucifixion-resurrection, then, needs to be supplemented as a basis for imagining the shift between the old and the new creations of God.

In the composition of a piece of music, if one wishes to change key (especially if one wishes to change into a relatively unrelated key) there are ways and means of doing so. One may, of course, simply change in a largely unannounced and unanticipated manner, causing a jarring to the sensibilities of the listeners who will very likely find it hard to link the two passages together at first. This is sometimes done for effect. But the more accepted and likely means of achieving the change is via a modulation or series of modulations in which one takes a chord belonging properly in the old key, but uses it in ways which are proper to a new key, thereby transforming its significance, and effecting a harmonious bridge between the passages. This same process may need to be effected several times in order to get from the original to the final desired key. Skilful composers may also smooth the transition by introducing already into the closing strains of the old passage melodic motifs which do not really belong there at all, but which point ahead of themselves to the new.

Moltmann's passing appeal to the model of 'conversion' indicates the need for the development of some such paradigm to set alongside that of crucifixion-resurrection in order to complement it dialectically, and hence accommodate the apparent evidence of God's skilful modulation from the key of death into the key of life. There is no need to turn to musicology for such a paradigm however. It is there already in the christological focus to which Moltmann himself directs us. But we need to cast our gaze back behind the event of the cross, and to remind ourselves that prior to this strikingly discontinuous irruption of the power of God's future into the present there had already been a whole life lived in which the power of this future was perceptibly locked in a struggle to the death with the powers of evil. The transformation or *palingennesia* of humanity did not begin on Golgotha, that is to say, but precisely in the womb of the virgin, and was effected through Jesus' Spirit-filled and enabled responsiveness to his father from moment to waking moment of his life *culminating* in the self-offering to death on the cross. In the events of Jesus' messianic ministry we find constant foreshadowings of the new order which constitute a genuine presence of the kingdom or rule of God in the midst of this order. As the one who furnishes Yahweh for the first time with a satisfactory covenant partner the Messiah is himself an embodiment of this rule in the world. And yet, the cross and resurrection, the decisive anticipation of the shift from old to new, are still to come. In all this we have a valuable paradigm for reflecting on how the power of God's future can be genuinely present and effective in the midst of a world which, as yet, cannot bear it. This, perhaps, is part of the theological significance of the gospel story of Jesus' transfiguration on the mountain, an eschatological moment in which the true meaning of Jesus' present is revealed to the three disciples through a vision of his post-resurrection glory, a glory discontinuous with the conditions of his historical ministry, yet genuinely present under the form of anticipations of it, and visible for those granted eyes to see. It is no coincidence that it is in the light cast by this event that Peter's stumbling confession of Jesus as the Messiah comes. Messianic history, we might say, is the context for the modulation from the conditions and potentialities of death to those of life in this world.

Transfigured and transfiguring imagination

The power of the future to transform the present lies chiefly in the capacity of God's Spirit to capture our imagination and to open up for us a new vision of God's promise and the present which it illuminates, thereby stimulating alternative ways of being in the world in the present, living towards the future. Imagination is thus a vital category in eschatology as in theology more generally.

Imaginative forms are rendered necessary rather than merely useful or ornamental precisely by the dialectical relationship between present and future about which we have already spoken. On the one hand some level of continuity and commensurability between the old and new orders is vital if we are to be able to say or think anything meaningful about God's future at all. The *novum ultimum* cannot be wholly lacking in analogy to the here-and-now, otherwise we are driven to silence, and can have no hope precisely because we can expect nothing, look forward to nothing, fashion for ourselves no imaginative horizon towards which to move. It is in terms of a transfigured present that we are able to speak and think about God's promised future. Yet the discontinuity and incommensurability about which we have said so much renders imagination absolutely necessary as the mode or capacity relevant to eschatological expectation and statement. Reason and science,

the tools of *logos*, in so far as they are orientated and accom-
modated to the familiar, the regular, the continuous, have no
means of penetrating beyond its limits.[18] It is precisely
imagination, the capacity which is able to take the known and
to modify it in striking and unexpected ways, which offers us
the opportunity to think beyond the limits of the given, to
explore states of affairs which, while they are radical and
surprising modifications of the known, are so striking and surprising as to transcend the latent possibilities and potentialities
of the known.

If, therefore, the promise of God is the source of hope, it
may be that we must pursue the suggestion that it is the
imagination of men and women to which that promise appeals,
which it seizes and expands, and which is the primary locus of
God's sanctifying activity in human life.

---

[18] It would be unfortunate if this were taken to mean that reason and science
had nothing whatever to do with the activity of imagination. Clearly this is not
the case, and no such crude separation is intended. The point here, however,
is simply that in so far as they are attending (as they often do) to the regularities
and predictable orderliness of this world, working deliberately within the
boundaries furnished by our shared experience of it, these tools as such are
unable to take us beyond those self-set limits into the limitless beyond of the
eschatological future. Here a different sort of imaginative activity is required.
At times science itself (in constructing hypotheses for example, especially ones
which involve moves towards a significant paradigm shift) is driven to utilize
imagination in similar ways. But for the most part its reliance upon imaginative
modes is of a more constrained sort, imagining within the limits (which might
be described as a form of reasoning – inference? deduction?) rather than
trespassing beyond them.

CHAPTER II/2

HOPE AND REALITY: CONTRADICTION AND CORRESPONDENCE

Response to Trevor Hart

JÜRGEN MOLTMANN

In his contribution, Trevor Hart deals mainly with my early *Theology of Hope* (1964; ET 1967). This gives me new courage, for 'back to the beginnings' has been the slogan of every movement for the renewal of church and society in Christian Europe. When life has become old and the spirit faint, it is in the beginnings that we again find the living springs from which the vital energies flow. That is why all the revival movements we know carry the prefix 're': reformation, revolution, risorgimento. When I read Trevor Hart's essay on imagination for the kingdom of God, I was reminded of a sentence written by the American theologian of the social gospel, Walter Rauschenbusch, which I liked to take as compass point when I was writing the *Theology of Hope*: 'Ascetic Christianity called the world evil and left it. Humanity is waiting for a revolutionary Christianity which will call the world evil and change it'.[1]

---

[1] In R. D. Cross (ed.), *Christianity and the Social Crisis* (New York, 1964) 91.

At that time I had a revolutionary Christianity of this kind in mind, a Christianity which would turn the wretched condition of the world into what was good, just and living by virtue of its hope. It was to be served by a theology which seeks the righteousness and justice of God in this world, and looks for the life of this world in the kingdom of God. Theology ought not to be just 'the doctrine of faith' – the title Schleiermacher gave to his exposition[2] – nor just *Church Dogmatics*, as in Barth. Including both these, and certainly not excluding either, it ought to be creative imagination for God's coming kingdom. Theology ought not merely to 're'-flect upon the Word of God that has already happened (Karl Barth). It should also think forward, following God's promise in that Word into the future of the coming kingdom.

God's 'kingdom' and 'righteousness' are alternative visions to everything we experience here and now as human Realpolitik or power politics, and as injustice and the oppression of the weak in our society.

It is this that gives rise to the problem to which Trevor Hart points so emphatically: are the experienced presence of God and God's hoped-for future commensurable or incommensurable? Are they two different conditions of this world, or are they two quite different worlds? Are there only qualitative contradictions between the two, or are there correspondences, analogies, parables and agreements as well? Or – as the question used to be put: does the kingdom of God stand in exclusive antithesis to this world according to Jesus' message, or is there a development of God's kingdom within this world in which we can co-operate? In other words, do we pray apocalyptically: 'May grace come and the world pass away', or do we 'pass our lives in the joyful confidence that this world will increasingly become the showplace for a people of God'? The man who asked this question was, of all people, Johannes Weiss, who in his book *Jesus' Proclamation of the Kingdom of God* (tactfully published only in 1892, two years after the death of his father-in-law, Albrecht

---

[2] F. Schleiermacher, *Glaubenslehre* [the doctrine of faith] (1821/2; revd edn 1830). The title of the published English translation is *The Christian Faith* (1928).

Ritschl)[3] rediscovered through his historical exegesis the apocalyptic character of the message about the kingdom of God, and in so doing became, together with Albert Schweitzer, the renewer of Christian eschatology in our century. But, running counter to his own exegesis, Weiss himself decided in favour of 'the joyful confidence' of the bourgeois Protestant world, with its credulous faith in progress, its missionary zeal for culture, and its imperialist Protestantism. Only twenty-two years later the terrible apocalypse of the First World War broke over humanity, ending in the mutual destruction of the Protestant powers of Great Britain and Prussian Germany.

Apocalyptic expectation of the kingdom of God or messianic hope for that kingdom? What faces us here is certainly anything but a merely abstract theological problem.

Drawing on George Steiner's book *After Babel* (1975; 2nd edn 1992), Trevor Hart finely brings out how our human capacity for hope and for an imagination of the future is deeply woven into the grammar of our language in the future tenses of our verbs. This is not the case in all human languages. With the help of future verbal forms we can look beyond the given present to a better state of affairs. We can talk about alternatives to existing reality, and can imagine counter-worlds. That is to say, we can confront the present we actually experience with a future anticipated in hope and creative imagination, and with the remembrances of our past; and these confrontations make us decide for hope contrary to experience, or for experience contrary to hope. At all events, our present, existing reality – even if it be no more than our personal existence – will be placed in the mode of possibility.

Turning to Ernst Bloch, Trevor Hart brings out the creative imagination which expresses itself in visions or utopias, but is nourished by the driving power of hope. But where does Bloch see this driving power of hope in human life coming from? We might say that the open future, like a land of unlimited possibilities, as it were, entices and fascinates human beings and makes them beings open to the world and ready for future. But from the viewpoint of the histories of civilization and religion

---

[3] First ET only in 1971 (London: SCM Press).

this is not true. It is in fact true only for the so-called Abrahamitic religions, which in worshipping the God of Israel also revere the exodus experience of Abraham and Sarah as a primal experience of God. And indeed Bloch too grounds the driving power of hope not only in the fascination of the open future, but also *mystically* in 'the darkness of the lived moment'.

In this dark moment – dark because spontaneously lived – something in our existence (*Da-sein*) 'ferments', 'thrusts' and 'drives' which has hitherto found no place and has not yet come to rest. Philosophically, Bloch later called this 'the Being which thrusts towards existence' (*Da-sein*) or 'the ground of existence' which is realized in ever new forms until it finds the felicitously successful form in which it comes to rest. But in his first book *The Spirit of Utopia* (1918, revd edn 1923, 246)[4] he still calls this inner driving power of hope 'the darkness of the lived God' and 'entry into the Holy Spirit'. At that time Bloch was thinking entirely in the categories of Jewish messianism, and by this 'God in us' he meant God's Shekinah: 'God will dwell in the midst of the Israelites', we read in Ezekiel. But where is God's dwelling if his people is in exile and imprisonment? God's Shekinah will then become the travelling comrade and the companion in affliction of his people, and in the exile of this hostile world longs for the 'homecoming' to God himself. In Christianity the divine Shekinah was called the Holy Spirit, which indwells our hearts, our bodies and the community of Christ, as the 'earnest' or pledge of glory.

At the end of his *Principle of Hope* (1959; ET 1986), Bloch means by this that 'home of identity' 'which shines out to everyone in childhood and where as yet no-one was'. In the exile of this world, the driving power of hope links the divine that dwells in us with God himself. If it were not for hope's yearning for home, we should not experience the conditions of this world as an exile, as godless or inhumane. We should simply come to terms with them: 'What can't be cured must be endured', as we say. But that means nothing less than that the real presence of hope in this estranged life is itself already a fragment of redemption and home.

---

[4] *Der Geist der Utopie*. The book has not been translated into English.

The mystical dimension is not always as clearly detectable in Bloch's work as the utopian dimension of hope. He himself based the utopian dimension on an 'ontology of not yet being', and hence suppressed the mystical dimension of eternity in 'the darkness of the lived moment'. Yet without this mystical dimension the ontology of the not-yet ends simply in an ontology of no-longer, and therefore literally leads 'to nothing'. It is at this point that my theological criticism begins: without a transcendental determination of future, the phenomenological future leads only into the past. Behind the past then stands the transcendental determination of time as transience. The rest is nihilism.

Trevor Hart has brought out very well the point that, according to the *Theology of Hope, the cross and resurrection of Jesus Christ* provides 'the paradigm for thinking about the relationship of old to new creation'. He is right. At that time I understood Christ's crucifixion in the contradiction between a world in contradiction to God and the human being corresponding to God. In this world in the shadow of the cross I saw the kingdom of God only beyond the cross, in the raising of the One crucified. The raising of Christ was for me like the daybreak following the long night of the eclipse of God (Rom 13:12). When this was used as paradigm for the relation between old and new, history and eschatology, the result was a rigid *dialectic of contrarieties*, of the kind maintained philosophically by T. W. Adorno in his *Negative Dialectics* (ET 1973).

But because this apocalyptic depresses and paralyses people, I then sought for 'the true life' in the midst of 'the life that is false', and found it along the path which Trevor Hart indicates: it is *the life of Jesus*, which certainly ends in earthly terms in his self-surrender on the cross, but only because he lived in the presence of God's coming kingdom among the poor, the sick, and sinners, so that he was rightly called 'the kingdom of God in person'.

This life which Jesus lived was imbued with, and guided by, the Holy Spirit, which had descended on him and 'rested' on him from the time of his baptism by John. That he was already conceived by the Holy Spirit belongs here too.

But Jesus' life remains incomprehensible unless we see that it was lived *among God's people*, Israel – indeed that – at least according to Matthew's Gospel – Jesus was also 'Israel in person'. The history of his individual life reflects the history of Israel with, running through it, the scarlet thread of God's promises, and with God's liberating real presences in the midst of the history of this world which passes away. On the other side of the raising of Jesus Christ we find the presence of his life in the real presence of the life-giving Spirit. When Paul talks about 'the life of Jesus' he always means the new life of the raised Christ. The raising of the crucified Jesus finds its analogies in the 'rebirth to a living hope' (1 Peter 1:3). Yet – as the story of Pentecost shows – this personal experience of Christ's presence in the Spirit was always understood as only the beginning of the universal outpouring of the Holy Spirit 'on all flesh'. 'All flesh' (Hebrew *kol basar*) means not just human life but all earthly living things. If we look at these wider circles, rippling out from the central happening of Christ's crucifixion and raising, then the dialectic of rigid antitheses cannot be the only way of thinking the 'transforming power' of the promised future of God's kingdom.

In my later 'systematic contributions to theology' from 1980 onwards, I used less inflexible, more living forms of dialectic. In *The Way of Jesus Christ* (ET 1990) I presented the central event of Christ's cross and resurrection in trinitarian perspectives: God the Father raises the dead Christ – the dead Christ then rises – the Holy Spirit in whose power Christ is raised and rises gives birth to him anew for eternal life in the pains of the cross (*The Way of Jesus Christ*, 247–249). With this, the event termed 'the raising of the crucified Jesus' also becomes a transition from death to life, and a metamorphosis from 'the form of a servant' to 'the form of the transfigured One'. Because in cross and resurrection Christ's identity is preserved, the forms he takes shift from the form or Gestalt of death to the form or Gestalt of eternal life. No other Christ takes the place of Jesus. The one exalted is the same as the one humiliated, the one raised the same as the one crucified. Where do we find the continuity in this discontinuity between death and life, end and beginning? I believe that this continuity in discontinuity can be seen in the presence of the Holy Spirit in Christ's life, death and resurrection. In Gethsemane and on Golgotha the Son feels forsaken by the Father but is sustained by the Holy Spirit.

If we move from this point to the problem of the continuity/ discontinuity or commensurability/non-commensurability between the old and the new creation, then the picture we have had hitherto changes.

According to the apocalyptic traditions, we talk about 'the time of this world which passes away', and 'the time of the world to come'. The two stand over against one another as mutually exclusive antitheses. That is why the apocalyptic prayer runs 'May thy kingdom come and this world pass away', and we are urged 'not to be conformed to this world' for 'the form of this world passes away' (1 Cor 7:31). It was in this sense that I said: 'This world "cannot bear" the resurrection and the new world created by resurrection' (*Theology of Hope*, 226, quoted by Trevor Hart). But these two apocalyptic aeons are not two different divine creations which exclude one another. They are *two world times* of God's *one same* creation. In 1934 the Barmen Theological Declaration of the Confessing Church made this distinction very well: 'Through him (Jesus Christ) we obtain joyful deliverance from the godless bondage of *this world* for free grateful service for *those he* (God) *has created*' (my italics). When we wait and hope for the new creation, we are not seeking another world; we are seeking for this world to be different. Eternal life is not a different life after death. Eternal life means that this mortal life becomes different. The continuity does not run from the old to the new, or from here to there, or from the past to the future; it runs from the new to the old, from there to here, and from the future to the past. 'Flesh and blood *cannot inherit* the kingdom of God', says Paul, in good apocalyptic fashion (1 Cor 15:50). But he also adds the good eschatological declaration: '*This* perishable nature must put on the imperishable, and *this* mortal nature must put on immortality' (1 Cor 15:53). In these two sentences is contained the whole eschatological dialectic.

If we look back from this vision of the new creation, we can detect continuities. The first of these is the identity of *the creation*

God has brought into being. Then we find the formula for
Israel's covenant: 'I will dwell with them and they shall be my
people' (Rev 21:3). The history of Israel's covenant and
God's faithfulness to his people stand in continuity to the
new creation. The history of *God's indwellings* in Israel, in Jesus
Christ (Col 2:9: 'In him all the fullness of the Godhead dwells
bodily'), in the experiences of the Holy Spirit, who 'dwells' in
believers and in the community of Christ, and in the *perichoresis*
in love of God and human beings (1 John 4:16: 'He who
abides in love abides *in* God, and God abides *in* him') – all
these things are in continuity with the new creation. In these
continuities the new creation of all things is already present,
and already determines the present. There is already true life
in the midst of the life that is false.

If we now follow the theological distinctions with a look at
experiences and actions in history: do the apocalyptic contradiction and the messianic correspondence of the kingdom of
God to the conditions of this world constitute mutually exclusive
ideas? Of course everywhere in Christianity we find apocalyptic
fundamentalists on the one hand and liberal modernists on
the other, apocalyptic sects which segregate themselves and cut
themselves off from 'the wicked world', and modern Christians
who want to keep up with every movement of 'the spirit of the
age'. But these differences are not the real problem. The real
problem is the prophetic recognition of the signs of the times –
of what hour has struck, and of the favourable moment, the
kairos.

Again and again there have been times when the people
of God have been persecuted, and martyrdom has been
enjoined. Then nothing more is possible in history. That is
'the night when no one can work'. Then all that is left is to
endure to the end, and in that endurance to be saved. Following
Shusako Endo's novel *Silence*, Trevor Hart has described just
such an apocalyptic situation which faced Japanese martyrs.
In situations like that the possibilities of history narrow
down, and all that remains is the sole decision: to confess or
to deny. These are experiences of the end of history – *finis*:
the whole world becomes meaningless – paradise lies beyond
death.

Yet again and again there have also been, and are, times of open doors and favourable opportunities for mission, for diaconal service to the poor, and for the liberation of the oppressed. Then we stand face to face with almost unlimited possibilities which can be realized, and we are filled with the 'joyful confidence' that this world can be made better, and that we can create juster and freer conditions for everyone: peace is possible – liberty exists – the kingdom of God is at hand – today is the day of salvation. Then hope turns into action, and we already anticipate today something of the new creation of all things which Christ will complete on his day. These are experiences of history's consummation – *telos*.

If we contemplate history under the aspect of the linear notion of time, that apocalyptic of the end and this messianism of the consummation are antitheses. But the linear notion of time does not fit the experiences of history: for us, history narrows down apocalyptically, and expands messianically. This is a question of God's providence, which leads us into experiences of the end, and into experiences of the beginning. The 'nearness' of God's kingdom and the 'nearness' of the end cannot be measured in temporal terms. They are *aggregate conditions of history* which we experience when we find ourselves in them. At times when history is open we have to know about history's end, and at times when history is closed we have to know about the new beginnings.

ESCHATOLOGY AND POLITICAL RADICALISM

The Example of Karl Barth and Jürgen Moltmann

TIMOTHY GORRINGE

Can Theology Contribute to Political Radicalism?

All theology is ideology. This is a tautology in the sense in which Marx introduces the concept of ideology as 'the production of ideas, of conceptions, of consciousness . . . what human beings say, imagine, conceive'.[1] For political radicals, however, it has often seemed to be a tautology in Marx's second sense of ideology, namely as false consciousness, the conscious or unconscious use of ideas to obfuscate reality and to preserve the social and political status quo. They can point to the undeniable fact that religion has time and again provided the sacred canopy for states and empires. This may happen overtly, as in Eusebius' lauding of Constantine as the new Solomon, or the Calvinist providentialism of seventeenth-century Holland or twentieth-century South Africa, or tacitly, as in Ritschl's or Harnack's theological summation of the virtues of Bismarckian or Wilhelmine Germany. All such theologies emanate from the

---

[1] K. Marx, 'The German Ideology', in Marx/Engels, *Complete Works*, vol. 5 (Moscow: Progress, 1976) 36.

ruling class and form part of 'the ruling ideas of the age', as the Communist Manifesto observed.

It goes without saying, on Marx's first, non-pejorative definition, that there may be liberative ideologies, products of thought and imagination designed to overthrow oppression and establish human freedom. To cite a rather dubious witness we recall how Carlyle was once reproached by a businessman with the rebuke: 'Ideas, Mr. Carlyle, ideas, nothing but ideas!' To which Carlyle replied: 'There was once a man called Rousseau who wrote a book containing nothing but ideas. The second edition was bound in the skin of those who laughed at the first.'[2] The famous eleventh thesis on Feuerbach is unintelligible without the third: 'it is human beings who change circumstances and . . . the educators must themselves first be educated'.[3] Since human beings, unlike bees or ants, do not have community 'by nature' they must shape it themselves. How this is to be done is the theme, in one way or another, of most 'ideology'. Put positively, it cannot be done at all without ideology, any more than it is possible to navigate complex terrain blindfold. Ideologies, in the neutral sense, are the maps which tell us what the lie of the land is like and therefore where we ought to go. That maps are not neutral but embody ideologies, as we see in the contrast between the Bartholomew and Peters projections, is the reason we have the second sense of ideology. Those ideologies are politically radical which incorporate the demand, which long predates the American and French revolutions, that polities must reflect in their concrete arrangements the fundamental equality of human beings. Since the 1970s political radicalism likewise takes on board a concern for the threatened earth.

Both in Belgium and England the socialist organizations Marx knew had a strong religious dimension which grounded their demand for equality, but he contemptuously dismissed Christian Socialism as 'the holy water sprinkled on the heart burnings of the aristocrat'. As so often in Marx here splendid rhetoric took

---

[2] Quoted in A. MacIntyre, *A Short History of Ethics* (London: Routledge, 1967) 183.

[3] Marx/Engels, *Complete Works*, vol. 5, 7.

the place of detailed argument. His conviction of the non-sense of theistic belief made him completely impatient with religion and he brushed it aside to get on to more important things. He ruled out the possibility of theology playing a liberative role because the religion he knew, which provided 'the heart of a heartless world', dulled the passion for change by fixing hopes for a better life beyond death. The footnotes to *Capital* document Andrew Ure's cynical use of the religion of the cross in precisely this sense in his *Philosophy of Manufactures*. But need religion and theology function like this?

The most superficial acquaintance with religion shows that it may often be opposed to the status quo and that it may be very concretely concerned with freedom. In terms of the Christian creed, any of its articles may have radical political implications, but the connexion between eschatological, apocalyptic or millenarian belief and political radicalism is especially well evidenced. When the soldiers of Cromwell's New Model Army marched against the forces of the King, for example, they sang marching songs which drew on the imagery of the book of Revelation:

> For God begins to honour us,
> The Saintes are marching on;
> The sword is sharp, the arrows swift
> To destroy Babylon.
> Against the kingdome of the beast
> Wee witnesses do rise . . .[4]

Cromwell's Puritans stood in an immense tradition of dissent stretching back to New Testament times in which marginal and often persecuted groups looked for the coming of Christ's kingdom to put the world to rights. This history, vividly sketched in Norman Cohn's *The Pursuit of the Millennium*, makes clear that it is often those without power in society, if not the downright oppressed, to whom such beliefs appeal. This is hardly surprising for there is an obvious critical potential both in the belief in a new heaven and a new earth which forms a contrast to the present world of injustice and suffering and in the imagery

---

[4] Quoted in E. P. Thompson, *Witness Against the Beast: William Blake and the Moral Law* (Cambridge: Cambridge University Press, 1993) 23.

of a coming judgment when the rich and mighty will receive their due. Eschatological hopes became fervently concrete in millenarianism and, as in the English Peasants' Revolt of 1381 or with the Ranters and Diggers of the 1640s, were often radically egalitarian. Whilst Cohn's study makes clear that the lunatic fringe of utopian politics is never far away in millenarian movements, at the same time it is undeniable that here ideology – in this case eschatological faith – functions to challenge those in power. Conversely we find an elective affinity between, say, the theology of Aquinas, part of whose job it was to oppose the dangerous radicalism of Joachim of Fiore, and Christendom, just as we do between Schleiermacher's *Whence of the feeling of Absolute Dependence* and the religion of the cultured middle class of the nineteenth century. It is instructive to set his remarks on the incapacity of the working class for religious feeling, in the first of his *Speeches*, alongside the work of his exact contemporary William Blake. Whilst Schleiermacher was writing the *Speeches* Blake was lashing Europe's lust for war, England's corrupt government, and the slave trade, with visions of the last judgment:

> riv'n link from link, the bursting Universe explodes.
> All things revers'd flew from their centres . . .
> Fathers and friends, Mothers and Infants, Kings & Warriors,
> Priests & chain'd Captives, met together in horrible fear;
> And every one of the dead appears as he had liv'd before,
> And all the marks remain of the slave's scourge & tyrant's Crown,
> And of the Priest's o'ergorged Abdomen . . .
> They see him whom they have pierc'd, they wail because of him,
> They magnify themselves no more against Jerusalem,
> Nor against her little ones.[5]

The difference of voice is partly accounted for by the difference of location: the printer and engraver, shortly to be put on trial for sedition because of his protests against the war on the one side, and the chaplain and theologian, welcome at the most exclusive literary salons of Berlin on the other. In the same way we may contrast Aquinas, the Vatican diplomat and teacher of

---

[5] W. Blake, *The Four Zoas*, Night the Ninth l.230ff., in *Blake: Complete Writings*, ed. G. Keynes (Oxford: Oxford University Press, 1969) 363.

the Schools, with the unknown painters and craftsmen of medieval Europe who time and again incorporated scathing political critique into their work, not least in the Chancel Dooms which showed Pope and Emperor being haled into hell. As the liberation theologians have insisted, the social site of the theologian is important. Equally, however, we find in both Aquinas and Schleiermacher that relegation of eschatology to an appendix which, as Moltmann remarks, 'has always been the condition that makes possible the adaptation of Christianity to its environment' (TH 41). Whilst political radicalism is not the exclusive preserve of eschatology within theological discourse, the complete omission of eschatology is probably always a politically reactionary sign.

Any religion's capacity to provide the sacred canopy for society depends on its overall credibility. Under increasing fire from the beginning of the eighteenth century on, the liberal Protestant version of this canopy withered in the trenches of Ypres and the Somme. This was the moment when politically radical eschatology was able to enter the theological mainstream, perhaps for the first time. We can follow the history of this move in the work of two Protestant theologians whose career spans virtually the whole of the twentieth century, Karl Barth and Jürgen Moltmann. Born in 1886, Barth grew up and went to university in the heyday of the 'Belle epoque' and his first significant theological writings appear at that period and reflect its ethos. His two great commentaries on Romans, effectively two rather different manifestos, were the theological marker to the disintegration of that age. He learned his craft as a dogmatic theologian in Weimar, and began his life work, the *Church Dogmatics*, in the context of resistance to fascism. The final volumes were written during the Cold War, and the last fragments from the age of affluence which followed that. Moltmann on the other hand, born forty years later in 1926, was a young soldier at the end of the Second World War, a prisoner of war, and began his theological output as Barth was ending his. His *Theology of Hope*, along with Barth's *Romans* one of the defining theological texts of the century, appeared two years after Vatican II had started, four years before Liberation theology found its voice at Medellin, five years before second

wave feminism became a major cultural force, before the
escalation of American action in Vietnam, and just under ten
years before the emergence of the Green Movement. All of his
later theology represents responses to these events and movements. In terms of cultural background, Barth's theology begins
in apocalypse and ends with relative stability; Moltmann begins
with relative stability and moves increasingly into the insecurity
signified by the preoccupation of present-day culture with
apocalypse.

Karl Barth

In the closing two decades of the nineteenth century and the
first two decades of the twentieth, the middle class, to which
Barth belonged, enjoyed general prosperity and the foundations
of civilization seemed solid. For Barth's generation of university
students it seemed, in Golo Mann's words, 'a harmless and care-
free age' – certainly not an age for millenarian enthusiasm.[6]
Harnack's *What is Christianity?*, with its 'simple gospel' of the
Fatherhood of God and the brotherhood of man, was its theological manifesto, and in this gospel cultural progress compre-
hensively takes the place of eschatology. This world went more
or less gaily to war in 1914. By 1918 it lay in ruins, though figures
like Hindenburg and Harnack never recognized that. Barth, by
contrast, not only saw the collapse but danced on the ruins, to
the piping of Overbeck.

Barth himself made much of the significance of the support
for the Kaiser by Harnack and his other theological teachers
in bringing about his break with liberalism, but equally as
important in this development, if not more so, was his crucial
meeting with the younger Blumhardt in 1916, and his growing
antagonism to Ragaz and Christian Socialism. It was the radical
edge which his eschatological faith gave him which ensured
that Christoph Blumhardt's involvement with Social Democracy
was never as unambivalent as that of Ragaz. He was concerned
to change the present, to find anticipations of the kingdom of

---

[6] G. Mann, *The History of Germany since 1789* (tr. M. Jackson; London:
Chatto & Windus, 1968) 280.

God here on earth, but the critical power of the coming kingdom made easy identifications with existing political programmes impossible. One could certainly argue that Christoph Blumhardt was Barth's single most important theological teacher. He took from him the mixture of concrete realism and eschatological tension and kept hold of it to the end of his life.

The new theology was, of course, not the product of the academy, but of the 'red pastor', instrumental in the formation of trade unions in his parish, a popular speaker at Social Democrat meetings. Where Schweitzer had done nothing with his rediscovery of eschatology, but retreated to the calmer waters of liberal theology and the edge of the primeval forest, in Barth eschatology became political. The first Romans commentary was completed in the heady days of 1918, when it seemed as if the Russian revolution might spread to Germany and the exegesis is frequently positively breathless.

For Barth in this commentary human beings are

> organs and agents of the power of God. The absolute necessity of our victorious offensive and defensive against the powers of the old world consists in the fact that God is no longer a stranger to us.

This God is no bare Idea, 'but in Christ God's reality (*Sache*) becomes our reality'.[7] The God who is not part of this universe is nevertheless at work in its very depths. God is not by us or against us but for us and with us as our 'nearest most intimate acquaintance', 'the pulse of our own organism' (Kutter), our own deepest, truest, freedom.[8] Taking up but quite transforming Durkheim's categories, Barth contrasts organic growth with 'mechanical' change, by which he seems to mean change that is man-made: 'The divine grows organically, and so needs no more mechanical building up.'[9] It is Christ's resurrection which brings us into this stream of organic life.

[7] K. Barth, *Der Römerbrief* (1st edn 1919), ed. H. Stoevesandt (Zurich: Theologische Verlag, 1985) (henceforth cited as RI) 313.
[8] RI 207.
[9] RI 90; 'The coming world comes not mechanically, but organically' (RI 21).

> We simply stand within this process . . . we want to be nothing other
> than an organic particle of the creation, bound up with the whole,
> which is now reconciled with God.[10]

It is return to the origin, through participation in the organism
or movement, which constitutes the 'process eschatology' of
this commentary.[11]

Organic growth means history: The germcell of life has once
again been planted in history and nature so that divine history
grows within human world history. Barth distinguishes between
'so called' history,[12] which human beings make for themselves,
and 'actual' history, the history God makes.[13] The two are
related: 'so called' history is the breakthrough point for actual
history. In the stream of so-called history the new element of
actual history which swims against this stream is visible.[14] God's
power, reality, kingdom, the new world – all 'break through'.
The breakthrough of God's power in Christ is not a 'historical'
event but the 'uncovering of the never still, necessary reality in
the cross section of time'.[15] To have faith is to be caught up in
God's movement, but this is not to be identified with left wing
projects such as pacifism and social democracy. Such things do
not represent the kingdom of God, wrote Barth, 'but the old
human kingdom in a new guise'.[16] By contrast Barth wanted
the 'absolute revolution of God'. Christianity

> does not agree with the State, it negates it – both its presupposition
> and its essence. It is *more* than Leninism! As far as Christianity is
> concerned it is 'all or nothing' in the sense that the fulfilment it
> expects is not . . . the goal or result of a development or a gradual
> 'ascent of man' but the discovery of a new creation or the substance
> of a new knowledge. *This* programme cannot be the object of any
> ethics.[17]

[10] RI 171.
[11] The term 'process eschatology' is Michael Beintker's: 'Der Römerbrief
von 1919', in G. Sauter (ed.), *Verkündigung und Forschung: Beihefte zu 'Evangelische
Theologie'*, 2 (1985) 24.
[12] RI 24.
[13] RI 66–67; 223–225.
[14] RI 66–67; 85.
[15] RI 106.
[16] RI 42.
[17] RI 505–507.

Barth takes it for granted that a Christian can have nothing to do with 'Monarchy, Capitalism, Militarism, Patriotism and Liberalism'. On the other hand, anticipating his Tambach lecture he writes: 'The divine may not be politicised nor the human theologised – not even for the benefit of democracy and social democracy.' Whatever is done against the present State can in no way represent the victory of God's kingdom.[18] Revolt against the ruling powers leads to the region of God's wrath.[19] This does not equate with quietism, as might appear, because the 'Spirit does not knock at the hard shell of politics. It bursts it from inside!'[20] Barth echoes Marx's call for permanent revolution, over against petty bourgeois haste to bring everything to a conclusion. The love of Christ remains faithful to 'the hope, the unquiet, the longing, the radical and permanent revolution'.[21] At the present moment (1918!) Spirit can be nothing other than revolution – 'precisely what we call revolution at the moment!'[22] Amidst the disappointments of contemporary socialism we look forward to the hour when the embers of Marxist dogma are newly kindled and 'the socialist Church will be resurrected in a socialist world'.[23] In terms which anticipate liberation theology he insists that the movement of the kingdom is

> fundamentally and one sidely a movement from below. Whilst I can be a Jew to the Jews and a Greek to the Greeks I cannot be a lord to the lords or an aesthete to the aesthetes . . . Over against everything which wants to be great I must take the standpoint of the small people, with whom God begins, not because they are virtuous but because *their* righteousness does not stand in the way, or at least, does less so.[24]

The belief in God's revolution is quite clearly not meant to be the disarming of 'real' revolution (which is part of 'so called' history), but part of actual (i.e. divine) history, which has concrete effects in the present.

[18] RI 507–509.
[19] RI 509–510.
[20] RI 512–516.
[21] RI 353 and the Marx citation there.
[22] RI RI 316.
[23] RI 444.
[24] RI 490.

This book was overtaken by events: the abortive socialist revolution in Germany and the emergence of the Weimar Republic. Barth was called to work in the Republic in 1922 and he spent the months prior to his move feverishly revising the commentary. 'The present situation in its complete concreteness is our starting point' he maintained.[25] This situation was the threat of anarchy on the one hand, and the failure of the 'so called revolution' on the other. If anything eschatology has a larger place in this commentary than in the first and it is spelt out in terms of a theology of hope. Exegeting Romans 8:24–25 Barth writes:

> A Christianity which is not wholly and completely and without reserve (*restlos*) eschatology has wholly, completely and without reserve nothing to do with Christ ... whatever is not hope is wooden, half baked, shackled, leaden and awkward, like the word 'reality'. It does not liberate but takes prisoner. It is not grace, but judgement and corruption. It is not divine leadership but fate. It is not God but an image of unredeemed human beings.[26]

Appealing in part to Barth's own later self-criticism Moltmann maintains that the eschaton in Barth's second Romans became a transcendental eternity,

> the transcendental meaning of all ages, equally near to all the ages of history and equally far from all of them. (TH 40)

Under the bane of the transcendental eschatology of Kant, Barth became preoccupied with the dialectic of time and eternity (TH 51). Marquardt puts this another way in arguing that in the second edition Barth carries out 'a sensational anti-revolutionary turn'.[27]

Now it is true that Barth here borrows Kierkegaard's language of 'the Moment' and maintains that the only possibility of fulfilling the law of love is in 'the Moment' between the times,

---

[25] K. Barth, *Der Römerbrief* (2nd edn) (Zurich: Theologische Verlag 1948) (henceforth cited as RII) 413; (tr. E. Hoskyns; Oxford: Oxford University Press, 1933) 427. The quotations given here are my own translation.

[26] RII 298. The English translation (314) is more than usually misleading.

[27] F. W. Marquardt, *Theologie und Sozialismus: Das Beispeil Karl Barths* (Munich: Chr. Kaiser, 1972) 142.

which is 'no moment in time'. This 'Moment' is 'the eternal moment, the *Now* – when the past and future stand still'.[28] Such language is still further sharpened in the commentary on Corinthians which appeared in 1924, and there is truth in the critique. But it is not the whole truth, for the teaching about the 'Moment' is not about the dialectic of time and eternity but a way of emphasizing the crisis with which the death and resurrection of Christ faces us, which makes any idea of 'progress' or normal movement impossible. Far from leading us into the fervid and privatized world of individualist decision, Barth refuses to identify eschatology with the lukewarm progressivism of Ebner's republic. He is arguing, as he did in the first edition, that Christianity is far more revolutionary than current 'revolutionary' programmes. The cross casts a shadow on all 'healthy' humanity, where our most secure standing place is shattered, set ablaze and finally dissolved.[29] The characteristic marks of Christianity are 'deprivation and hope' rather than having and being.[30] The gospel is not there to give comfort but to witness to the power of God who raises the dead. 'It is the alarm cry, the fire bell, of a coming new world.'[31] In his self-critique written some sixteen years after this edition he noted that those who tried to make a fresh start at the original departure point of the older Blumhardt

> felt compelled to press beyond all temporal expectations ... to the view of a pure and absolute futurity of God and Jesus Christ as the limit and fulfilment of all time. It was due to the inner and outer circumstances of these years that the divine No of judgement, now understood as a No directed to both religious and cultural developments, had to be expressed more loudly, and certainly more clearly heard, than the gracious Yes that we believed we genuinely heard ... In the critical form in which it was presented, this could not unjustly be connected with the spiritual shaking experienced by Europeans through the world war.[32]

[28] RII 481 (tr. 497).
[29] RII 221 (tr. 239).
[30] RII 12 (tr. 36).
[31] RII 13 (tr. 38).
[32] K. Barth, *Church Dogmatics* (ET, Edinburgh: T. & T. Clark, 1936–1969), II/1, 634.

Barth's eschatology, then, remained radically political in the second commentary on Romans despite the lurid Kierkegaardian borrowings. For him Romans remained 'unmistakeably revolutionary'.[33] Where in the first commentary the target was principally legitimism, here the revolutionary is more in mind. 'It is highly unlikely that anyone will become a reactionary on the grounds of having read Romans!'[34] The danger, rather, is that the reader will take from the letter a 'Titanism of revolt and upheaval and renovation':

> Revolutionary Titanism is far more dangerous and godless than the reactionary kind because in its origin it is so much closer to the truth.[35]

As in the first commentary, Barth insists that evil is never the answer to evil. Before Hannah Arendt he was well aware that revolutions devour their own children. The true revolution is forgiveness of sins and resurrection of the dead, but the revolutionary chooses hatred and insubordination. This choice is worse than the legitimist option for satisfaction, security and usurpation because 'by it God is far better understood, but so much the worse abused'.[36] What then? An endorsement of the status quo? Not at all. In place of the first commentary's denial of legitimacy, we have 'the great positive possibility':

> Not a single act but the bringing together of all positive (protesting!) ethical possibilities . . . We define love as the 'Great Positive Possibility', because in it the revolutionary aspect of all ethics comes to light, because it is actually concerned with the denial and breaking up of the status quo (*das Bestehende*) . . . in so far as we love one another we cannot wish to uphold the present order as such, because in love we do the new thing which brings the old crashing down.[37]

Love is the denial and demolition of the existing order which no revolt can bring about, the destruction of everything which is – 'like God'.[38]

---

[33] RII 468 (tr. 484).
[34] RII 461 (tr. 478).
[35] RII 462 (tr. 478).
[36] RII 465 (tr. 481).
[37] RII 476–477 (tr. 493).
[38] RII 480 (tr. 496).

In both commentaries on Romans, then, we have an eschatology which is politically exceptionally radical, though it is open to argument that what is proposed in the second commentary is impossibly utopian, and careless of realization.

But we need to press on and ask what happened to this radical eschatology when the red pastor became the professor. Many commentators on Barth's eschatology stop with the second Romans, or perhaps with the commentary on Corinthians. As early as the 1930s former comrades in arms like Gogarten alleged that Barth became a prisoner to his theological system, an allegation encouraged by the notorious remark in 1934 that it was important to do theology 'as if nothing had happened'. Does the political radical fired by an eschatological, if not millenarian, hope for a new world become the academic chiefly concerned with dogmatic minutiae? Was Barth, after 1922, or at least after 1942 when the fusillade of writings encouraging resistance to fascism stops, imprisoned in an ivory tower? Of course, detailing the eschatology of the *Dogmatics* does not provide a comprehensive answer to that question, but, given the force of the eschatology in the two books which made his name, we might expect it to give us a clue, and in fact it does so. It is clear that had Barth lived to complete volume five of the *Dogmatics* we would have many hundreds of pages on eschatology, as we see from paragraph 12 of the *Dogmatics*, on God as Redeemer, but even without this there remains a great deal. In terms of the questions with which eschatology normally deals we have extended treatments of death and the last judgment, of hope and promise, of God's glory and eternal joy, of the kingdom of God, and Barth himself drew attention to his account of threefold time and the threefold parousia of Christ as significant contributions to eschatology.[39] It is true that the *Dogmatics* is not 'wholly and completely' eschatology as the second Romans required theology to be, but eschatology is never far away either. Contrary to what is often implied, Barth's theology never became de-eschatologized.

[39] K. Barth, *Letters 1961–1968* (tr. G. Bromiley; Edinburgh: T. & T. Clark, 1981) 176.

At the deepest level what marks the eschatological cast of Barth's theology is his understanding of God's historicity.

> God is historical even in Godself, and much more so in God's relationship to the reality which is distinct from Godself. God is the Lord of God's kingdom, deciding, acting, ruling, doing good, creating peace, judging, giving joy, living in God's will and acts . . . It is the kingdom which God sets up in the course of a historical movement which has a beginning, middle and an end. It is the kingdom which comes from heaven to earth.[40]

This historicity of God led Barth to redefine eternity in terms of God's pre-, post- and supra-temporality. Eschatology corresponded to post-temporality, taught above all by the Blumhardts, who emphasized this aspect of the divine reality in their teaching on Christian hope. Writing in the period immediately before the Second World War, Barth believed that it was now necessary to re-emphasize other aspects of God's temporality. To focus too completely on eschatology is to fail to do justice to the living God, active and knowable here and now.

> Such interesting concentrations in theology must be completely avoided if we are not to come under the domination of compelling ideas . . . The doctrine of the living God will not tolerate any such concentrations . . . There can be no vitality and freshness in theology where there is only one insight.[41]

It was doubtless this conviction which led him to describe the God of *Theology of Hope* as 'rather a pauper'.

The hope which was a key part of the Blumhardts' gospel was likewise a key part of Barth's. He emphasizes again and again that Christian life is essentially a life in hope. 'Christian hope is a present being in and with and by the promise of the future.'[42] Human being in Christ is in its totality teleologically directed, 'an eschatological being'.[43] By contrast traditional Protestant teaching had 'a very this worldly, immanentist, even middle class appearance'. It is living under the promise which makes human life radical. We must distinguish great and small

---

[40] K. Barth, *Church Dogmatics* IV/1, 112.
[41] K. Barth, *Church Dogmatics* II/1, 636.
[42] K. Barth, *Church Dogmatics* IV/1, 120.
[43] K. Barth, *Church Dogmatics* IV/1, 109.

hopes. Christ is the content of the great hope, but there are also penultimate and provisional hopes, and it is in these many little hopes that the Christian lives from day to day.[44] Our constitution in hope is the work of the Spirit.

> Grounded in God, namely, in the God who acts in Jesus Christ, and orientated on him, Christian hope is an uninterrupted and unequivocally positive expectation of the future.[45]

Christian hope makes the believer 'more restless than the most restless, more urgent than the most urgent revolutionaries in his immediate or more distant circle'.[46] Christian existence in hope also means that ethics is eschatological. In an early essay Barth even insisted that ethics was necessarily millenarian, and that it was about the abolition of class, nation and war.[47] In the *Dogmatics* he insists that the command of God has in human life 'an urgency which is not so apparent from other standpoints and which may be rightly described as eschatological'.[48] We live in the time between Christ's knocking and his entering. It is this which means that every human act must be measured and tested by the question whether it is a seizing or neglecting of the unique opportunity each person is given. Finally, this eschatological nature of ethics is reflected in the gospel of the kingdom. The kingdom is not identical to the community but

> As the kingdom of God is on the way from the first to the last revelation, it is the community. As the kingdom or rule of God is engaged in this movement, it creates the sphere corresponding to it and it is to be found on this way too.[49]

Barth returned to the theme of the kingdom, and to the Blumhardts, in the draft of what was to have been paragraph 78 of the *Dogmatics*, which he never prepared for publication. We have to be clear that we cannot make the kingdom a utopia,

---

[44] K. Barth, *Church Dogmatics* IV/1, 121.

[45] K. Barth, *Church Dogmatics* IV/3, 910.

[46] K. Barth, *Church Dogmatics* IV/4, 201.

[47] K. Barth, 'The Problem of Ethics Today', in *The Word of God and the Word of Man* (tr. D. Horton; London: Hodder & Stoughton, 1928) 158.

[48] K. Barth, *Church Dogmatics* III/4, 579.

[49] K. Barth, *Church Dogmatics* IV/2, 656.

but on the other hand it 'certainly calls for human righteousness and order amid all human unrighteousness and disorder'.[50]

> As they pray for the coming of the kingdom of God, they call upon God to accept and have mercy on erring and confused humanity by establishing right and righteousness in the land in the definitive manifestation and revelation of the King raised up by him.[51]

Prayer for the kingdom issues in *fiat iustitia*, though not *et pereat mundum*.

It is fair to say that at no point in the *Dogmatics* is eschatology entirely forgotten. The impression that Barth is not true to his original eschatological intent arises partly from his Christology and partly from his view of revelation. There is undoubtedly something in Bonhoeffer's allegation of christomonism, which Barth disliked so much. Of course, Christian eschatology is grounded in Christ, but in Barth Christ becomes the *content* of eschatology.

> Nothing which will be has not already taken place on Easter Day – included and anticipated in the person of the one man Jesus . . . Strictly speaking there are no 'last things,' i.e. no abstract and autonomous last things apart from and alongside Him, the last One.[52]

Barth agrees with Tertullian that Christ is the kingdom.

> Jesus Christ is the new thing. *He* is the mystery that cannot be imprisoned in any system of human conceptuality but can be revealed and known only in parables. *He* is God acting concretely within human history . . . *He* is the total and definitive limitation of human unrighteousness and disorder, of the interim demonic world of unchained powers: the conqueror of this world, the victorious enemy of all the enmity of men against God, one another and themselves.[53]

It is this tendency of the figure of Christ to fill the entire horizon which gives the impression that the *Dogmatics* lacks a real

---

[50] K. Barth, *The Christian Life* (tr. G. Bromiley; Grand Rapids: Eerdmans, 1981) 239–240.

[51] K. Barth, *The Christian Life*, 261.

[52] K. Barth, *Church Dogmatics* III/2, 489–490.

[53] K. Barth, *The Christian Life*, 252.

eschatological dimension. His treatment of the resurrection is linked to this. The resurrection is the revelation of the truth about Jesus, the 'verdict of the Father'. But then, as Moltmann rightly sees, this treatment of the resurrection dehistoricizes it. It is 'no longer an eschatological happening. It is simply and solely the transcendent endorsement of the redemptive significance of the cross of Christ' (WJC 231). The agenda of *Theology of Hope*, centred on promise, revelation and history, was precisely to remedy this problem.

Jürgen Moltmann

In his brief autobiographical recollections Moltmann writes that the '60s were brimming over with movements of hope and experiences of rebirth and renewal', and suggests that this is why the *Theology of Hope* found the resonance it did in 1964 (EG 12). On the other hand, there was also the apocalyptic moment of the Cuban missile crisis in 1962, in which 'human hearts failed them for fear', and hope and renewal were certainly not the whole story. Daniel Bell, Edward Shils, Seymour Lipset and Raymond Aron were all proclaiming the end of ideology at the very moment that Bloch finally published *The Principle of Hope*.[54] Their thesis was that the great ideologies forged at the end of the eighteenth and nineteenth centuries, and above all Marxism, had shown themselves to be morally bankrupt. The history of the twentieth century showed only too clearly that ideologies were fantasies of the intellectuals, totalizing, utopian, dogmatic and naive. They generated terror, propaganda and the camps. What was needed instead was modest, pragmatic reformism, not revolution but a mixed economy and the welfare state. Theologically, 1962 saw the publication of the all time theological best seller, J. A. T. Robinson's *Honest to God*, a garbled account of Bonhoeffer, Tillich and Bultmann which sold 200,000 copies, and which led no less a reviewer than Alasdair

---

[54] D. Bell, *The End of Ideology* (Glencoe, Illinois: Free Press, 1960); S. Lipset, *Political Man* (London: Heinemann, 1959); E Shils, 'Ideology and the Intellectual', in *Sewanee Review* 66 (1958) 450–480; R. Aron, *The Opium of the Intellectuals* (London: Secker & Warburg, 1957).

MacIntyre to conclude that the bishop was for certain an atheist.[55] From this point of view *Theology of Hope* was counter-cultural in that it appealed to all kinds of utopian impulses from the standpoint of a robust faith in the God revealed in Scripture.

Moltmann begins *Theology of Hope* with a programmatic state-ment which echoes Barth's affirmation of eschatology in the second Romans:

> The eschatological is not one element of Christianity, but it is the medium of Christian faith as such, the key in which everything is set, the glow that suffuses everything here in the dawn of an expected new day. (TH 16)

The energetic way in which this programme was carried through prompted Barth to write that it made theology too much a matter of eschatological principle: 'You know that I too was once on the edge of moving in this direction, but I refrained from doing so.'[56] This was an unfair comment to the extent that *Theology of Hope*, like both *Romans* commentaries, was an attempt to right the boat, or perhaps better to set it on a new course, rather than to provide a substitute for the *Dogmatics*.

The principal polemical front in the book is directed at the 'epiphany of the eternal present', and the attack on natural theology may be understood as part of that. Moltmann showed, more clearly than Barth, the way in which these two forms of theology supported the status quo. His contrast of the wayfaring God YHWH with the God of Parmenides has drawn fire from the word go, but continues to be persuasive.[57] The religion of the epiphany of the eternal present, which takes ever new guises in various forms of sacramental theology, mysticism, and 'transcendental meditation', is the religion of the sacred canopy. It was, as Moltmann notes, not the delay of the parousia but the idea that all our hopes are *fulfilled* which led to the acute hellenization of Christianity (TH 157). Against this he insists

---

[55] A. MacIntyre, 'God and the Theologians', in *Against the Self Images of the Age* (London: Duckworth, 1971).

[56] K. Barth, *Letters 1961–1968*, 175.

[57] The sharpest attack I know of is in H. McCabe, 'The Involvement of God', in *God Matters* (London: Chapman, 1987). Though I would like to appropriate Aquinas for the radical left, I remain unpersuaded.

again and again that the job of faith is to unsettle us, to provide a disturbance. The one who hopes becomes

> homeless with the homeless, for the sake of the home of recon-ciliation. He becomes restless with the restless, for the sake of the peace of God. He becomes rightless with the rightless, for the sake of the diviner right that is coming. (TH 224)

The promise which keeps history on the move is a *promissio inquieta* which could never be satisfied with the pragmatism of the end of ideology (TH 88). Christian theology is, then, as Peter Winzeler described Barth's theology, *Widerstehende Theologie*, a theology of resistance.

> In practical opposition to things as they are, and in creative re-shaping of them, Christian hope calls them in question and this serves the things that are to come. (TH 330)

As strongly as Barth, Moltmann insists that eschatology is grounded in Christology: 'Christian eschatology is at heart Christology in an eschatological perspective' (TH 192). The key difference is the insistence that everything is not yet completed, that there are promises outstanding: 'With the raising of Jesus all has not yet been done' (TH 163). In a way which recalls the 'great and little hopes' of *Romans*, Moltmann insists that the believer hopes not just for God but for 'this and that'. Faith

> does not merely hope personally 'in him', but has also substantial hopes of his lordship, his peace and his righteousness on earth. Otherwise hope itself could unobtrusively change into a kind of fulfilment. (TH 119)

For Barth, as for the Old Testament scholar Zimmerli, God in Godself is the content of the future, but to this Moltmann rightly objects that it 'is not the name that is the object of knowledge, but the claim to power contained in it' (TH 115). Because this is so 'the world is the correlate of hope' – the place where real possibilities can be fleshed out (TH 289). At the same time the answer to Barth's question whether Moltmann had not simply baptized Bloch's principle of hope is that it is the grounding of Christian eschatology in Christ and *his* future which provides the touchstone to distinguish the spirit of eschatology from that of utopia (TH 17). In other words, the hoped for future is given a quite definite shape by our knowledge of the crucified and risen Christ. This Christ-shaped future is what we call the kingdom of God, 'in which all things attain to right, to life, to peace, to freedom, and to truth', and in which, above all, in contradistinction to Bloch, death is conquered (TH 224, 220).

On the cover of the first edition of *Theology of Hope* appeared Gollwitzer's criticism that the book gave no concrete guidance on eschatological ethics. Five years later this kind of criticism was developed by Rubem Alves, who opposed to Moltmann what he called 'a theology of human hope'. His charge was twofold. First, that Moltmann was essentially idealist, believing that it is promise which keeps the future open as opposed to concrete human experiences of suffering.

> The pattern for the historical movement which Moltmann offers is . . . basically platonic. It is eros . . . which creates the *cor inquietum*. And more than that: God becomes the *primum movens*, as with Aristotle, pulling history to its future, but without being involved in history.[58]

As opposed to this political idealism Alves believes that human beings are aware of the pain of their situation simply because they are human beings and feel in their flesh the inadequacy between world, self and community. Secondly – and this was a criticism suggested by Barth – Alves believes that Moltmann fails to do justice to the present reality of God. The biblical communities

> did not know a God whose essential nature was the future, the *primum movens* ahead of history. The Old and New Testaments speak about the historical present of God. The pure futuricity of God is a new form of Docetism in which God loses the present dimension and therefore becomes ahistorical.[59]

Alves anticipated a good deal of criticism from what shortly became liberation theology, which found the *Theology of Hope* too abstract and insufficiently engaged with concrete political issues. Moltmann himself recognized the validity of this criticism

[58] R. Alves, *Theology of Human Hope* (New York: World Publishing, 1969) 59.

to the extent that, with Johann Baptist Metz, he began to develop a 'political theology' at this time. But once again we have to ask in what a politically radical theology consists. Returning to the third thesis on Feuerbach we have to insist on an inescapable dialectic between theory and praxis. It is not idealism to claim that the contribution of ideas to political change is indispensable. It is idealism to focus only on ideas and not, in Marx's words, to see that they come from 'real, active human beings as they are conditioned by a definite development of their productive forms'. The famous formulation, which Alves is following, that it is not consciousness that determines life but life that determines consciousness is inadequately dialectical. Liberation theology's relentless insistence on beginning with praxis, throughout the 1970s, ran into great difficulties because of its failure to respect this. In Juan Luis Segundo, for example, it involved the paradoxical insistence that faith had no content.[60] But what is faith which does not believe in this or trust in that? Segundo started his hermeneutical circle with the experience of oppression, but this fails to do justice to Freire's perception that oppression is internalized, and that consciousness-raising education is needed to enable people to see oppression for what it is. When Moltmann speaks of the *promissio inquieta* he is talking about the way in which telling the story of the crucified and risen Messiah raises consciousness, stirs up trouble, by contrasting the present godless situation with the promised future. The claim that Moltmann's theology fails to acknowledge God's present reality in turn fails to see that God is present in and through the promise. To illustrate what this means we can see that there is all the difference in the world between the eucharist which is really a glorified form of benediction, focused on the 'real presence' of Christ in the elements, and the presence of God in word and sacrament which strains after the kingdom of God. There is nothing docetic, nor ahistorical, about this. And what about the frequent charge that this theology is too abstract? Barth noted that *Theology of Hope* was not so much an eschatology as prolegomena to an eschatology and an eschatological ethic.

---

[59] Alves, *Theology*, 94.
[60] J. L. Segundo, *Faith and Ideologies* (Maryknoll: Orbis, 1984).

It is clear that it is important to detail theological responses
to concrete situations, as, for example, Ulrich Duchrow has
done for the world economy, and Moltmann himself with the
State. At the same time, in the fine phrase of Ellul, there are no
Christian ethics, but only the ethical inventiveness of Christians.
Theology of Hope feeds that ethical inventiveness, and it feeds it
in the direction of political radicalism, of making all things new,
of refusing to be satisfied even with the 'never had it so good'
status quo of Europe in 1964.

The moment at which *Theology of Hope* appeared was the
prelude to a profound cultural revolution, affecting the
northern hemisphere countries in the first instance, but,
through 'globalization', the whole world thereafter. The
arrival of an age of affluence for the majority in the northern
hemisphere nations, huge advances in medicine, and especially
in contraceptive technique, in media and communications
technology, in the industrial balance of power between East
and West, have all played their part in this revolution. In the
course of it the sexual contract, and our understanding of
gender, have been renegotiated as never before in human
history; detraditionalization has spread to most parts of the
earth; class politics have been replaced by the micro-politics of
gender and new social movements. In the North the discourse
of secularization has been replaced by that of postmodernity
with its 'incredulity towards metanarratives', in Jean François
Lyotard's now celebrated phrase, aversion to grand social
designs and all forms of political engineering, and acceptance
of the irredeemable plurality of the world. What happens to
political eschatology in this context?

'Every theology undoubtedly has its historical context',
Moltmann warned in 1975, 'but the context is not yet the *text*
itself' (EH 44). What is important is the concern of theology
itself. But the hallmark of a contextual theology is the attempt
to speak theologically to the situation of the day, not at the
level of the ephemeral, but of the fundamental, and Moltmann's
theology has in this sense always been contextual. We have, then,
to understand Moltmann's work, since the appearance of his
second great book, *The Crucified God*, in 1972, as situated against
the background of this cultural revolution. As compared with

Theology of Hope there are three theological developments of especial significance. The first is that Moltmann develops a far more positive appreciation of apocalyptic, the second that the dialogue with twentieth-century Judaism becomes more overt, the third that it is now much clearer that 'kingdom eschatology' makes no sense without cosmic eschatology.

In a sense the possibility of a humanly induced apocalypse was announced on 6 August 1945, and the Peace Movement of the 1950s and 1960s was the response to that possibility. It is remarkable, however, how the image of apocalypse has gripped the creative imagination in the 1980s and 1990s in a way which it did not in those earlier decades. (One thinks, for example, of Francis Ford Coppola's *Apocalypse Now* [1985], Julian Barnes' *History of the World in ten and a half chapters* [1989], Joseph Heller's *Closing Time* [1994].) What happened at 1.23 a.m. on 26 April 1986 at Chernobyl immensely reinforced the apocalyptic sense. It leads Moltmann to insist that we can no longer have any certainty that the earth will continue to survive. As opposed to the situation in 1964 we have to learn not just to hope, but to hope in danger.

> In view of the deadly dangers threatening the world, Christian remembrance makes present the death of Christ in its apocalyptic dimensions, in order to draw from his resurrection from the dead hope for 'the life of the world to come', and from his rebirth to eternal life hope for the rebirth of the cosmos ... Life out of this hope then means already acting here and today in accordance with the world of justice and righteousness and peace, contrary to all appearances, and contrary to all historical chances of success. (CoG 234).

In the thirty years between his two essays on eschatology biblical scholarship has rediscovered apocalyptic literature as the literature of resistance, and Moltmann has appropriated this in the new, ultimately threatening situation. Against the 'eat, drink, for tomorrow we die' mentality of a consumerism terrified to face reality, a politically responsible theology is a theology of care for the threatened earth. Because the ecological crisis is, as Moltmann has said, 'a religious crisis of the paradigm in which people in the western world put their trust and live', we need an apocalyptic spirituality which combats apathy and cynicism and teaches us to 'lift up our heads' for God's new beginning (CoG 211, 230).

Although Ernst Bloch appeared only seven times in the footnotes to *Theology of Hope* (as compared to copious references to Barth and Bultmann), Moltmann always acknowledged that it was reading *The Principle of Hope* which was the spark for the book. In the series of works which began in 1980, Rosenzweig, Scholem, Adorno and Walter Benjamin have been increasingly important partners in a way that they have not been for Moltmann's peers, and never were for Barth, whose bemused response to Rosenzweig appears constantly in the correspondence with Miskotte. The impact of this dialogue has been to keep his theology very firmly anchored both in the reality of day-to-day history and in the terror of history. Of course, kabbalistic Judaism could be speculative, and Moltmann has often enough been criticized for borrowing the idea of the *tsimtsum*, but by and large it has always been much more down to earth than Christian theology. We can see the difference this makes very clearly in his Christology. Where Barth's Jesus is always the Christ – trailing clouds of ontological glory – Moltmann thinks of him as the Messiah. The primary categories are not the an- and enhypostasia, but historical and social ones known in the Messianic movement and the Messianic *façon de vivre*. In the same way, to learn eschatology from Jewish thinkers is to learn, as he puts it, 'redemption from the power of history' but within history (CoG 45). A messianic interpretation of eschatology looks for an interruption in the 'laws' of the market and the 'compulsion' of competition.

> [A]nother future becomes perceptible. The laws and forces of the past are no longer 'compulsive'. God's messianic future wins power over the present. New perspectives open up. The deadliness of progress towards the economic, ecological, nuclear and genetic catastrophes is recognized; and the modern world's lack of future is perceived. The way becomes free for alternative developments. (CoG 45)

Millenarianism, the so-called *opinio judaica*, plays a role in the second book, against what is clearly perceived as a much darker horizon, which it did not in the first. Bloch's 'where deliverance is near, danger also grows' is frequently quoted. Rejecting both political and ecclesial millenarianism he advocates an eschatological millenarianism which, again, is concerned with inculcating a spirituality of resistance.

> The Thousand Years' reign of Christ, 'the kingdom of peace', is hope's positive counterpart to the Antichrist's destruction of the world in a storm of fire, and is indispensable for every alternative form of life and action which will withstand the ravages of the world here and now. Without millenarian hope, the Christian ethic of resistance and the consistent discipleship of Christ lose their most powerful motivation. (CoG 201)

The third major change is the greatly increased prominence given to cosmic eschatology, again partly in response to the ecological crisis. Too anthropocentric a theology, focusing exclusively on the kingdom, fails to respect the rights of the non-human creation, and likewise fails to understand that human being is 'bound up with rocks and stones and trees' and that the non-human creation is not simply there at human disposal.

In considering Moltmann's contribution to a radical political theology in a postmodern environment, it is worth noting two other points which are not strictly speaking part of his eschatology. One of the leading interpreters of postmodernity, Frederic Jameson, identifies its religious and theological correlate as fundamentalism, *tout court*.[61] One can see the point, for fundamentalism is essentially a defensive reaction to an aggressive pluralism of beliefs and lifestyles. Moltmann's response to this has been, since *The Church in the Power of the Spirit* (1975), to lay stress on the openness of the church, on a lifestyle of open friendship, on the openness of world process, grounded in a Trinity which is open to otherness. In attempting a theology which is radically trinitarian and open in this way Moltmann has taken up the challenge Barth set him on reading *Theology of Hope*.[62] By accepting the doctrine of the immanent trinity, Barth said, it would be possible to give the eschata full

---

[61] F. Jameson, *Postmodernism, or, The Cultural Logic of Late Capitalism* (London: Verso, 1991) 388.

[62] K. Barth, *Letters 1961–1968*, 175–176.

weight whilst giving honour also to the kingdoms of nature and grace. A theology of open process is not only the necessary non-fundamentalist response to the situation of postmodernity, but it reads the whole of creation, including human nature, in terms of possibility. This is opposed to both the fatalism of the market and to any determinism of gender.

It is also interesting to observe the correlation between the agenda for a future radical politics of contemporary secular left thinkers such as David Miliband and Anthony Giddens with Moltmann's proposals in *The Spirit of Life* (1991).[63] Moltmann shares with them a focus on new social movements – peace groups, environmental groups, Third World groups and self-help groups and on the realization of participatory democracy. To put words into his mouth, what emerges as a liberative politics is a feminist, Green socialism. In theological terms this translates into the affirmation (in which he differs most decidedly from Barth!) of the feminist movement as part of an eschatological experience of the Spirit and of a church orientated towards the kingdom of God (SL 241, 248).

Eschatology and Transformative Praxis

Behind some of the criticism of Moltmann's political theology, especially that which emanates from Latin America, lies suspicion of the academy and the ivory tower, of experience insufficiently grounded in praxis. It is difficult to know how to respond to this other than with Gollwitzer's *Denken kann auch Dienen*, or the remark of Lenin which all students in the 1960s learned that 'the first duty of the revolutionary is to study'. Marquardt's thesis that it was socialist praxis which produced Barth's first, truly socialist commentary carries with it the implication that the move to the academy produced a different kind of theology. Georges Casalis, Peter Winzeler and more recently Sabine Plonz have all sought to counter this

---

[63] Cf. A. Giddens, *Beyond Left and Right: The Future of Radical Politics* (Cambridge: Polity, 1994); D. Miliband (ed.), *Reinventing the Left* (Cambridge: Polity, 1994); H. Wainwright, *Arguments for a New Left* (Oxford: Blackwell, 1994).

implication.[64] In Moltmann's case his passionate concern for both the Third World and the environment is transparent. In any case, exactly the same questions may be put to Bloch and Adorno, to William Blake and even, to some extent, to Marx. Activism is not the only, or even the most important, form of political service. The crucial transition from ideas to policies and action is carried out, for the most part, not by individuals but by movements, groups and parties. Moltmann in particular has understood the church as just such a movement. Most of us who are part of this movement will share Alves' reaction that the church we know is hopelessly compromised, straggling along in the moralistic rear rather than leading the revolutionary shock troops. If we stay with it it is because of a conviction that what it takes to make and to keep human life human is inadequately grounded in Alves' political humanism, and that the death and resurrection of Christ focuses what is essential in a way that nothing else does. If this commitment is something more than escapism it is in virtue of eschatology, which we have learned from both Barth and Moltmann is the hope which is loyal to the earth, and which represents the refusal of all complacency. Under the impact of this eschatology Christian mission has been reconceived. When Barth was a student, as he noted later with characteristic irony, well meaning people had in view the evangelization of the world in this generation. Though that was never part of his horizon, his account of the church's task remained confined to witness to Christ and, in *Dogmatics* IV/3, took very 'churchy' form. Moltmann puts more insistently the questions of what the implications of faith in Christ are – the 'this and that' of the kingdom. Christian mission, then, includes resistance to the idolatry of consumerism, of the market, and of the arms trade which is bound up with it. It involves, in other words, a radical politics. Both theologians find in eschatology not only the source of unending disquiet with the status quo but even more importantly the critique which prevents revolutions devouring their own children, which challenges the hubris which has been the fatal flaw of all

---

[64] P. Winzeler, *Widerstehender Theologie* (Stuttgart: Alektor, 1982); S. Plonz, *Die herrenlosen Gewalte* (Mainz: Grünewald, 1995).

revolutionary projects since the eighteenth century. What the eschatology of these theologians offers us is not just the courage of despair but the courage of faith in the God who raised Jesus from the dead. The task of the church, they teach us, in an increasingly apocalyptic scenario, is to live by the messianic politics of resistance and hope.

WHAT HAS HAPPENED TO OUR UTOPIAS?

1968 and 1989

Response to Timothy Gorringe

JÜRGEN MOLTMANN

Tim Gorringe's account of eschatology and political radicalism in Karl Barth and in my own work is so good and unerring that I can only agree with it entirely, and can find nothing to criticize, and no point for even the slightest reservation. But there was one theologian who linked me with Barth in a special and very personal way. Tim Gorringe names him. It was Helmut Gollwitzer, during his Berlin period. Gollwitzer was Barth's best pupil and his friend, and from 1971, in the companionship of the editorial board of the periodical *Evangelische Theologie*, he became my friend too, and my teacher in the practical questions of political theology which impinged on us in divided Germany, with its immense arms build-up. After Ernst Wolf's death, I had suddenly to take over the editorship of this important journal of the Confessing Church. Helmut Gollwitzer was my ally whenever controversial theological-political decisions had to be made. We introduced Jim Cone and his 'black theology' to Germany, and were the first to take up the challenges of the liberation theology of Latin America. In the situation posed by the build-up of nuclear armaments, we fought for a theological

declaration on peace which would not fall below the level of
the Barmen Theological Declaration. As a result, some members
of our editorial board left the journal, but new members came
to take their place. After the turning point of 1989, in remembrance of Gollwitzer's eschatological visions and his political
commitment, I wrote the following justification of practical
utopian thinking, in the face of the sneers of conservative
proponents of Realpolitik. I believe that it is with this contribution that I can best enter into Tim Gorringe's concern.

1

Ever since the undramatic collapse of the eastern bloc and
'socialism as it really exists' in 1989–1990, 'the end of utopia'
has been dramatically proclaimed in the West. In 1991 Joachim
Fest wrote the book on this neo-German trend under the title
The Ruined Dream – the End of the Utopian Era.[1] He began with
the peculiar assertion that with 'the end of socialism' utopias in
general had 'died the death', and that in future 'the ballyhoo
of utopias' was something people would have to live without.
Life without utopia, he maintained, was now simply 'the price
of modernity'. He ended up burying a whole era from 1789
onwards, for the French Revolution was 'the first emotionally
loaded attempt to put utopian ideas into practice'. Carried away
as he was by his enthusiasm over the end, it escaped him that
he was also throwing on to the scrap heap of history the
Universal Declaration of Human Rights, the democratic constitutional state, and 'the American dream' – in fact the whole
'modernity project'; and that by so doing he was announcing
nothing less than *the end of the future.* So must we in future exist
without a future?

Let us cast our minds back. In the 1960s a new utopian
rejoicing undoubtedly prevailed among us. After the restora-
tions and stagnations of the postwar period – 'No experiments!'
– everywhere we saw new voyages setting forth for new shores,
with practical utopias. With Willy Brandt we wanted 'to risk more

---

[1] *Der zerstörte Traum – vom Ende des utopischen Zeitalters* (Berlin, 1991; no
English translation).

democracy'. With Vatican II the Catholic Church began a great leap forward, in a few years catching up with Reformation and Enlightenment, in order to bring them into the present. In the United States the civil rights movement achieved widespread influence, and surmounted white racism in both structures and ways of thinking. The peoples of the Third World were seeking their independence and their dignity. In Latin America, the liberation movements and liberation theologies were springing up. In Czechoslovakia, 'socialism with a human face' developed, a democratic socialism contrary to its dictatorial predecessor. All these new beginnings in the direction of a new future developed specific utopias – counter-images to a present fixated on the past, counter-histories to the history of violence and terror.

It will immediately be clear that these were not primarily social utopias. In the context of their particular situation, they were for the most part utopias of democratic human rights. The 'long trek through the institutions' was supposed to reform those institutions in such a way that state, society and churches could once more become authentic and could live up to their own claims. Their world was to be changed, so that their proper image might emerge, and their corrupt disfigurement be overcome. The legitimation crises of state, society and religion were to be surmounted.

2

As we know, the great teacher of hope in the West Germany of the 1960s was Ernst Bloch, who had fled from East Germany in 1961. His three-volume, encyclopaedic work *The Principle of Hope* (Frankfurt 1959, East Berlin 1960, ET 1986) led out of the postwar psychological climate of existentialism and the religion of 'consoled despair'. He lent us a guiding passion and a moral vision. His philosophy gathered into a generous pattern the loose threads of our experiences and our expectation.

When I asked him at our first meeting: 'But Herr Bloch, you are a Marxist, aren't you?' he replied coolly: 'I have incorporated Marxism into my system.' But then what is the Leitmotif of his system? It is demonstrably Jewish and (influenced by his first wife Elsa) Christian *messianism*. That is why Bloch drew the religions into his criticism and his visions, and in the messianic hope for home and identity found the scarlet thread running through the religious and the atheistic. From Bloch we learnt the inalienable unity of *social utopias* and *utopias of justice*. 'No socialism without democracy – no democracy without socialism', Rosa Luxemburg had proclaimed. For liberty cannot be achieved without equality, or equality without liberty. The modern world begins with the acknowledgment of human rights – that all human beings are created free and equal. 'The social utopias painted in advance of time conditions in which there are no weary and heavy laden; natural law constructed conditions in which the humiliated and despised are no more', wrote Bloch in 1961 in his book *Natural Law and Human Dignity*[2] with good biblical echoes. But neither social utopias nor natural law can be implemented without a covenant with nature, the still hidden subject. Without just concurrences with nature there is no just human society, he wrote, long before there was any Club of Rome or any Green parties. On the other hand, all his books end with religious vistas – towards a church as a 'power-free teaching power of conscience', towards a church 'as a ship without superstition, ever voyaging forth', towards a 'religion as the retrospective bond with our poverty-stricken fragmentariness of a whole forward-looking dream', and towards that 'kindness' which as brotherliness and sisterliness is able to hold in equilibrium those two principles of liberty and equality. If anything is missing, it is the great Christian *resurrection hope* – death swallowed up in victory – and the vision of the new heaven and the new earth from which death, sorrow, pain and crying will disappear.

3

The real changeover from utopian rejoicing to a bleak apocalypse without hope did not take place in 1989. It already began in 1968, when the troops of the Warsaw Pact put a brutal

---

[2] ET tr. D. J. Schmidt; Cambridge, Massachusetts/London: MIT Press, 1986. This quotation is translated directly from the German.

end to 'socialism with a human face', when the papal encyclical *Humanae vitae* blocked the reforming spirit of Vatican II, when Martin Luther King was murdered, and Rudi Dutschke shot, and the carpet bombings of the Vietnam war started. At that time we came to understand the future as by no means open, or an antechamber of unlimited possibilities, but as occupied by counter-forces and counter-utopias. 'I was full of enthusiasm for utopia and found consolation in the apocalypse', wrote the Rumanian writer Cioran in Paris at that time. He was speaking ironically, for – unlike the Jewish and Christian apocalypses – the apocalypses of the modern world have no hope at all, and are totally devoid of consolation. The 'nuclear Armageddon' about which Ronald Reagan talked so darkly means annihilation of the world without the kingdom of God. The ecological end of the world which many people are afraid of, and not without cause, means the destruction of nature without a new creation. The genocides and mass annihilations which our century of violence has perpetrated are crimes against humanity, exterminism without God. It is no wonder that in the face of the power of annihilation which has fallen into human hands, the dreaded terrors are interpreted apocalyptically.

But a new *apocalyptic terrorism* has developed too. 'Without destruction there can be no construction' was Mao Tse-Tung's order to the cultural revolution. It cost the lives of millions, and reduced China's finest cultural treasures to rubble. In Cambodia, the mass murderer Pol Pot took Mao's watchword seriously. Two million dead were left on the killing fields. Apocalyptic terrorism can lead to the mass suicide of sect followers: in 1978 in Jonestown, Guyana, it was 912 members of the People's Temple commune; in 1993 in Waco, Texas, seventy-eight adherents of the Branch Davidian group, and in Vietnam fifty-two members of an end-of-the-world sect; in 1994 fifty-three members of the Solar Temple sect in Switzerland and Canada; in 1997 thirty-nine adherents of a Ufo death cult in San Diego, California; and so on. Their motive was to achieve 'translation' from this world, which is hopelessly approaching its end, into a better one. Apocalyptic terrorism can also lead to the mass murder of people in this wicked world for the sake of a purer future. The people responsible for the Oklahoma bombing and the American militia men believed something like that. The poison gas sect of Shoko Asahara who are facing trial in Tokyo were evidently convinced that they were called to 'the final struggle'. 'Rather an end with terror than this terror without end' was the phrase used by many people in Germany in the final year of the war. The person for whom the present, his own life, the hustle and bustle of other people, and 'the whole system' is nothing but a horror without hope, will be prepared to press for 'the end' in just this way. The more the cynicism of the powerful provokes the resignation of the powerless, the more desires for annihilation will spread. Then the end of the future will unexpectedly become the end of the world.

Many hopes which were vested in practical utopias in the 1960s underestimated the powers of evil and death, and came to grief accordingly. 'Can hope be disappointed?' asked Bloch when he came to Tübingen, and answered: for hope, it is a point of honour that it can be disappointed; but it can also be born again. The modern apocalypses of annihilation, on the other hand, can be confuted only through active intervention on behalf of life. All is not yet lost. People who love life liberate the future from fear of the world's end, and from the death wishes of apocalyptic terrorists.

4

If the proclaimed 'end of the utopias' is not to be followed by these apocalyptic utopias of the end, we must be clear about the utopias we live from, and to which we are prepared to commit ourselves.

The *utopia of justice* is more alive than ever it was: human dignity and the right to walk with head held high, universal human rights and democracy. In the last twenty years, most military dictatorships have vanished as ingloriously as they deserved; the Universal Declaration of Human Rights of 1948 and the Human Rights pacts of 1966 are generally accepted; everyone possesses not only the civil rights of the country he or she lives in, but human rights too. That is why violations of civil rights in individual states are condemned universally, and provoke the imposition of international sanctions; the international court of justice in The Hague is bringing charges against those responsible for war crimes in Bosnia; the Socialist party dictatorships in the former eastern bloc, and the racist dictatorship of South Africa's apartheid regime were ended without bloodshed. What was once one of humanity's utopias has meanwhile become the justice of a growing society embracing all humanity, and the foundation of a developing 'global ethic'. Human rights give us grounds for condemning inhumanity, but they are not grounds for losing heart.

The *social utopias* of human equality, on the other hand, have got left behind. The globalization of the economy and the total marketing of everything is producing ever-greater social inequalities, and is endangering political democracy in the process. These things are threatening the welfare state, which we can allegedly no longer afford; they are reducing the dignity of human beings to their market value; they are making an increasing number of men and women 'surplus people'. The more these discrepancies grow, the greater the need to develop new social utopias which envisage a society deserving of the name 'humane'. And these utopias will give rise to new social, or socialist, movements – movements, perhaps, simply springing up among the people.

But the most important thing of all seems to me to be a new *love for life*. The more men and women acquire power over life, the stronger their reverence for life must be. We can expect from the Christian faith new courage to live in the face of human violence and possible destruction. We can expect from the Christian community respect for the dignity of others and recognition of them in their otherness – which means kindness, brotherliness and sisterliness. The churches are not there for their own sake. They are there for God's coming kingdom and its righteousness and justice. But God's presence means life, the abundance of life, fulfilled life, resurrection. The utopias are coming – the apocalypses are going: this hope remains.

CHAPTER IV/1

THE MILLENNIUM

RICHARD BAUCKHAM

Moltmann's extensive discussion of millenarianism in chapter III of *The Coming of God* concludes: 'Christian eschatology – eschatology, that is, which is messianic, healing and saving – is millenarian eschatology' (CoG 202). It is a discussion notable for the seriousness (rare in a contemporary theologian) with which he treats the Christian millenarian tradition, for his use of millenarianism as a key category for interpreting Christian and Western history, for the fresh perspectives which he thereby sheds on the history of eschatological thought and praxis, and for his own advocacy of millenarian hope as an essential part of Christian eschatology. Moltmann brings the millennium in from the margins to which the mainstream theological tradition has assigned it and fully into the sphere of properly theological concerns and assessment. In this chapter I shall focus primarily on Moltmann's historical and theological arguments rather than on the exegetical issues, though I shall make some comments on Moltmann's treatment of the latter in a final section. The exegetical issues have been frequently and thoroughly debated in the literature, whereas Moltmann's contribution has been to open up fresh theological angles from which to assess the millenarian tradition and consider the role which the millennium should have in a Christian eschatology. While I have found myself unable to agree with him that Christian eschatology must be millenarian in the sense he argues, as the following engagement with his proposals will show, nevertheless I have found

123

this part of *The Coming of God* highly challenging and productive of fresh insights.[1]

A Millenarian Reading of History

It will be helpful to begin with Moltmann's interpretation of millenarianism in Christian and Western history. Crucial to his argument – and a relatively novel contribution to this subject – is the distinction he makes and the relationship he envisages between two kinds of millenarianism, which he calls 'eschatological millenarianism' (*eschatologische Chiliasmus*: e.g. CoG 146, 192, 193) and 'historical millenarianism' (*historische Chiliasmus*: e.g. CoG 146, 192, 193) or (sometimes) 'presentative millenarianism' (*präsentische Millennarismus*: e.g. CoG 148, 154; cf. WJC 32). Eschatological millenarianism is what in the Christian tradition has usually been called millenarianism (or millennialism or chiliasm), that is, the expectation of the universal kingdom of Christ and the saints on earth in the final future of this world, as a kind of this-worldly, historical transition to the new creation at the end of history. This eschatological millenarianism flourished in the patristic period down to the fourth century, but then, especially under the influence of Augustine, largely disappeared until the late Middle Ages in

---

[1] The following quotation from a dictionary article on millenarianism which I wrote before Moltmann's discussion of millenarianism was published will indicate the extent to which I am likely to concur and to appreciate this aspect of *The Coming of God*:

> Finally, there is a sense in which the whole project of the modern West, in its quest for a more perfect world through technology and political change, has been a kind of secular millenarianism. The ambiguity of what this project has achieved has never been more apparent. But the millenarian impulse seems hard to escape: some of the most radical ecological protest groups promise a return to paradise not unlike the millenarianism of the early church. The challenge to the contemporary church is to formulate the Christian hope in a way which (with the postmillennial tradition) promotes responsible and hopeful activity, but (with the premillennial tradition) avoids the dangerous Utopianism of believing that humanity can design and build the kingdom of God itself.

('Millenarianism', in P. B. Clarke and A. Linzey (eds), *Dictionary of Ethics, Theology and Society* [London: Routledge, 1996] 568.)

the West, when it re-emerged especially in the form of the Joachimist tradition and then in various forms in the Reformation period and especially in post-Reformation Protestantism. Two essential characteristics of it are that it envisages the future reign of Christ as an alternative to the present, a time of fulfilment and unambiguous triumph of all that is good, by contrast with the sufferings and evils of the present, and also that it connects this future reign of Christ within history closely with the end of history and the new creation of all things (146).

Those who interpret the thousand years of Revelation 20 not as a period in the future, but as a period of history in which the present belongs, have usually been called amillenarians (or amillennialists), i.e. those who do not believe in a millennium.[2] Augustine, for example, following the Donatist theologian Tyconius, influentially took the millennium of Revelation 20 to be the age of the church, inaugurated by the resurrection of Christ and continuing until the reign of Antichrist at the very end of history. Such a view can be called amillenarian if the millennium is defined as necessarily a period in the future. Moltmann, however, prefers to call this kind of view 'historical' or 'presentative millenarianism', in order to draw attention to the fact that it conceives the present as the earthly reign of Christ and the saints and as the last age of history. In other words, it is a kind of realized millenarianism,[3] which finds the fulfilment

---

[2] Moltmann himself defines amillenarianism thus: 'the denial of any millennium at all. Occasionally this takes the one-sided form of denying only a future millennium . . . but generally the time-eternity dialectic takes the place of historical dynamic' (CoG 147). In fact, because the term is usually used to distinguish one form of interpretation of Revelation 20 (which cannot deny that the text speaks of some kind of millennium), it usually designates what Moltmann here says it only 'occasionally' designates (cf. S. J. Grentz, *The Millennial Maze* [Downers Grove: InterVarsity Press, 1992] 150–151). His point about the 'time-eternity dialectic', however, is important, and could have been integrated into his reading of millenarian history. Some medieval eschatology could be seen as tending, in one direction, to this Platonically influenced emphasis on eternity rather than the eschatological future, and, in the other direction, to what Moltmann calls historical millenarianism, but these two aspects were not perceived as alternatives.

[3] This idea of realized millenarianism is already adumbrated in IK 29–30; HTG 108–109; WJC 25–26, 31–32.

of the millennial hope already in the past and the present. The definition can be extended a little to views which do not refer specifically to the thousand years of Revelation 20, but express a triumphalist sense of the goal of history already being realized in the present. Moltmann's point is that such views do not rule out a future millennium merely on exegetical grounds, but because their understanding of the fulfilment of Christ's kingdom on earth already in the present is incompatible with the hope for a qualitatively better future within history. Futurist millenarianism, by insisting that the reign of Christ and the saints is still to come in the future, threatens historical millenarianism's idealization of the present, and this is why it has so often been condemned: 'The condemnations of eschatological millenarianism always have their basis in a historical millenarianism' (CoG 193). Moltmann finds in Christian history, therefore, an oppositional relationship between eschatological and historical millenarianism. Hope for a future millennium, as an alternative to the present, provides the eschatological proviso that qualifies the present as not yet the rule of the saints and the last age of history, whereas the triumphalist claim to the universal rule of the saints with Christ already in the present must outlaw eschatological millenarianism.

Of this realized millenarianism Moltmann says: 'It is not the disappointment that was for two thousand years Christianity's chief problem; it was the fulfilment' (CoG 148). The extent of the problem becomes clear as he discusses three forms of historical millenarianism: political, ecclesiastical and epochal.

(1) Political millenarianism began when Constantine and his successors adopted Christianity as the political religion of the empire, and Eusebius of Caesarea and others portrayed the Christian empire as the universal kingdom of Christ on earth.[4]

---

[4] In fact even Eusebius 'stops short of pressing the implications of this messianic conception to its limits: Constantine is not actually the Saviour, nor is his Empire actually the Kingdom of Christ. Hellenistic conceptions of kingship here come to his aid and have enabled him to represent the emperor as the image of the Logos, his empire as the *image* of Christ's kingdom' (R. A. Markus, *Saeculum: History and Society in the Theology of St Augustine* [Cambridge: Cambridge University Press, 1970] 50). Strictly speaking, therefore, Moltmann somewhat overstates the case when he states, as Eusebius' view: 'The Roman

Moltmann finds this political millenarianism continued in the East in Byzantinism and Tsarism, and in the medieval West in the Holy Roman Empire, with its mission to subjugate the nations to Christian rule (160–167). Among modern examples he pays most attention to America's self-image as the redeemer nation with a God-given universal mission.

(2) The church in the medieval West and the Roman Catholic church down to modern times, with its papal centralism and hierarchical structure, epitomize ecclesiastical millenarianism. In this development the church

> ceases to see itself as the struggling, resisting and suffering church; it is now the church victorious and dominant. It no longer participates in the struggle and sufferings of Christ, but already judges and reigns with him in his kingdom. The hierarchical concept of the church is a millenarian concept of the church. (179)

The hierarchical church's claim to rule and judge the nations reveals, says Moltmann, 'a triumphalist, illusory and presumptuous ecclesiology' (184) which can be understood only as realized millenarianism. So, by contrast with the general view that the millenarianism of the early church petered out around the fifth century, partly in consequence of Augustine's exegesis, Moltmann holds that millenarianism did not die out, but was taken over by the realized millenarianism of empire and church:

> it was transformed into a political and ecclesiastical self-confidence and sense of mission. Once the Christian imperium and the Christian empires themselves become millenarian, they can obviously no longer tolerate any futurist millenarianism; they are bound to see this as profoundly calling in question their own existence, and put an extinguisher on such hope as heretical. (181)

(3) Epochal millenarianism is Moltmann's term for the secularized millenarian dream of the modern world which stems

---

empire which had now become Christian was itself nothing less than the universal kingdom of Christ' (CoG 161). For an account of Eusebius which supports Moltmann's interpretation broadly but nuances it, see B. E. Daley, *The Hope of the Early Church* (Cambridge: Cambridge University Press, 1991) 77–78.

from the Enlightenment (134–135, 184–192). He makes the important, though not novel claim,[5] that the Enlightenment's teleological concept of history is a humanistic transformation of the Christian millenarian tradition.[6] Only the latter provided the idea of a goal of history which will be attained within history. In its sense of the modern world as the last age of history, a qualitatively new period in which progress toward the ultimate goal of history is already under way, the Enlightenment's and the modern West's self-understanding is a form of historical or presentative millenarianism.[7] Its millenarian dream has three elements: imperialism (universal rule over the rest of the peoples of the world, first political, now economic), scientific and technological subjugation of nature, and the project to make human beings the sole subject of history (185–186, 190). Like the historical millenarianism of the triumphalist church and the Christian empires, the modern ideology of progress is a presumptuous illusion, subject to the disappointments of history. But it is worse than illusory: it justifies violent domination in the realization of universal rule, and leads to the catastrophes – nuclear, ecological and economic – which threaten the modern world.

While historical millenarianism is an ideology used to legitimate power, eschatological millenarianism is a form of resistance to the powers of this world: 'a necessary picture of hope in resistance, in suffering, and in the exiles of this world' (192). Typically, as in the early church, it is the theology of

---

[5] It was first argued at length by E. L. Tuveson, *Millennium and Utopia: A Study in the Background to the Idea of Progress* (Berkeley: University of California Press, 1949).

[6] M. Grosso, *The Millennium Myth* (Wheaton, Illinois: Theosophical Publishing House, 1995) 60, claims that the Italian Renaissance of the fifteenth century was 'the first great secular form of the [Millennium] Myth'. There is some truth in this claim (and certainly the promethean utopianism of the modern age has its origins in the Renaissance), but it is not clear that Christian eschatology played more than a minor role in the thought of Marsilio Ficino and Giovanni Pico della Mirandola, though some other Italian Renaissance thinkers were influenced by Joachimism (see M. Reeves, *Joachim of Fiore and the Prophetic Future* [London: SPCK, 1976] chapter 4).

[7] Cf. already the use of the term 'millenarianism', as well as 'messianism', in TH 261–265, 293–295.

martyrs (139, 152–153, 194–195). However, Moltmann acknowledges that it can also be a form of spiritual escapism, as in
modern American dispensationalism (153, 159):

> If the call is no longer to resistance against the powers and their
> idols, but if instead escapades into religious dream worlds are
> offered in the face of a world destined for downfall . . . the meaning
> of the millenarian hope is turned upside down. (153)

He calls this dispensationalist millenarianism 'apocalyptic flight
from the world' (159), though he does not explain how it can
be consistent, as he observes it is, with political involvement in
the American right.

Some Critical Comments

Moltmann's millenarian reading of history seems to me
broadly convincing and genuinely illuminating. The following
critical comments imply merely that at some points it requires
refinement or elaboration:

(1) Moltmann's argument that the decline of futurist
millenarianism in the early church and the suspicion with
which it has often subsequently been viewed were solely due to
the historical millenarianism of church and empire is one-sided.
The pre-Constantinian church was by no means unanimously
millenarian,[8] and those who did not hold millenarian views
in this period certainly did not hold a triumphalist view of
church or empire. The popular view that the martyrs ascend at
death to be with Christ in his heavenly kingdom may have
seemed incompatible with the expectation of an earthly
kingdom and may have led to a non-millenarian reading of
Revelation 20 already in the pre-Constantinian period, anticipating Augustine's exegesis of the reign of the martyrs as their
present rule in heaven (*De Civ. Dei* 20.9).[9] Those who explicitly

---

[8] See the table in C. E. Hill, *Regnum Caelorum: Patterns of Future Hope in
Early Christianity* (Oxford: Clarendon Press, 1992) 194–195. Note that in the
second century Justin makes quite clear that many orthodox Christians did
not share his millenarian views, though many did (*Dial.* 80).

[9] This is argued by Hill, *Regnum Caelorum*.

rejected millenarianism in the pre-Constantinian period (notably Gaius of Rome, Origen and Dionysius of Alexandria),[10] found the millenarian expectation of an earthly paradise too crassly physical and earthly to be appropriate as a Christian hope. The influence of Platonism must be detected here, especially in Origen. This objection to millenarianism as materialistic, taken up also by Jerome[11] and Augustine (*De Civ. Dei* 20.7)[12] continues through to the Reformers and the Protestant confessions (CoG 155), such that (as Moltmann recognizes: CoG 157) futurist millenarianism could only gain respectability in the Protestant traditions in the seventeenth century by carefully characterizing the blessings of the millennium as spiritual rather than worldly.[13] (In this respect it followed the lead of the Joachimist tradition.)

Moltmann maintains that in the post-Constantinian period, 'presentative millenarianism' outlawed futurist millenarianism,[14] and in consequence 'all that was left . . . was hope for souls in the heaven of a world beyond this one' (CoG 147; cf. 182). This latter characterization of medieval eschatology is not strictly

---

[10] Hill, *Regnum Caelorum*, 119–120, 127–132, 141–143; Daley, *The Hope*, 49, 60–61; H. Bietenhard, 'The Millennial Hope in the Early Church', *SJT* 6 (1953) 20–23.

[11] Bietenhard, 'The Millennial Hope', 26–27.

[12] Augustine here says that futurist millenarianism 'would be in some degree tolerable' if the rewards it promised the saints in the millennium were spiritual (he himself had held this kind of millenarianism in his youth); the kind of millenarianism he condemns unreservedly is materialistic.

[13] Cf. R. Bauckham, *Tudor Apocalypse* (Appleford: Sutton Courtenay Press, 1978) 211.

[14] A point of detail in Moltmann's historical account that should be challenged is his comment on the Council of Ephesus: it was 'quite logical that in 431 the imperial Council of Ephesus should have condemned this hope for the millennium, maintaining – contrary to 1 Cor 15:28 – that the lordship of Christ, which is now already a hidden reality, "is eternal" and without end' (154). The statement that Christ's kingdom is without end had already appeared in the Niceno-Constantinopolitan Creed (381), where it was aimed not against millenarianism but against the teaching of Marcellus of Ancyra, who interpreted 1 Corinthians 15:24–28 to mean that the distinction of Father and Son in incarnation will cease when 'God is all in all'. The statement that Christ's kingdom is without end can hardly be deplored as a contradiction of biblical testimony, since it is in fact virtually a quotation from Luke 1:33 (cf. also Rev 11:15; Dan 7:14).

accurate, since the expectation of bodily resurrection was always firmly maintained, but it is true that the eschatological expectation was dominantly other-worldly and 'spiritual'. What Moltmann misses is that this spiritualizing tendency in the Christian eschatological tradition derives primarily from the strong Platonic influence in the tradition and was itself a reason for the rejection of millenarianism. In other words, in highlighting the historical relationship between 'presentative millenarianism' and futurist millenarianism Moltmann has focused on only one side of the picture, the other side of which is the relationship between futurist millenarianism and the understanding of final destiny or new creation.

(2) Moltmann's critique of historical millenarianism is more thorough and convincing than his account of eschatological millenarianism. We need more examples of the latter to show that in the medieval and modern periods it has functioned as a theology of resistance and suffering. Since non-millenarian eschatological hope has also functioned in this way (e.g. for the Protestant martyrs of the Reformation period),[15] the question needs to be probed whether eschatological millenarianism is inherently better suited to function in this way than non-millenarian eschatology is. And since Moltmann recognizes that eschatological millenarianism can function both authentically as a form of resistance and inauthentically as a form of escapism, the roots of these alternative functions need investigation.

(3) Moltmann fails to distinguish between the two types of futurist millenarianism: premillenarianism and postmillenarianism (or premillennialism and postmillennialism). He does use the term 'postmillenarianism', but not in its well-established sense. He uses it rather in the same sense as 'presentative' or 'historical millenarianism' (CoG 147, 153, 194), apparently treating all futurist millenarianism as premillenarianism. This is not just terminologically confusing; it also deprives him of a distinction between two kinds of futurist millenarianism which is essential to an accurate reading of the Christian millenarian

---

[15] Bauckham, *Tudor Apocalypse*, chapters 3 and 6.

tradition and its relationship to the secular eschatologies of the modern period.

As Moltmann correctly states, premillenarianism is the expectation of a millennium to follow the parousia of Christ, while postmillenarianism is belief in a millennium prior to the parousia (CoG 147). He also correctly notes that the distinction is very important (148, 153). What he fails to notice is that, as normally used, the term 'postmillenarianism' refers to expectation of a millennium in the *future* before the parousia.[16] Thus, for the most part, the Joachimist tradition was (in this sense) postmillenarian, as were Johann Heinrich Alsted, Campegius Vitringa and Johann Albrecht Bengel, whom Moltmann correctly sees as important figures in the development of seventeenth- and eighteenth-century Protestant millenarianism, but misleadingly classifies as premillenarians (CoG 157). He does not notice that, whereas in seventeenth-century Protestantism premillenarianism was more popular than postmillenarianism, in the eighteenth century post-millenarianism became increasingly dominant. It is primarily this Protestant *postmillenarianism* which lies in the background to the American political messianism which Moltmann describes and assesses at length (168–178) and to the secularized millenarianism of the nineteenth-century idea of progress.[17]

---

[16] Cf. A. W. Wainwright, *Mysterious Apocalypse* (Nashville: Abingdon, 1993) 80: 'Typical postmillennialism expected the millennium to begin in the future. But strictly speaking, the term *postmillennial* could be applied to thinkers like Augustine, who believed that the millennium began with the first advent of Christ and would extend until his second coming.'

[17] Cf. R. Bauckham, 'Chiliasmus IV: Reformation und Neuzeit', *Theologische Realenzyklopädie*, vol. 7 (Berlin: de Gruyter, 1981) 741–742; E. L. Tuveson, *Redeemer Nation: The Idea of America's Millennial Role* (Chicago: University of Chicago Press, 1968); J. B. Quandt, 'Religion and Social Thought: The Secularization of Post-Millennialism', *American Quarterly* 25 (1973) 390–409; J. W. Davidson, *The Logic of Millennial Thought: Eighteenth-Century New England* (New Haven/London: Yale University Press, 1977); Wainwright, *Mysterious Apocalypse*, 77–81, 177–181; C. Burdon, *The Apocalypse in England: Revelation Unravelling* (Studies in Literature and Religion; London: Macmillan/New York: St Martin's Press, 1997) 105–119. A very well-known example of American postmillenarianism is Julia Ward Howe's 'The Battle Hymn of the Republic' (1862). But the contrasts between premillenarianism and postmillenarianism should not be absolutized (cf. Davidson, *The Logic of Millennial Thought*, 33).

Premillenarianism tends to envisage the arrival of the millennium as an event for which believers can only hope and pray, since the visible coming of Christ is to be a sheerly supernatural event of powerful divine intervention, rupturing the historical process and bringing about a radically novel state of affairs through cataclysmic transformation of the world. Postmillenarianism, on the other hand, expects the millennium to come about through the activity of the Holy Spirit prospering the preaching of the Gospel and other kinds of human activity in history. Postmillenarianism is therefore more open both to the role of human activity in bringing about the millennial kingdom and to envisaging the arrival of the millennium as a gradual historical process, taking place through natural causes rather than through supernatural intervention.[18] Premillenarians may believe the parousia to be imminent, but postmillenarians may well think the millennium to be already dawning in the movements of the Spirit in which they themselves have an active part to play. In this sense only does real postmillenarianism come close to what Moltmann calls 'presentative millenarianism', but nevertheless the two forms of thought are distinct. Though postmillenarians have often thought the process which will bring in the millennium to be already underway, they have rarely, if ever, thought of it as already present.

It will readily be seen that postmillenarianism comes much closer than premillenarianism to the secular millenarianisms of the Enlightenment and the modern period. Whereas premillenarianism enjoyed a major revival in the early nineteenth century as a reaction against the French Revolution and the

---

[18] More precisely one could say that the theological background to the idea of progress lay in postmillennial expectations combined with the conviction that God works providentially in human history through natural causes rather than miraculously, progressively rather than discontinuously. (Note, for example, William Smith quoted in Davidson, *The Logic of Millennial Thought*, 264: 'Except in extraordinary cases the Supreme Being seems to conduct all his operations by general laws; and both in the Natural and Moral world, the advances to Perfection are gradual and progressive.') It is an easy step from this theological model to a secularized view of progress as the law of nature.

anti-Christian aspects of Enlightenment ideology,[19] religious forms of postmillenarianism, especially in nineteenth-century America, increasingly approximated to their secular equivalents. The role of affliction and apostasy in the path towards the millennium, which had had a significant place in the older postmillenarianism, was now played down in favour of a simple and steady process of improvement, and the role of human activity in achieving the millennium was played up. In this way nineteenth-century postmillenarianism merged into liberal theology's faith in human progress.

My contention, then, is that Moltmann's millenarian reading of Western history would be considerably improved were he to recognize futurist postmillenarianism as a significant category.

Must Christian Eschatology Be Millenarian?

As we noted at the outset, Moltmann's claim is that 'Christian eschatology – eschatology, that is, which is messianic, healing and saving – is millenarian eschatology' (CoG 202).[20] Whereas the attempts at premature realization of the millennium within history which he calls 'historical millenarianism' have been disastrous, eschatological millenarianism 'is a necessary picture of hope in resistance, in sufferings, and in the exiles of this world' (192). We must now consider the theological reasons which lead Moltmann to think the hope of a millennial reign of Christ on earth necessary for Christian eschatology, and ask whether these reasons are entirely conclusive ones.

The fundamental question we shall have to ask is whether the idea of the millennium fulfils a theological need which Moltmann's understanding of the new creation of all things cannot fulfil. It is important to recall that, from *Theology of Hope* onwards, Moltmann has insisted that Christian hope is not for another world but for the eschatological transformation of this

---

[19] Bauckham, 'Chiliasmus', 742–743; W. H. Oliver, *Prophets and Millennialists: The Uses of Biblical Prophecy in England from the 1780s to the 1840s* (Auckland: Auckland University Press, 1978); J. F. C. Harrison, *The Second Coming: Popular Millenarianism 1780–1850* (London: Routledge, 1979).

[20] Cf. already HTG 96, 109; IK 27: 'no eschatology without chiliasm'.

world (e.g. TH 21: Christian hope 'sees in the resurrection of Christ not the eternity of heaven, but the future of the very earth on which his cross stands'). The 'integrative eschatology' of *The Coming of God* – in which it is a principle that the new creation is the eschatological destiny of all things, material and spiritual, human and non-human – surely makes this even more clear and emphatic. It seems odd that Moltmann can say that when the churches excluded the hope of a future millennium, 'all that was left to them was hope for souls in the heaven of a world beyond this one' (CoG 147). Why should the exclusion of hope for a future millennium not leave us with hope for the new creation as Moltmann envisages it – not a purely spiritual other world, but precisely this world renewed and transfigured in all its material as well as spiritual reality?[21] In most of Moltmann's earlier theology, the millennium goes unmentioned,[22] but the eschatological motivation and direction of Christian praxis in the present appears to be supplied by the hope of the eschatological new creation of all things. It seems that Moltmann now thinks only the millennium, as a this-worldly future prior to the new creation, can supply such motivation and direction: 'Without millenarian hope, the Christian ethic of resistance and consistent discipleship lose their most powerful motivation' (CoG 201). The question we must ask is: what theological

[21] Moltmann's 1982 article, 'Christian Hope – Messianic or Transcendent? A Theological Conversation with Joachim of Fiore and Thomas Aquinas' (HTG 91–109), seems to be important for the development of his thought here. He sees Joachim's eschatology (immanent, messianic and millenarian) and Thomas' eschatology (transcendent and heavenly) as two complementary sides of the Christian hope. His engagement in the controversy between Joachim and Thomas seems to have made him see the eschaton itself, the new creation, in a more transcendent way, focused on the beatific vision rather than the earthly kingdom of God, so that the need for an earthly fulfilment of history has to be met by millenarianism. My question would be: Why must these two sides of the Christian hope be kept apart, the millennium being the focus of one of them, the new creation the focus of the other? Does not Moltmann's concept of the new creation, as the eschatological future of *this world* in the immediate presence of God, in fact combine the messianic and the transcendent, the earthly kingdom and the beatific vision?

[22] For references to the millennium before CoG, see IK 26–32 (published in 1980); TKG 235 n. 44 (first published in 1980) and HTG 96, 108–109 (first published in 1982).

function does the millennium fulfil which the new creation cannot?

Moltmann does not systematically set out his reasons for thinking a future millennium theologically necessary, but it is possible to glean a series of such reasons from his discussion. I shall explain and discuss three of them:

(1) From Moltmann's millenarian reading of history it is clear that a major function of futurist millenarianism is to supply the eschatological proviso which qualifies all forms of church, state and civilization in the present as at best provisional and penultimate. In particular, this relates to the issue of rule. By maintaining the hope of the universal earthly rule of Christ and his saints as a future, eschatological prospect, millenarian hope qualifies the present as the time in which Christ and his saints do not yet rule on earth. Thus the claims of Christian empires and states to embody Christ's rule, with the implications of absolutism, domination and aspirations to universal dominance which such claims entail, are exposed as presumptuous by the millenarian hope. The claim of a centralized, hierarchical church to embody Christ's earthly rule, with the authoritarian, theocratic and triumphalist implications of this, is exposed as presumptuous by the millenarian hope:

> Before the millennium there is no rule of the saints. Only in the millennium will the martyrs rule with Christ and judge the nations. Before the millennium, the church is the brotherly and sisterly, charismatic, non-violent fellowship of those who wait for the coming of the Lord and in the power of the Spirit, who is the giver of life, enter into Christ's struggle and bear their cross in his discipleship. (CoG 184)

Finally, the modern secular millenarian project of domination – the West's domination of the rest of the world and its subjugation of nature – is exposed by the millenarian hope as a kind of eschatological hubris, an attempt to achieve eschatological salvation by the seizure of power. In all three cases the premature usurpation of millennial rule is deadly and destructive. The millenarian ideology serves to justify domination and violence. The claims to universal rule have to be enforced, and the need to maintain the illusion of a golden age achieved requires the suppression of dissent and the silencing and forgetting of the victims of power.

We can observe here a significant continuity between Moltmann's millenarianism and his long-standing rejection of civil religion and national or state churches. The idea of a Christian society in which the church is coterminous with civil society is realized millenarianism, since it is only in the millennial reign of Christ that

> the Christian spirit [will] abandon its special form of life in the church, and acquire its universal political form of living. Only in the messianic kingdom will the body politic become the body of Christ. (166)

Eschatological millenarianism therefore has as its corollary the kind of ecclesiology Moltmann developed in *The Church in the Power of the Spirit*: the messianic fellowship of committed disciples, a provisional reality whose role is to serve the coming universal kingdom of God.[23]

While realized millenarianism allies or assimilates the church to the systems of power and violence that perpetuate the dominance of the powerful, futurist millenarianism offers an alternative to the present which enables Christian resistance to the powers of this world. We might say that realized millenarianism is the expression of a theology of glory, while futurist millenarianism is the eschatological corollary of a theology of the cross (cf. 194–195).

This argument seems to me of considerable value, but I would make two comments on it:

(*a*) The issue of when Christ's earthly rule with his saints occurs – now or in the future millennium – needs supplementing with a discussion of the nature of that rule. Otherwise Moltmann's argument is in danger of suggesting that while it is premature for Christians to attempt to exercise absolutist and violent domination over the world now, they will exercise such domination in the coming millennium. This is a significant issue because some millenarian groups – or their leaders – clearly

---

[23] See R. Bauckham, *The Theology of Jürgen Moltmann* (Edinburgh: T. & T. Clark, 1995) chapter 6.

entertain dangerous aspirations to power, dreaming of ruling in place of the powers that currently rule, and can, with a kind of eschatological impatience, end up trying to put these aspirations into immediate effect. The Anabaptist kingdom of Münster in the sixteenth century is the textbook illustration,[24] to which we may now add the Japanese cult of Aum Shinrikyo, which in 1995 came close to succeeding in killing thousands of people in a kind of trial-run for Armageddon.[25]

(*b*) I am not convinced that the function of providing an alternative to the present which enables resistance and supplies the eschatological proviso can only be fulfilled by the hope of a millennium, and not by the hope of the new creation, if the latter is envisaged as the eschatological future of this world. After all, according to Revelation, it is not only in the millennium that the saints rule (20:4) but also in the New Jerusalem (22:5). Moltmann argues that the realized millenarianism of the post-Constantinian church resulted in the reduction of eschatology to a purely spiritual, other-worldly hope (CoG 182). But the remedy which Moltmann's own eschatology has always offered for a purely spiritual, other-worldly hope is not to retain such a hope as final destiny, while adding a this-worldly millennium as the penultimate expectation. The remedy is to understand the new creation itself as the destiny of the whole of this present creation, taken into God's immediate presence and transfigured with his glory. Once the new creation is understood in this way, it is not clear why a millennium is necessary.

(2) According to Moltmann only the millennium supplies a 'goal of history' (133–134, 137, 193, 197). He does not think of this goal in the sense of a completion of the historical project of the dominant, a prolongation of the present, as the secular millenarianisms that stemmed from the Enlightenment did.

---

[24] N. Cohn, *The Pursuit of the Millennium* (2nd edn; London: Paladin, 1970) chapter 13. Though generally regarded, even in their own time, as millenarians, it seems that the Münsterites actually expected not a transitional period (millennium) but Christ's eternal reign on earth, which he would soon come to establish with the help of his people.

[25] See the account in D. Thompson, *The End of Time: Faith and Fear in the Shadow of the Millennium* (London: Random House, 1997) chapter 11.

Rather it is the goal for those who participate in Christ's struggle against the powers, especially the martyrs (194), for whom the millennium represents the hope of participating in his resurrection (195). It is also the goal for Israel, for whom the millennium represents resurrection and redemption, the fulfilment of the messianic promises (182, 197–198).[26] It is the goal of the moral struggle for justice, freedom and love: at least, Moltmann quotes a passage of Barth, evidently with approval, to this effect. For history to have a goal, Moltmann appears to argue, it must have a goal within history. The eschaton itself is not the goal but the end of history.[27] The millennium consummates history; the eschaton ends history. The millennium is future history; the new creation is the future of history (197). But why must history have a goal within history? Why should it not have its goal in the new creation? I can think of two possible reasons: (a) Since the new creation ends history, it cannot also be its goal. (This, I think, is what Moltmann means in CoG 197.) But this is surely a confusion. The new creation ends the temporal process of history, but it does not end the content of history, i.e. all that has existed and happened within the temporal process. In Moltmann's view, all that has lived and happened in history is gathered up into the new creation, redeemed and transfigured. Why should this not be seen as the goal of history? (b) The new creation is not the goal of history in the sense that history – human action in history – achieves or produces it. But nor is the millennium, in Moltmann's understanding, the goal of history in this sense. It is the *God-given* consummation of history. I do not see why the new creation cannot be seen as the goal of history in this sense.

I suspect that at this point it is the development of the secular millenarianisms of the modern period that has influenced Moltmann's thought. (Barth's reference to Kant in the passage Moltmann quotes in CoG 193 may suggest this; cf. 188–189.)

[26] On Moltmann's treatment of Israel, see S. R. Haynes, *Prospects for Post-Holocaust Theology* (AAR Academy Series 77; Atlanta, Georgia: Scholars Press, 1991) chapters 3 and 5 (138 on millenarianism).

[27] This distinction is probably influenced by Walter Benjamin, as quoted in WJC 303: 'the kingdom of God is not the *telos* of the historical dynamic; it cannot be made the goal. For historically it is not a goal; it is the end.'

For such secular millenarianisms, the goal of history has, of course, to be within history. It is the immanent *telos* to which human history itself leads, as human action progresses in that direction. For such secular thought, there is in any case no new creation beyond history. But for Christian eschatology which does envisage such a new creation, I do not see why history should not have its goal beyond itself, in God's fulfilment and transfiguration of history in eternity.

(3) A different way in which Moltmann represents the theological necessity of the millennium is to see it as transitional.[28] It 'mediates between world history here, and the end of the world and the new world there' (201). It is 'the eschatological mediation between history and eternity' (156). This gives it a coherent place in the more general picture Moltmann paints in this book of an eschatological *process* which began with the resurrection of Jesus and will end in the new creation (see chapter I/1 section 4 above).[29] But that is not enough to demonstrate the necessity of this particular transitional phase. Moltmann claims that if 'we leave out this transition [the millennium], as the non-millenarian eschatologies do, then world history will end – according to modern fantasy – with an abrupt Big Bang', to which he attaches the terms 'Hiroshima images' and 'catastrophe' (201–202). But (*a*) God's act of new creation does not destroy; it is not catastrophic; it redeems and renews and transfigures. It ends history – the temporal process; but it does not end the world. (*b*) Even if Moltmann's millennium is rather more like the new creation than the world at present is, the new creation must still represent a radical transformation. In principle there cannot be a kind of smooth evolution from this world to the new creation. Even the world

[28] The idea of the millennium as transitional between this world and the new creation goes back to Irenaeus (*Adv. Haer.* 5.32.1; 5.35.1–2).

[29] Moltmann's idea of transitional stages in the eschatological process probably owes something to Joachim of Fiore's three overlapping *status* of world history: see HTG 96 for a formulation of the stages of transition as Moltmann understands them, influenced by Joachim. In TKG, on the other hand, he appropriated Joachim's trinitarian scheme of *three* status, but differed from Joachim in refusing to see them as three *successive* stages (209).

history that reached its goal in Moltmann's millennium would end with 'an abrupt Big Bang', if that were the appropriate way to conceptualize the end.

In relation to Moltmann's idea of transition, there is a seeming contradiction in Moltmann's thought. When, in chapter II, he discusses the idea, advanced by several modern Catholic theologians, of a resurrection at death, he argues that this would mean the perfecting of individual persons before the perfecting of the world (103). But then

> our bodily solidarity with this earth would be broken and dissolved. But is not every grave in this earth a sign that human beings and the earth belong together, and will only be redeemed together? Without 'the new earth' there is no 'resurrection of the body'. Only the new earth offers possibilities for the new embodiment of human beings. (CoG 104)

Yet in Moltmann's millennium there are precisely human beings risen to new embodiment without the new earth. The idea of transition seems here to be in tension with the idea of our solidarity with the earth. However, the problem can be solved by taking up Moltmann's hints that the earth itself participates in a cosmic transformation during the millennium (144, 277–279).[30] In that case during the millennium the earth is already new along with the resurrected saints. But it is difficult to see how the ideas he takes up from J. T. Beck's ideas about 'the new world-organism' (277–278) can refer to a transitional form of renewal of the earth prior to the eschatological new creation itself, since Beck is explicitly interpreting 1 Corinthians 15:28 (which in Moltmann's own understanding of 1 Cor 15:20–28 as an eschatological process brings the process to its

---

[30] On p. 144, Moltmann reports as the view of 'many millenarians' the expectation of a sabbath of nature, restoring paradise, in the millennium, but he does not there accept or reject the view for himself. On pp. 277–279 he takes up, in response to ecofeminism, his nineteenth-century Tübingen predecessor, J. T. Beck's ideas of 'a new world-organism'. But it is not clear that the passage refers to the millennium rather than the new creation. In conversation Moltmann has told me that it does, but both its context and its content would probably suggest to most readers that it refers to the new creation (after the millennium).

final goal beyond the millennium in the new creation [CoG 335]). Moltmann's millenarianism here has the problem which all millenarianism has: how to characterize the millennium in such a way as to make it intelligible as transitional rather than final.

In conclusion, it seems to me that for the most part the functions of the millennium in Moltmann's eschatology could be understood as relating to a particular *aspect* of the Christian eschatological hope, but not necessarily an aspect which has to be understood as an interim period in the eschatological process. Moltmann quotes Paul Althaus who said that millenarians rightly stress the 'this-worldly character of the Christian hope', and Walter Kreck who observed that millenarianism 'wards off a docetism in eschatology which abandons the earth' (CoG 193). These, according to Moltmann, 'are not genuine acknowledgements of millenarian eschatology; they are actually a dismissal of it in various polite forms' (193). But it seems to me they are near the mark. What the millenarian hope does is to focus on the eschatological hope in its more immanent and this-worldly aspect, as the fulfilment of human and historical goals and as the ideal form of the life we live on this earth in this age. This focus is the appropriate one to provide motivation and direction for some aspects of Christian life now, both positively as goal and negatively as eschatological proviso. Other aspects of the eschatological hope, such as the beatific vision and the glorification of all creation in the immediate presence of God, are by comparison more transcendent and in a sense other-worldly. In the millenarian tradition these two sides of the Christian hope have been assigned respectively to the millennium and the eternal state. In the non-millenarian Christian tradition, as Moltmann complains, the more immanent and this-worldly side has been neglected, while in the secular millenarianisms of the modern age, the more transcendent and other-worldly side has been left aside completely. Christian eschatology needs both sides of its traditional hope, and it needs the millenarian tradition to remind it of the immanent and this-worldly side. But it does not seem to me necessary to follow the millenarian tradition in its temporal distinction between the new creation in eternity and a this-worldly kingdom of Christ which precedes it. If the new creation is understood as God's new creation precisely of this world and this reality, as it is a merit of Moltmann's theology to insist, then it is an eschatological conception in which the this-worldly and the other-worldly are not incompatible but are the two aspects of the one eschatological reality. Since most eschatological thought is a necessarily imaginative picturing of the un-imaginable, we may have to use alternative images to represent different aspects of the eschatological hope, but we can understand these images as different angles on the one eschatological reality. Irenaeus' earthly paradise, Augustine's heavenly city, Dante's beatific vision, the restored Israel of the dispensationalists, the classless society of Karl Marx and the ecological reconciliation of the Greens – all these and many more are complementary angles on the eschatological reality, each relating in a different way to the Christian imperative of living hopefully now.[31]

Some Exegetical Issues

The strength of Moltmann's discussion of millenarianism is theological rather than exegetical. He does not engage at length with the relevant biblical texts and the complex exegetical debate that has surrounded them (especially, of course, Revelation 20:1–10). But he does advance some interpretations of biblical texts which are of interest and deserve comment.

Moltmann argues that life in community with Christ leads to participation in his resurrection life in a 'special and messianic' resurrection at the beginning of the millennial kingdom. This resurrection of Christian disciples is to be distinguished from the 'universal and eschatological' resurrection at the end of the millennium (CoG 194–195). This distinction between two resurrections would be most obviously based on Revelation (20:4–5; cf. CoG 151–152, 196), but Moltmann is more concerned to root it in Pauline theology (CoG 150–151, 194–195). He observes the difference between the two terms 'resurrection

---

[31] I have developed the ideas in this paragraph further in my article 'Approaching the Millennium', forthcoming in *Anvil* (1999).

from the dead' (used in Phil 3:11)[32] and 'resurrection *of* the dead'. Just as Jesus was raised *from* the dead, that is, from among the dead, while the rest of the dead remain dead, so those who share his mission and sufferings will also rise *from* the dead, while the rest of the dead remain dead until the general resurrection *of* the dead. This distinction in meaning between the two phrases is valid, though rarely noticed.[33] The terms 'resurrection from the dead'[34] and 'to rise/be raised from the dead'[35] seem invariably to indicate selective resurrection. For the most part they refer to the resurrection of Jesus, but in a few cases to the future resurrection of the people of God (Mark 12:25; Luke 20:35; Acts 4:2; Phil 3:11; cf. Eph 5:14). Moltmann is also correct to understand the similar phrase 'life from the dead' (Rom 11:15)[36] in the same way (CoG 151, 198).[37] In no case do these phrases including 'from the dead' refer to the general resurrection of all people, for which they are obviously unsuited.

However, it is by no means necessarily the case that those texts which use such a phrase with reference to Christian believers presuppose a chronological interval between their resurrection and that of the rest of the dead. It is clear that for

---

[32] Moltmann notes that Luther's version has 'resurrection *of* the dead', as does the 1611 (King James) English Bible (added in the English translation of Moltmann's work), and comments: 'probably deliberately so, in order to exclude millenarianism' (CoG 195). But this is not a case of misleading translation (as in Acts 4:2 NRSV: 'resurrection of the dead'), but of a variant text. The Received Text, usually followed in sixteenth-century translations, has τῶν νεκρῶν in place of the better reading ἐκ νεκρῶν.

[33] See R. H. Lightfoot, *Saint Paul's Epistle to the Philippians* (London: Macmillan, 1868) 151; J. W. Mealy, *After the Thousand Years: Resurrection and Judgment in Revelation 20* (JSNTSS 70; Sheffield: JSOT Press, 1992) 246–247 n. 2.

[34] ἀνάστασις ἐκ νεκρῶν: Luke 20:35; Acts 4:2; ἐξανάστασις ἐκ νεκρῶν: Phil 3:11.

[35] ἀνίστημι ἐκ νεκρῶν: used nine times of Jesus; also: Mark 12:25; Luke 16:31; Eph 5:14. ἐγείρω ἐκ νεκρῶν: used twenty-four times of Jesus, also of Lazarus (John 12:1, 9, 17), John the Baptist (Mark 6:14; Luke 9:7) and Isaac (Heb 11:19).

[36] ζωὴ ἐκ νεκρῶν; cf. also ὡσεὶ ἐκ νεκρῶν ζῶντας (Rom 6:13), which also has a selective meaning.

[37] Moltmann takes it to refer to Israel's resurrection in advance of the general resurrection. More likely Paul means that Israel's 'acceptance' will lead, in the sequence of end-time events, to the resurrection of all believers (cf. J. D. G. Dunn, *Romans 9–16* [WBC 38B; Dallas: Word Books, 1988] 657–658).

Paul at least resurrection is a soteriological concept: resurrection to new and eternal life. In 1 Corinthians 15, even though he uses the more general term 'resurrection *of* the dead' (15:12, 13, 21, 42), he refers only to the resurrection of Christian believers to glorious and imperishable new life. In this chapter he does not consider the fate of others at all. Outside the Pauline literature, there is occasional reference to the resurrection of the unrepentant (John 5:28–29; Acts 24:15; Rev 20:5), but for the most part, although they are expected to appear at the last judgment and receive sentence of condemnation, they are not said to rise. Resurrection suggested salvific participation in the eternal life into which Jesus Christ rose. Therefore the phrases 'resurrection from the dead' and 'to rise/be raised from the dead', when used of God's people, imply that only they rise in the proper sense, to new life,[38] whereas the rest of the dead do not, either at the same time or at any other time.

These comments presume that, in Paul's thinking, those who are not raised 'from the dead' do not rise to eternal life. Moltmann, on the other hand, reads Paul in a universalistic sense, such that resurrection to eternal life is a process in three stages: the resurrection of Christ as 'the first fruits', the resurrection of 'those who belong to Christ' at his parousia (1 Cor 15:20, 23), and the general resurrection which he supposes comes at 'the end' (15:24) when death itself is destroyed (15:26) (CoG 196). This is not the place to discuss Moltmann's general argument for universal salvation (CoG 235–255). A case can certainly be made for this exegesis of 1 Corinthians 15 on the basis of verse 22,[39] and a case can also be made for a rule of Christ which intervenes between the parousia and 'the end'.[40] But it seems that the sequence that really matters to Paul here

---

[38] The context in all these cases (Mark 12:25; Luke 20:35; Acts 4:2; Phil 3:11; Eph 5:14) is important in establishing this meaning.

[39] E.g. M. C. de Boer, *The Defeat of Death: Apocalyptic Eschatology in 1 Corinthians 15 and Romans 5* (JSNTSS 22; Sheffield: JSOT Press, 1988) 112–113, 126.

[40] E.g. L. J. Kreitzer, *Jesus and God in Paul's Eschatology* (JSNTSS 19; Sheffield: JSOT Press, 1987) chapter 3, who discusses earlier treatments of the kingdom of Christ in 1 Cor 15:20–28. While arguing that Paul may here refer to a messianic kingdom between the parousia and the last judgment, he finds this inconsistent with Pauline eschatology outside this passage.

is: the resurrection of Christ, the resurrection of 'those who belong to Christ' at his parousia, and Christ's destruction of death itself at the end. The sequence corresponds to Revelation's (20:4, 14), but there is no other reason for supposing that Paul here envisages a temporal period of Christ's reign between the second and third stages of his sequence. Paul elsewhere pictures the parousia as the first of an immediate sequence of eschatological events (1 Thess 4:16–17).

However, besides the specific and disputed exegetical issue of precisely how Paul portrays the nature and sequence of the end-time events, there is a broader hermeneutical issue, which applies also to Revelation 20:1–10, the principal text from which even Moltmann's notion of the millennial rule of Christ and the saints derives (cf. CoG 151–153). Despite his criticism of this chapter for its 'legalistic, apocalyptic ideas of judgment' (CoG 196), he correctly understands and approves its portrayal of the millennium as a hope for martyrs, empowering their resistance to the idolatrous power of Rome (152). In the conflict between the beast and Christ's faithful followers, as Revelation portrays it, the beast appears to reign victoriously and to wield the absolute power it claims, while the martyrs, those who witness to the rule of God and Christ, appear to be defeated. When at the parousia the truth of things becomes finally evident, the beast must be seen to be defeated and Christ must be seen to reign. But also the martyrs must be seen to be not defeated, but victorious, participating in Christ's kingdom.[41] Everything Revelation 20:1–10 says about the millennium seems designed for this single function: to demonstrate the triumph of the martyrs in Christ's kingdom.[42] As Moltmann says:

> John wants to say that the martyrs of the Roman empire will be justified by God. His [sic] Thousand Years' empire is the pictorial presentation [die bildliche Darstellung] of their justification and the divine counter-image for godless Rome. (152)

[41] That Revelation 20 portrays the millennium as consequent on and following the parousia is agreed by most modern exegetes. For exegetical discussion of alternative approaches, see Mealy, *After the Thousand Years*, chapters 2–3.

[42] R. Bauckham, *The Theology of the Book of Revelation* (Cambridge: Cambridge University Press, 1993) 106–108.

But if the passage in Revelation is a 'pictorial presentation' of the vindication of the martyrs at the parousia, why need we suppose that the eschatological reality to which it points must be a temporal period? Moltmann has perhaps not given sufficient recognition to the fact that biblical eschatological pictures and narratives are imaginative construals of the eschatological expectations which cannot be told as though they were already history. When Paul portrays the end-time events in a narrative sequence and when John tells a story about a thousand-year reign of Christ and the saints following the parousia, they put aspects of the meaning of the parousia and the end into imaginative story form. Because John *portrays* the eschatological vindication of the martyrs as a *period* of rule with Christ, consequent on the parousia, we need not suppose that, for his prophecy to be true prophecy, there must be such a *period*.

The point is not that we can simply replace with theological abstractions the imaginative portrayals in which the biblical writers express the eschatological hope. But fully recognizing that they are precisely imaginative portrayals allows us to avoid the unnecessary puzzles which arise from taking the notion of a millennial period literally,[43] and to restrict the symbol of the millennium to the restricted function it actually has in Revelation 20, as millenarians have rarely been able to do. The other hopes which millenarians – and, to some extent, Moltmann himself – have invested in the millennium are not thereby discarded, but, as we have already suggested, can be fully acknowledged as aspects of the eschatological hope of new creation.[44]

---

[43] Bauckham, *The Theology of the Book of Revelation*, 108.

[44] A shorter version of this chapter was given as the Tyndale Christian Doctrine Lecture for 1997 at the Tyndale Fellowship Triennial Conference, Swanwick, Derbyshire, July 1997, and has been published in the proceedings of the conference as 'Must Christian Eschatology be Millenarian?: A Response to Jürgen Moltmann', in K. E. Brower and M. W. Elliott (eds), *'The reader must understand': Eschatology in Bible and Theology* (Leicester: Apollos, 1997) 263–277.

THE HOPE OF ISRAEL AND THE ANABAPTIST ALTERNATIVE

Response to Richard Bauckham

JÜRGEN MOLTMANN

Richard Bauckham has a profound knowledge of English and American millenarian traditions. I am grateful for his erudite and penetrating contribution, which rounds off the total picture of Christian millenarianism. I regret all the more, of course, that he finds himself unable to agree with me that Christian eschatology has to include the expectation of a millennium for the transition from the time of history to the eternity of the new creation – just as, conversely, every expectation of Christ's kingdom of peace which has a Christian motivation must be integrated into eschatology, if it is not to be sectarian and secularized. I should therefore like to put forward my reasons once more, for I have the impression that Richard Bauckham has not addressed them sufficiently. They evidently have a different cogency for me from the weight they have for him.

1. Does Christianity Have a Hope for Israel?

Whenever Christianity put itself in Israel's place, seeing itself as 'the new people of God' – and that was the case throughout history – there was no Christian hope for Israel; nor was there any recognition of Israel's theological right to exist, parallel to Christianity – the synagogue side by side with the church, and the Jews side by side with Christians. The sole Christian hope for Israel was that Israel be converted to Christianity. The church viewed itself as Israel's future. The result was the antisemitic enactments of the emperors Theodosius and Justinian and the decrees of the Fourth Lateran Council in the Middle Ages, as well as the antisemitic writings of Martin Luther's later years. Even Schleiermacher, in his 'written opinion' on the emancipation of the Jews in Prussia, still demanded the surrender of their hope for the Messiah. Right down to the present day, there is no Christian creed which expresses an eschatological hope for Israel, and with that the recognition of Israel's divine calling, apart from the church.

I was confronted with these disagreeable facts at the beginning of the 1970s, when I began to take part in the Christian–Jewish dialogue and, with the help of the Dutch Hervormde Kerk's Confession 'Fundamenten en Perspektieven van Belijden' of 1949, addressed myself to the revision of the relationship between the church and Israel. I found that in the confessional documents of the Reformation period, Israel is mentioned in only a single, tiny passage, where the expectation of Christ's thousand years' kingdom of peace at the end of time is rejected as a 'Jewish dream' (Augsburg Confession XVII: The Return of Christ for Judgment).

This designation of the millennium as a Jewish dream is generally explained historically: it is supposed to have been due to movements within the Judaism of the time. But I understand it theologically. Christ's kingdom of peace is evidently associated with hope for Israel's future in the fulfilment of God's promises to Israel in the kingdom of the Son of man (Daniel 7). But for Christians this kingdom of the Son of man is identical with Christ's kingdom of peace at the end of time.[1] If, with Ernst Käsemann, I read Romans 9–11 correctly, Paul means by the

---

[1] I agree with Berthold Klappert on this point. See B. Klappert, *Worauf wir hoffen. Das Kommen Gottes und der Weg Jesus Christi. Mit einer Antwort von Jürgen Moltmann*. Kaiser Taschenbuch 152 (Gütersloh, 1997) 48–52.

apocalyptic 'mystery' in 11:25–32 that all-Israel has been smitten with blindness by God so that they cannot recognize in Jesus the Christ of Israel 'until the full number of the Gentiles has come in'. Then 'all-Israel will be saved'. 'As regards the gospel *they are enemies for your sake*, but as regards election they are beloved for the sake of their forefathers.' Paul justifies his mission to the Gentiles, which he wanted to pursue to the ends of the earth, on the grounds of all-Israel's rejection of the gospel: that is the starting point; while all-Israel's acceptance and salvation through the One 'who will come from Zion', the Christ of the parousia, is the final goal. His mission to the Gentiles is the detour he is making for the purpose of Israel's redemption. Israel's future does not lie in the church. It is to be found in the kingdom of the Messiah / Son of man, as God has promised Israel. Paul describes this End-time 'timetable of salvation' geographically, and according to our terminology this also means within history. That is to say it has in view already the end of time, not just the eternity of the new creation.

Right down to the present day, Christian millenarianism has had a clearly detectible affinity to Israel. It is only here that the theological recognition of Israel's enduring vocation, and the hope for Israel's future, are really preserved. The forms may be debatable. But for the watchful Christian church, the millennium and Israel evidently belong together. This does not mean surrendering the universalism of salvation in Christ. On the contrary: 'For God has consigned all men to disobedience, that he may have mercy upon all.' The historical paths are separate and individual, the eschatological goal universal. Up to now I have seen no positive Israel theology on the Christian side which fails to integrate Christ's chiliastic kingdom of peace into the eschatology. In the German tradition, the rejection of this expectation led to a disregard and dismissal of the 'unbelieving Jews' such as we see in Paul Althaus' eschatology, *The Last Things*.[2]

---

[2] P. Althaus, *Die letzten Dinge*, Gütersloh, 1922; 7th edn 1957; no English translation. Chapter 7c: 'The Intermediate Kingdom' (297–313): 'Israel no longer has any special position in the church and for the church, nor has it any special "salvific vocation" for "Christ is also the end of the Messiah"' (309).

Luther's eschatology consisted essentially of an apocalyptic expectation of an imminent Last Judgment – and the older he became the more this was the case. Right down to the nineteenth and twentieth centuries, Lutheranism followed him in this view of eschatology and the Jews. The apocalyptic tradition in England, on the other hand, developed a theology of hope for the Jews, because it was aligned towards the resurrection and God's coming kingdom. Hand in hand with expectation of the overthrow of the Antichrist went the expectation of Israel's redemption and the establishment of Christ's thousand years' empire. This apocalyptic discussion acquired a practical application when it became a question of the readmission of the Jews to England, after Menasseh ben Israel's petition *Spes Israel* (1650) and in the Whitehall debates (from 1655). Here the close connection between a Christian hope for Israel and the universal eschatology of 'the renewal of the world' is unmistakeable. I am indebted to Avihu Zakai[3] for providing proofs for my historical hypothesis, which I had hitherto expressed merely as a supposition.

2. Christ's Kingdom of Peace

My second orientation towards *Christ's kingdom of peace* derives from the left wing of the Reformation, the so-called Anabaptists, and the ethics of the religious social movement of Leonhard Ragaz and the early Karl Barth.

The Anabaptists of the Reformation period rejected for themselves both infant baptism (which is the foundation of an established church incorporating the whole of a people) and the sword (which is the foundation of the state). With this they cast aside the two sustaining pillars of the *Corpus Christianum*. What hopes impelled them, and what eschatology did they develop?

---

[3] Avihu Zakai, 'Reformation, History, and Eschatology in English Protestantism' in *History and Theory* 26 (1987) 300–318; also 'The Poetics of History and the Destiny of Israel: The Role of the Jews in English Apocalyptic Thought During the Sixteenth and Seventeenth Centuries,' *Journal of Jewish Thought and Philosophy* 5 (Amsterdam, 1966) 313–350.

They evidently saw in Christ's coming kingdom of peace an alternative future, over against the present power of the *Corpus Christianum*. They lived in this counter-image of the future as contrast to the present they experienced, and this alternative counter-image moved them to adopt believers' baptism on the one hand, and a life of non-violence on the other. We can see this from the Anabaptist Schleitheim Confession of 1527. Their resistance to church and state in the *Corpus Christianum* was 'suffering obedience', for most of the Protestant martyrs in the Reformation period were Anabaptists. It is easy to understand how the persecutions by Catholic and Protestant rulers and cities, and the martyrdom endured, gave rise to millenarian expectations of an imminent End.

Richard Bauckham thinks 'the Anabaptist kingdom of Münster in the sixteenth century is the textbook illustration' for the millenarian danger, which is 'to exercise absolutist and violent domination over the world now'. Unfortunately he cites as parallel the Japanese poison-gas sect Aum Shinrikyo. I consider this to be completely misleading, historically speaking. Here Richard has been taken in by the polemic in Catholic and Protestant textbooks against 'the kingdom of God in Münster'. Merely to compare the articles on this in the Catholic *Lexikon für Theologie und Kirche* and the Protestant *Religion in Geschichte und Gegenwart* with the account in the *Mennonite Encyclopaedia* (III, 777–782), is enough to show that the polemic against the Anabaptists is still alive today, more than 450 years after events! According to my own findings, it was only the pressure of the Catholic bishop's siege of Münster and the hopelessness of their situation which evoked the extravagant excesses of Jan van Leyden and his followers. But the mass murders of the peaceful Anabaptists were perpetrated by those who claimed that the *Corpus Christianum* was the millennium, and who accordingly nipped every alternative hope in the bud – the hope of Jews as well as the hope of the Anabaptists.

It was only in the nineteenth century that the hope for Christ's coming kingdom of peace once more became relevant for ethics, in the Blumhardt movement, in the religious social movement, and in the peace movement. Here the vision of Christ's coming kingdom of peace again offered an alternative future, as well as

alternative action in that *Corpus Christianum* which, as a
'Christian world' in 'a Christian era', considers that it itself is
the millennium, a conviction sufficiently evident from the
fathers of the Enlightenment down to the last supporters of
German cultural Protestantism.

TIME AND ETERNITY

RICHARD BAUCKHAM

This chapter comprises two distinct but related parts. The first part analyses and discusses the relationship of time and eternity in Moltmann's theology, especially in *The Coming of God*. The issue is at the heart of Moltmann's eschatology, determining the kind of eschatology he develops in *The Coming of God*, especially as defined in contrast to the immanent eschatology of historical progressivism in the modern period. The second part of the chapter proposes an eschatological aesthetic, in which Moltmann's understanding of the relation of time and eternity will enable certain kinds of art to be seen as implicitly anticipations of the new creation. The concept of the *moment* provides the most important link between the two parts. In chapter I of *The Coming of God* Moltmann traces the 'rediscovery of the present as a *moment* which towers out of the continuum of the times' (44) in the Christian and Jewish theologians of the period between the two World Wars. In this same period, the *moment* appears as a key concept in literature in the work of Virginia Woolf and in painting in the work of Claude Monet. These therefore furnish the examples of which the second part of the chapter offers an eschatological reading.

I. Moltmann on Time and Eternity

The relation of time and eternity is a preoccupation of *The Coming of God*. Arguably it is the critical point in Moltmann's

155

enterprise of defining a truly *eschatological* eschatology in contrast
to what he regards as the de-eschatologized eschatologies of
the modern period. These include the Christian theological
interpretations of eschatology in the first half of the twentieth
century (CoG 7–22), in contrast to which he had already defined
his eschatological approach in *Theology of Hope* (I). They also
include the secular eschatologies of the modern period. His
differentiation from these had been by no means so clear in
Theology of Hope, with the result that his position was at that time
often misinterpreted as aligned with precisely the features of
the modern ideology of progress which he is concerned to
expose as disastrous illusion in *The Coming of God*. The secular
millenarianism of the modern period shares with the secular
apocalypticism which has often succeeded it the erroneous and
fatal attempt to 'draw eschatology into history'. Millenarianism
has done this in a positive sense, apocalypticism in a negative
sense, but both threaten to destroy the world (CoG 5). The
disastrous failure of the modern attempt to appropriate
eschatology by reducing it to history, by identifying it with an
immanent historical process, is a pervasive background for
Moltmann's thought in *The Coming of God*, just as it was for
German theological eschatology from dialectical theology
onwards. The impression which many of those who read *Theology
of Hope* rather superficially in the context of the late 1960s
gained, that Moltmann was dissociating himself from dialectical
theology's break with all historical progressivism in order to
seek a new kind of theological alignment with historical
progressivism (albeit in a dialectical, quasi-Marxist way), was
always a mistaken impression,[1] but must be unequivocally shown
to be such by *The Coming of God*. Moltmann's difference with
Barth and Bultmann is not over the need for decisive rejection
of all forms of modern historical progressivism (not just the
culture-Protestantism of the nineteenth-century German
Liberals), but over what constitutes a genuinely eschatological
alternative to it. Therefore, in *The Coming of God*, he turns – in a

---

[1] This is not at all to deny Moltmann's critical solidarity with western
Marxists, or even the points of real convergence between his theology of hope
and a Marxist view of history (cf., e.g. FC 11), but these do not imply his
acceptance of any kind of dogma of inevitable historical progress.

fully explicit way for the first time – for precedent to the Jewish thinkers, especially Franz Rosenzweig and Walter Benjamin, who rejected modern progressivism under the impact of the same horrors of twentieth-century history as precipitated Christian theology into new thinking about history and eschatology.

We might say that over against all forms of historical progressivism that collapse eschatology into history, Moltmann insists on the *transcendence* of the *eschatological* future over history,[2] whereas, against the early Barth, the early Althaus and Bultmann, he insists on the transcendence of the eschatological *future* over history. The eschatological future is not a goal of history that will be reached along a continuous temporal line drawn from the past through the present to the future. On the necessity to break this continuity between history and eschatology, on which all historical progressivisms rest, Moltmann is in full agreement with Barth and Bultmann, as with Rosenzweig and Benjamin. But he rejects the dialectical theologians' rendering of eschatology as the supra-temporal presence of eternity that impinges on all time without entering it. Rejecting this transcendent abstraction from history, as well as progressivism's immanent completion of history, he looks, with Rosenzweig and Benjamin, for the redemption of history. This requires conceiving the eschatological as both future (unlike dialectical theology) and transcendent (unlike progressivism). The eschatological future is related to history as future, but transcends all history. It is not future history, but the future of history.[3] Its transcendence can be expressed in the biblical category *novum*, which designates the eschatological as wholly other, non-analogous, transcendently new. It is what does not develop out of the old, but transforms, re-news the old, creates the old anew (CoG 27–29). Historical time cannot produce it, but nor is it unrelated to historical time: it comes to time to transform it. More properly, God, in his eschatological coming, comes to transform and to renew: 'With the coming of God's glory, future time ends and eternal time begins' (CoG 26).

---

[2] For the use of the idea of transcendence to define the truly eschatological future, see already Moltmann's early essay, 'The Future as a New Paradigm of Transcendence' (RRF 177–199 = FC 1–17, first published in 1969).

[3] So already FC 15.

Much depends then on the distinction and relation between historical time with its future and the 'eternal time' which is the future *of* time. We can call these time[4] and eternity provided we make clear from the outset that the distinction is between, on the one hand, the time characteristic of this world, 'historical time' or, as Moltmann sometimes calls it, 'transitory time', and, on the other hand, the 'aeonic time' or 'eternal time' of the new creation, which is not the absolute eternity of God but a kind of relative eternity of the creation which reflects and participates in the divine eternity (see especially WJC 330–331; CoG 295). But, in order to understand the way Moltmann re-eschatologizes eschatology, it is certainly not enough to say that he adds an eschatological future which transcends historical time to the historical future as envisaged by the historicized eschatology of the modern age. He does not merely add eternity to time as we all understand it. For there is no 'time as we all understand it'. The understanding of time is itself at issue in the issue of the eternal future of time.

I.1. The modern myth of time

It will be as well to begin with the understanding of time which Moltmann rejects, the modern time myth.[5] By this is meant not a concept to be found in specific major thinkers, so much as a set of broad cultural assumptions about time which have deeply affected both thought about and experience of the temporal process in the modern West. Of course, there have been many who have thought differently, in part or in whole, and almost certainly most have experienced time in some ways which do not really cohere with this particular model of the nature of

---

[4] The use of the word 'time' is potentially confusing, but Moltmann and others use it in the sense of time as it inheres in the whole temporal process of the world, rather than in the sense of a bare or abstract time which would still, as it were, be there even if nothing happened in it. A broad use of the word 'history' sometimes has a similar sense, but the word normally refers to the past to the exclusion of the future.

[5] In the following three paragraphs I am expounding what Moltmann indicates only more briefly.

time, but nevertheless the myth we shall attempt to describe has had a considerable cultural dominance. (Though Moltmann does not often speak of postmodernity, the term 'modern' here does not mean 'contemporary', but the period from the Enlightenment, whose intellectual characteristics are now being superseded by others. The modern time myth is the one which was characteristic of the nineteenth and early twentieth centuries, but has been declining more recently, though it is still significantly influential. Thus, for example, a description of it is not intended to take account of the important implications of recent developments in physics for understanding time.)

It will not do to characterize the modern time myth simply as linear or quantitative time, though Moltmann does sometimes give the impression that this is a purely modern creation (CoG 138: 'a modern scientific category'; cf. GC 127). All historical societies (including biblical ones)[6] have for some purposes measured time in numbers of days, months and years.[7] All use calendar time, which is in some sense linear and quantitative, although calendars incorporate cyclical elements, in the form both of the natural cycles of time (day and night, the moon, the seasons)[8] and of annually recurring festivals which usually give access to non-linear time.[9] But the issue is the extent to which the linear and the quantitative dominate. Mechanical clocks[10] (which measure hours and minutes in stable quantities as ancient societies usually

---

[6] S. J. DeVries, *Yesterday, Today, and Tomorrow: Time and History in the Old Testament* (London: SPCK, 1976) 343–345.

[7] Perhaps there are tribal societies that do not: cf. R. Banks, *The Tyranny of Time* (Exeter: Paternoster, 1983) 140–141.

[8] For linguistic recognition of this kind of cyclical element in time in the Old Testament, see J. Barr, *Biblical Words for Time* (SBT; London: SCM Press, 1962) 141.

[9] W. Benjamin (quoted in S. Mosès, *L'Ange de l'Histoire: Rosenzweig, Benjamin, Scholem* [Paris: Éditions du Seuil, 1992] 160) notes that for this reason calendars do not measure time in the way clocks do.

[10] On the late medieval origins and later development of mechanical clocks and their effect on time-measurement, see D. L. Landes, *Revolution in Time: Clocks and the Making of the Modern World* (Cambridge, Massachusetts: [Belknap Press of] Harvard University Press, 1983).

did not),[11] the prevalence of calendars, along with the decline in importance of cyclical elements in the calendar, and the introduction of standard time,[12] have increased the role of the linear and the quantitative in the modern Western world's sense of time. Also very important is the adoption of dating AD (instead of local eras and dating by regnal years of monarchs) in regular and common use especially from the sixteenth century. This gives a sense of all time as a continuous process, measured in regular units of years and centuries, encompassing a single universal history, and stretching into the indefinite future. Finally, the Newtonian understanding of time in relation to the physical world[13] encouraged an analogously quantitative understanding of time in relation to human history and experience. It is important to note that the linear image of time as it appears in the modern time myth, with all times in past, present and future located along a single line, is not simply a way of representing the irreversibility of the time process. When dominant in the understanding of time, it promotes the sense of the future as no more than a prolongation of the past and the present, and the present no more than a transition from past to future, thereby obscuring the openness of the present and the future to unpredictable possibilities, including the radically new. It also encourages the purely quantitative sense of time, in which events in time are related to each other only via the measurable length of time which separates them on the time line.

These developments are certainly not ideologically neutral. They accompanied the growth of the modern historicist,

[11] In much of the ancient world the hour was not a constant quantity of time, but a twelfth of the period of daylight or the period of darkness, however long these might be. It is salutary to consider how inconvenient we should find it not to have hours of fixed length: strictly quantitative time is woven into the way we live as it was not for ancient people.

[12] S. Kern, *The Culture of Time and Space 1880–1919* (London: Weidenfeld & Nicolson, 1983) 11–14.

[13] B. Adam, *Time and Social Theory* (Cambridge: Polity Press, 1990) 50–51, quoting Isaac Newton: 'Absolute, true, and mathematical time, of itself, and from its own nature, flows equally without relation to anything external, and by another name is called duration . . . All motions may be accelerated or retarded, but the flowing of absolute time is not liable to change' (cf. also Kern, *The Culture of Time*, 11).

progressivist myth of time, seen at its purest in Hegel and at its most typical in the nineteenth-century Liberal and Marxist versions of the idea of inevitable historical progress. In Stéphane Mosès' account[14] of the way this progressivist myth of time was rejected and replaced in the thought of Rosenzweig, Benjamin and Gershom Scholem, it has three features. There is the idea of continuity, in which time is conceived as a homogeneous process, advancing in a single rectilinear movement. There is the idea of causality, in which history is understood on the analogy of physical causality in Newtonian mechanics. What happens afterwards is determined by what happened before it in a continuous causal and temporal sequence. Thirdly, there is the idea of progress, according to which this continuous, long march of history across the centuries, measured in quantifiable stages like a long-distance journey, amounts to a cumulative progress, continuously approaching ever-nearer the utopia that lies in the indefinite future. This whole picture of time[15] combines the influence of the Christian providential understanding of history as ordered by divine purpose to an end, transmuted into the notion of an immanent telos of historical movement, with that of Newtonian science, on which nineteenth-century historical science strove to model itself.[16]

This is a very simple sketch of the dominant modern myth of time, lacking all the qualifications and complexity which would be required in another context. It has been intended primarily as a basis for understanding how and why Moltmann differs from this broad approach to time which is characteristic of the modern era. He is critical of it on several counts:

(1) First, the homogeneity of past, present and future and the purely quantitative difference between them (the future

[14] S. Mosès, *L'Ange de l'Histoire: Rosenzweig, Benjamin, Scholem* [Paris: Éditions du Seuil, 1992]. Moltmann's account of these three Jewish thinkers in CoG 33–41 is considerably influenced by Mosès' book (he refers to the German translation: CoG 344–346), though he knew and was influenced by the work of all three before he read Mosès.

[15] Of course, it is a generalization: there have been ways of viewing time in the modern period which share some of the key features outlined here but not others.

[16] Mosès, *L'Ange de l'Histoire*, 21, 76, 89, 156–167.

differs from the past only in the quantity of calendar time that separates them) contradict the qualitative difference of past and future which is essential to Christian faith's 'own messianic understanding of time' (GC 123; cf. CoG 26, 138–139). This qualitative difference of past and future 'is the very opposite of setting them on a single line' (GC 124). Rather than thinking of past, present and future along an undifferentiated line, he follows Georg Picht and Ernst Bloch in assigning the three modes of time to modes of being that are different in kind: 'future is the sphere of the possible, past the sphere of the real [what has passed from potentiality into actuality], present the frontier on which the possible is either real-ized or not real-ized' (CoG 286). As the sphere of potentiality, the future exceeds the past (CoG 26; cf. 287). Because of the difference in modalities of being we deal differently with past and future: we recall historical experiences, we project expectations of the future (286–287, 288–289).

The notion of historical time as a single line moving into the future generally presupposes either a deistic theological view of history, as the mere implementation of a divine plan wholly determined in advance (cf. CoG 13), or the quasi-scientific view of historical causality, according to which the past determines the future. For Moltmann, the future is not the prolongation of the past, but the sphere of indefinite possibilities which may or may not be realized in the present and become past. On this view, historical time is certainly irreversible: once the potential has become actual as past it cannot again become unrealized potential (CoG 286–287; cf. 282–283). In fact, this way of thinking makes the irreversibility of time intelligible in a way that the mere image of the straight line, so often thought to be implied by the notion of the irreversibility of time,[17] does not. Only a particular view of purpose or causality in history can explain the irreversibility of time as represented in the rectilinear concept. (In passing, it is worth noting the sense in which, according to Moltmann, time will be reversed in the transformation of time at the

---

[17] E.g. E. Brunner, *Eternal Hope* (tr. H. Knight; London: Lutterworth, 1954) 43.

eschaton [CoG 294–295].[18] It is not, of course, the movement from potentiality to actuality which will be reversed, but the movement in which reality passes into the past and is no longer present reality. In other words, not time's creativity, but time's transience will be reversed. Whereas in time everything passes away and is lost, in eternity everything that has passed away will be recovered so that nothing is lost.)

Although the modern myth understands time as orientated to the future as goal, it cannot give to the future the kind of ontological priority that is postulated in the view Moltmann adopts, since the future can do no more than develop the potential of the past. It is no more than the prolongation of the line that runs from the past through the present. The radically and qualitatively new cannot be expected from it (cf. CoG 25; WJC 158–159). The view Moltmann adopts gives the future priority as 'the source from which time springs' (CoG 287), though at this point he distinguishes future time, which will actually occur in the future and follow every previous time into the past, from the transcendent future which, transcending all historical time, is the source of time (CoG 26, 287; cf. GC 129–130). This understanding of the future as the source of time coheres with his privileging of the concept of the future as *adventus* (what is coming) over the concept of the future as

---

[18] A. J. Torrance in H. D. Regan and A. J. Torrance (eds), *Christ and Context: The Confrontation between Gospel and Culture* (Edinburgh: T. & T. Clark, 1993) 199, criticizes Moltmann on the grounds that 'there is no movement in time at all . . . time does not run forward any more than it runs backward' (cf. also A. J. Torrance, *Persons in Communion: An Essay on Trinitarian Description and Human Participation* [Edinburgh: T. & T. Clark, 1996] 312; and most fully in 'Creatio ex Nihilo and the Spatio-Temporal Dimensions, with special reference to Jürgen Moltmann and D. C. Williams', in C. E. Gunton (ed.), *The Doctrine of Creation* [Edinburgh: T. & T. Clark, 1997] 92–99). Moltmann's response (*Christ and Context*, 207–208) is reasonable: 'I still believe that one is allowed to speak about future, present and past, and that there is a certain irreversibility because future can become present and then past, but past cannot become future again.' Much of our talk about time uses spatial metaphors, of which 'movement' is an example. It seems almost impossible to talk about our experience of temporal successiveness without such metaphors. But it is one thing to point out that they are metaphors, another to claim that when we use such metaphors we are not saying anything true about time.

futurum (what will be).[19] (Unlike Latin, neither German nor English have two nouns embodying this distinction, but nevertheless both ways of thinking about the future are familiar in ordinary speech. The future not only 'will be', but also 'is coming'.) *Futurum* is appropriate to the linear conception of homogeneous time: the future will be, and, like everything else that is in time, will subsequently cease to be. *Adventus*, the future that comes to meet us, enables one to think of God as exercising the power of the transcendent future over time,[20] and as the God whose eschatological coming[21] to the world is also the transcendent *novum* (GC 132–134; CoG 25–26).

There are two key differences here from the modern time myth. First, because the source of time is the transcendent future, historical time is genuinely open to the future, rather than determined by the past. It is open to the unpredictable and the genuinely new that are not prolongations of the past and the present, but come from the potentiality of the future. This point is also recognized in views of time which have this much in common with Moltmann, but which do not go along with him in his second main difference from the modern time myth. However, this first point is very characteristic of Moltmann's thought, and the second point could not be

---

[19] As Moltmann points out (FC 180 n. 53), theological use of this linguistic distinction seems first to have been made by Brunner, *Eternal Hope*, 25:

> In fact the "future" [Zukunft = *adventus*] itself, as also its Latin [*sic*] equivalents *avenir*, *avenire*, etc., are of Christian origin. Humanity has a future because it awaits the coming of the kingdom of God in the future coming of its Lord. The life of the world to come as distinct from *futurum* is an eschatological concept; it suggests the realization of hope through an event which springs from the beyond, from the transcendent; not like *futurum*, something which grows out of what already exists.

(It is true that *adventus* does not have the meaning 'future' in classical Latin, but less clear that the idea of the future coming originates only in Christian contexts.) Moltmann first used the distinction in 1966 (FC 29–31; cf. 180 n. 53).

[20] This point is already made in FC 27 (first published in 1966), which Moltmann echoes in CoG 24.

[21] 'God's being is in his coming, not in his becoming' is Moltmann's repeated correction of Jüngel (FC 180 n. 53; GC 133; CoG 23).

true if the first were not. The second point is that, although the modern time myth resolutely attempts to subordinate transience to progress, in fact the transience which is inherent in historical time cannot be transcended without transcendence *of* historical time. Every future to which purely linear time can lead will pass away. Everything that is not yet must one day be no longer. But if the God of the transcendent future comes, then the transcendence of transience in the transformation of time is conceivable.

In the concept of the future just expounded Moltmann is very close to Pannenberg,[22] by whom he has certainly been influenced, but in his rejection of the homogeneous and quantitative concept of time he is also close to Rosenzweig and Benjamin, even though his thinking here developed largely independently of them. Against the homogeneity and continuity of time, Rosenzweig and Benjamin stress the discontinuities of history and the qualitatively different moments that compose it.[23] The present moment is not a mere transition from past to present in an undifferentiated sequence of cause and effect, as the purely linear image of time suggests. It has significance in itself which is not exhausted by its relationship to its immediate past and its immediate actual future. Each moment is qualitatively unique[24] and opens towards a variety of possible futures. At any such moment, the radically new, even messianic redemption could

[22] W. Pannenberg, *Theology and the Kingdom of God* (ed. R. J. Neuhaus; Philadelphia: Westminster Press, 1969) chapter 1; idem, 'The God of Hope', in *Basic Questions in Theology*, vol. 2 (tr. G. H. Kehm; London: SCM Press, 1971) 234–249.

[23] The critique of homogeneous time through appeal to the qualitative differences in the lived experience of time appears earlier in H. Bergson, *Time and Free Will* (tr. F. L. Pogson; London: George Allen [3rd edn.], 1913), first published in French in 1889. Some degree of influence on Rosenzweig and Benjamin seems likely. For criticism of homogeneous time at the beginning of the twentieth century, see Kern, *The Culture of Time*, 16–20. For Benjamin's understanding of time, see especially P. Osborne, 'Small-scale Victories, Large-scale Defeats: Walter Benjamin's Politics of Time', in A. Benjamin and P. Osborne (eds), *Walter Benjamin's Philosophy: Destruction and Experience* (London: Routledge, 1994) 59–109.

[24] Comparable with this is Moltmann's appeal to the 'kairological interpretation' in which 'the flux of time is non-homogeneous: there are favourable and unfavourable times' (CoG 291).

enter history.[25] We shall return to the key concept of the discontinuous moment. But we note that although Moltmann's account of the ontological priority of the future is distinctive in this context, he shares with the Jewish thinkers the rejection of historical continuity and necessity and the openness of each present to a wide field of future possibilities. As in Rosenzweig, it is this which makes even the coming of the eschatological new, the absolute other of redemption, capable of being envisaged.[26]

(2) As well as the qualitative difference of past and future, Moltmann has two other key ways of denying that historical time can be adequately envisaged as a single temporal line. First, although it is clearly true that the flow of time is irreversible, it is not true that past, present and future are related in a simple sequence of before and after. Each present has its own past and future, such that, for example, it is possible to take up in the present the future of the past, meaning not the future that became actual but the unrealized possibilities of a past time. (This is Moltmann's rather frequently repeated notion that there is 'future in the past': e.g. TH 269; GC 123, 126, 131–132; WJC 240; CoG 140, 289. The idea probably derived originally from Bloch [cf. GC 339 n. 50], but the influence of Benjamin's *Theses on the Philosophy of History* is also notable [cf. TH 268; GC 339 n. 46].)[27] Such processes create a complex interlacing of the times (cf. GC 124):

---

[25] Mosès, *L'Ange de l'Histoire*, 21–24, 76–78, 88–91, 153–167, 180. Benjamin, for whom messianic redemption is a symbol of the possibility of revolutionary change, the radically new, sees in each moment a conflict between the principles of continuity, which would continue the past unchanged, and of unpredictable rupture, in which the radically new would break in. Both he and Rosenzweig see the messianic redemption (despite their different interpretations of it) not as the goal of a process or the distant end of the historical sequence, but as a possibility for each unique moment, so radically undetermined is the historical process. On Benjamin, see also S. A. Handelman, *Fragments of Redemption: Jewish Thought and Literary Theory in Benjamin, Scholem, and Levinas* (Bloomington/Indianapolis: Indiana University Press, 1991).

[26] See especially Mosès, *L'Ange de l'Histoire*, 77–78. On Rosenzweig's understanding of time and eternity, see also R. Gibbs, *Correlations in Rosenzweig and Levinas* (Princeton: Princeton University Press, 1992) chapters 5–6.

[27] For Benjamin's thought on this topic, see Mosès, *L'Ange de l'Histoire*, 152–153.

> The concept of linear time covers only simple series of events. But if these series of events are woven into a network of inter-relations and multiple effects, networks of time have to be developed, in which linear and cyclical temporal concepts are combined. (GC 129)

The effect is, once again, to open up history to multiple possibilities for which the idea of a simple causal sequence, analogous to Newtonian physics, cannot allow. Also, in the important idea of the past's own future, with the consequent need to understand the past in the light of its own hopes and the opportunity to take up the discarded and suppressed possibilities of the past, there is also the implication of a kind of community with the past in hope (TH 269; GC 132). Whereas the linear time of the modern time myth can only leave the past in the past and confines hope for the future to the future, the more complex interlacings of past, present and future which Moltmann describes cohere with the expectation of a trans-cendent future which will be the future of every present:

> Interaction with those who are past and dead is necessary in the name of the common future in the resurrection of the dead – necessary, and an expression of a community not merely in transience but in coming too. (CoG 140; cf. WJC 238–240)

(3) The third key way in which Moltmann rejects the adequacy of the picture of historical time as a linear sequence is that the irreversible flow of time is interrupted by the rhythmic recurrence of sabbaths (CoG 138, 283; cf. GC 286: the Sabbath 'brings interruption, interval and rhythm into human temporal experience'). (The point here is not merely the rhythmic element itself, which linear concepts of time easily subsume, but the rhythmic *interruption*. At intervals the time which moves forward in a progressive sequence is interrupted by time which is treated quite differently, so that it is experienced as other than the forward-moving flow of time to which the other six days of the week belong.) Moltmann explicitly opposes this role of the Sabbath to the nineteenth-century and still current notion that the effect of eschatology on the experience of history has been to make history a purposeful process leading inexorably to its eschatological goal. This progressivist view sees the end of

history one-sidedly as history's goal, in effect reducing eschatology to history, whereas the Jewish and Christian eschatological traditions have equally seen the end of history as what ends history. In other words, the eschaton is not history's immanent completion so much as its transcendent redemption. If the eschaton is to be seen as both goal and end of history, then its effect on the structure of historical time can be best seen in the 'rhythmicization' of time which the Sabbath (together with the sabbatical and jubilee years) effects. The forward-moving purposive time of work-days is cyclically interrupted by the times of Sabbath rest and celebration which prefigure the eschatological Sabbath of God's rest in his creation in eternity, the Sabbath which is both the goal and the end of history. Because the Sabbath was given in creation and anticipates the eschaton,[28] it is not the experience of God's action in history (like the exodus celebrated in passover) but the experience of the eternal presence of the God who is, in which, beyond the losses and achievements of history, creation will be glorified in its eschatological eternity (cf. GC 287). (The Christian Sunday, rather differently from the Jewish Sabbath, also rhythmicizes time [CoG 138]: it anticipates the new creation as new beginning, and so in its own way also resists the one-sided understanding of eschatology as the goal of a continuous linear process [GC 294–296].)

It is worth noting, as Moltmann does not,[29] that the modern concept of time as homogeneous has increasingly operated to remove the rhythmical elements in public time in Western societies. The standardization and commercialization of life can no longer tolerate weekly interruption, and so the laws which gave Sunday a publicly different character have been progressively repealed. With the theoretical notion of homogeneous

---

[28] It is important to note that the Sabbath is not one of cycles of nature which structure calendar time in a partly cyclical way (day and night, the month, the year): 'the sabbath is defined simply by the creation story, not by any natural cycle' (GC 285; cf. F. Rosenzweig, *The Star of Redemption* [tr. W. W. Hallo; Notre Dame: Notre Dame Press, 1985] 291).

[29] In CJF 87, he protests against the availability of Saturday and Sunday for flexible working hours, but does not explicitly relate this to concepts of time.

time as the ideological context, public time has been in practice homogenized. There is, indeed, much to be said for the view that economic considerations ('time is money') have played a dominant role in promoting the notion of linear time,[30] just as the axiom of economic growth has proved the most enduring aspect of the idea of progress.[31]

Though Moltmann's thinking about the Sabbath derives in general from his appreciation of Jewish theology (GC 276–290), there is no doubt that Rosenzweig is here especially influential. Moltmann's use of Rosenzweig's major work, *The Star of Redemption*, is extremely selective, but the passage on the Sabbath[32] is one to which he frequently refers, though only in his later work (1985 onwards).[33] Rosenzweig argued that the Jewish people, who have lived a kind of alternative history on the margins of Western society, have experienced temporality quite differently from the way time has been experienced in the historical consciousness of the modern West,[34] with its dominant model of linear progress, which Rosenzweig takes to be the Christian model. The Jewish people have lived a kind of immobile history, a sacred time structured by the annual

[30] So P. Eicher, 'Temporalisation de l'éternité: Le Seigneur du temps et l'origine de la modernité', in J.-L. Leuba (ed.), *Temps et Eschatologie* (Paris: Éditions du Cerf, 1994) 231–232. B. Adam, *Time and Social Theory* (Cambridge: Polity Press, 1990) 139, following H.-W. Hohn, traces the notion of time as quantitative and the future as controllable to economic developments in the late middle ages: 'with the emergence of world trade in conjunction with city states the future became an entity, a quantity to be allocated, budgeted, controlled and utilised for exchange. It became equated with money.'

[31] Cf. C. Lasch, *The True and Only Heaven: Progress and Its Critics* (New York: Norton, 1991) chapter 2.

[32] Rosenzweig, *The Star of Redemption*, 308–315.

[33] For Moltmann's explicit allusions to this passage, see HTG 195 n. 15; GC 277, 278, 280, 290; WJC 27; CoG 35.

[34] Especially at this point, Rosenzweig's work has been highly controversial for subsequent Jewish thinkers. For savage criticism of Rosenzweig, whom, ironically in our present context, he accuses of christianizing Judaism, see E. Berkovits, *Major Themes in Modern Philosophies of Judaism* (New York: Ktav, 1974) 37–67, who reads Rosenzweig very differently from the much more sympathetic treatment by Mosès. Moltmann's own use of Rosenzweig, it has to be admitted, generally consists of a rather opportunist appropriation of particular themes and favourite quotations abstracted from their context in Rosenzweig's highly distinctive philosophical version of Judaism.

recurrence of the festivals. In place of the long march of history towards the ever-receding utopia, Jews anticipate redemption in the non-historical, symbolic time of the festivals and rites.[35] Of these the Sabbath is primary: 'it attracts the eternal into the Today, not just by analogy but in reality'.[36]

It will be seen that in the above points (1), (2) and (3) Moltmann is engaged, in various ways, both in understanding historical time as open to the truly eschatological, i.e. transcendent future, and also in envisaging that future as related to time not as the end-point of historical time conceived as a rectilinear process, but as the transcendent power of the redemption of all historical time. A fourth idea, that of the moment of eternity experienced in time, which is related to these three and has a similar effect, is reserved for special treatment in section I.4 below.

(4) The modern time myth can be seen as an ideology of the powerful, for whom a future continuous with the present represents the continuation and extension of their position of dominance and privilege. (Here the critique can be applied to the time myth only in its liberal progressivist, not its Marxist revolutionary form.) A model of time which requires the future to be extrapolated from the past and the present, which denies alternative possibilities, radical changes, real novelty, unpredictable irruptions in the historical process, is a model in the interests of those who must suppress alternative possibilities if they are to maintain their own power in the future. It is the ideology which justifies their own power to determine the future (GC 134; CoG 45, 135; cf. FC 43, 56). Thus the one-sided secular millenarianism of the modern world is a myth of power which provokes among the powerless and the dominated the hope of an apocalyptic end to the present order and an alternative future (CoG 135–136). This perspective coheres with an argument about eschatological transcendence which Moltmann already adopted in an essay of 1969:

---

[35] Cf. Mosès, *L'Ange de l'Histoire*, 63–67, 85–86.
[36] Rosenzweig, *The Star of Redemption*, 192.

[T]he more [Christian faith] interprets this eschatological transcendence in Christian terms – that is, with its eyes on the crucified
Jesus – the more it will become conscious that the qualitatively
new future of God has allied itself with those who are dispossessed,
denied and downtrodden at the present day; so that this future
does not begin up at the spearheads of progress in a 'progressive
society', but down below, among society's victims. It will have to
link hope for the eschatological future with a loving solidarity with
the dispossessed. (FC 17)

More consistently and fully, Moltmann now sees the 'progress'
of the modern world as the project of the powerful to control
and to create the future, and the time myth of the modern world
as the ideology of this project of domination.

At this point Moltmann is closest, among the Jewish messianic
thinkers he looks to as precedents for his eschatology, to
Benjamin, for whom the past seen from the perspective of the
present continuous with it is the story of the victors, while the
story of the vanquished, which can be brought to new life, is
that of hopes for disruptions and alternatives. Against the
dominant myth of the present as mere transition from the
past to a future that follows inexorably from it, Benjamin saw
the present as the scene of conflict between the alternative
possibilities of continuity and discontinuity, repetition of the
past and revolution, the unchangeable and the genuinely new.[37]
There are also correspondences here with Rosenzweig, who saw
Hegel's philosophy of history as a form of absolute legitimation
of the ambitions of the nations whose destinies were said to
achieve the meaning of history.[38]

(5) Finally, I add a point which is wholly consistent with
Moltmann's approach but at which he explicitly only hints. The
concept of time as continuous and homogeneous disguises the
negative features of the transience which is a prime characteristic
of historical time. The myth of inevitable and interminable
progress, occurring cumulatively as historical time moves ever
onward, 'spreads the veil of an illusionary immortality over the

[37] See Mosès, *L'Ange de l'Histoire*, 152–156.
[38] Mosès, *L'Ange de l'Histoire*, 70–71, 77–78.

modern West' (CoG 159) – illusionary because it does not surmount transience. Future progress is of no value to those who have died in the past. Moreover, every immanent achievement of the historical process will itself be subject to transience (cf. CoG 6, 13, 19, which make this point generally about the transposition of eschatology into time). Eschatology reduced to an immanent process of history cannot in the end resist the trend of transient time to universal death and nothingness (284). By postulating endless time the modern myth of progress has propagated an illusory sense of eternity, but in reality endless historical time, endless *transient* time, cannot lead to true eternity, the transcendence of transience, but only to universal death. The illusion is sustained by a picture of time from which transience is removed. That this is a misleading picture of time can easily be seen by contrasting with it the model of historical time, found both in the Bible and in most traditional societies, which represents the passage of time in the succession of the generations. In this model the continuity of history is represented in a way that equally acknowledges the discontinuity incurred by death.[39] By contrast, the typically modern practice of representing the passage of time by numbered centuries ignores death and all forms of discontinuity, giving only the impression of mathematically cumulative advance. The point is that one form of representation takes account of death, while the other does not. Of course, the people who use it have some degree of consciousness of death and discontinuity, but the fact that their way of representing time itself does not include recognition of this, as representation by a sequence of generations does, functions to minimize awareness of loss and discontinuity as intrinsic to the experience of historical time.

The suppression of transience in the modern concept of time belongs to its character as a kind of immanent theodicy, designed to justify the course of history by means of its immanent meaning. The course of history is justified by its future goal, but this means that the meaning of history benefits future rather than past generations, and the victors of history rather than the

---

[39] Cf. Mosès, *L'Ange de l'Histoire*, 88, 160.

victims of progress. Only if transience and evil are minimized can this appear a credible theodicy. This is, of course, in part why the horrors of twentieth-century history dealt such blows to the myth of progress and were the crucible in which alternative views of time have been proposed. They demonstrate the enormity of the evils with which the idea of progress can deal only by forgetting the victims – and by forgetting especially that many were the victims precisely of progress.

In conclusion, it may be illuminating to contrast the modern time myth with the eschatological understanding of time which Moltmann proposes in the following way. For Moltmann, historical time is characterized by the negative and the positive sides of its susceptibility to change: on the one hand, transience, which brings all things in time to nothing, and, on the other hand, openness to God's future (CoG 283–284). It is only because this positive potentiality is openness to the transcendent eschatological future that it is possible to hope for redemption from transience. By contrast, the modern myth of homogeneous linear time tends to suppress both the negative and the positive sides of temporality: it emphasizes continuity at the expense of transience and loss, and it emphasizes continuity at the expense of the unpredictable possibilities of radical novelty. If it is to sustain the sense of meaning in history which has been characteristic of the modern world, it must do both these things at once. Once transience and tragedy are allowed full recognition, only transcendence can give meaning to history. Only eschatological transcendence can keep the theodicy question open, refusing to forget the dead and the victims in hope of their resurrection and glorification in the transcendent future which is the future of all history. Thus our exploration of the criticisms Moltmann makes of the time myth of modern progressivism reinforces the overriding importance of eschatological transcendence to his project in *The Coming of God*. Only with an eschatology that is truly eschatological, that is, that speaks of the future that transcends history, can Christian faith respond adequately to the contemporary crisis in which the project of modern historical progressivism, though deeply discredited, has still the power to bring about the catastrophes to which it is leading.

I.2. Theological options

The contrast we have explored between Moltmann's eschatology of the transcendent future and the myth of time that has sustained the secularized eschatology of modern historical progressivisms will also help us to understand the way Moltmann positions himself in relation to the eschatological options that arose in Christian theology and in Jewish theological and philosophical thought in the first half of the twentieth century (CoG I). The two broad theological options he rejects are 'the transposition of eschatology into time' and 'the transposition of eschatology into eternity'. The former includes, as its forerunner, the 'prophetic theology' of seventeenth- and eighteenth-century Protestantism (CoG 7; treated in more detail in TH 69–76), the 'consistent eschatology' of Albert Schweitzer and Johannes Weiss (CoG 7–10; see also WJC 316–317; TH 37–39), and the 'salvation-history' theology of Oscar Cullmann (CoG 10–13; cf. also FC 19–20). The latter is represented by the early work of Karl Barth (CoG 13–16; see also TH 50–58), the first edition of Paul Althaus' eschatology (CoG 16–19; cf. also FC 20–23),[40] and Rudolf Bultmann (CoG 19–22; see also TH 58–69; and, on all three, WJC 317–318). Against these two trends he defines his own position as 'the eschatology of the coming God' (CoG 22–29), and then finds precedent and inspiration for this in the rebirth of messianic thinking in Jewish thinkers of the first half of the century (CoG 29–46).

It will be clear now that the first option, 'the transposition of eschatology into time', as it appears in twentieth-century theologies, depends on the modern time myth and represents the same kind of reduction of eschatology to historical time as do the secular millenarianisms of the modern period. This helps to account for the severity with which Moltmann dismisses the representatives of this theological option. But it is also the case that the second option, 'the transposition of eschatology into eternity', also essentially takes the modern conception of time

[40] Althaus' position shifted from an 'axiological eschatology' in the first edition of his *The Last Things* (1922) to a combination of this with a 'teleological eschatology', which gives weight to a future dimension, in the third edition (1933). CoG 16–19 focuses on the former, FC 20–23 on the latter.

for granted (cf. CoG 135 on Bultmann). The time–eternity dialectic of these theologians adds a vertical dimension of eternity to the horizontal linear dimension in such a way that the former constantly impinges on the latter, encountering believers in a way that detaches them from historical time. It is not that time itself is in any way differentiated, but that eternity breaks into time in a non-temporal, supra-historical moment. Time and history are abolished in the believer's encounter with the eternal in the moment, but they continue to run their course in the world. Modern progressivism is countered simply by declaring this course to be of no theological concern. This is bound to be the case for a theology that rightly insists on eschatological transcendence, but still takes for granted the modern myth of linear and homogeneous time.

The classification of the theological options is valuable, but it is arguable that Moltmann has distinguished his own position from each of the other two a little too sharply. In the case of 'the transposition of eschatology into eternity', it is not only in the assertion of transcendence against the immanent eschatology of historical progressivism that this position approaches his own. This is also true, in a certain sense, of the immediacy of eschatological eternity to every time that the assertion of transcendence entails. For example, he quotes Althaus:

> Every time is immediate to judgment, immediate to completion. In this sense every time is last time. All time, not just the last time, will be perpetually ended and gathered up by eternity. (CoG 17)

Yet Moltmann himself holds that the eschatological coming of God which will end historical time occurs simultaneously to all time (WJC 328). He can say that

> This last day in time is at once the present of eternity to all times. This 'last day' is 'the day of days'. There is no other way of thinking of the day of resurrection. In content it is defined as 'the day of the Lord', to which all times are simultaneous. (CoG 279–280)

He can say that, 'In the eternal creation all the times which in God's creative resolve were fanned out will also be gathered together' (CoG 292). The difference Moltmann sees is that, for

Althaus and Barth, the immediacy is that of God's non-temporal eternity to time, whereas for Moltmann it is that of God's eschatological coming to time to end and to transform it. The former abolishes time, the latter transforms it. Nevertheless there is real resemblance, in the common claim that the eschaton is not related to time merely as an occurrence in the historical future, but has an immediate relationship to all time. The resemblance is such as to provoke the question: Why does Moltmann speak of the simultaneity of the eschaton to all times when he discusses the eschatological moment (as in the quotations above), but not in relation to the experience of living in historical time? (See his debate with Barth: CoG 292–294.) Of course, this would not mean that the eschatological moment occurs in every moment (CoG 293). But it should mean that every moment confronts immediately – that is, without the mediation of historical future – the eschatological moment which will gather it into eternity. Moltmann does not seem to have faced the problem of how the simultaneity of the eschaton to all time can be understood from the perspective of a moment within historical time, which would somehow have to be understood as *both* a moment within the flow of time *and* as in immediate relationship with the transcendent future in which it will be transformed into eternity. The concern to retain real eschatological futurity in distinction from 'the transposition of eschatology into eternity' (cf. WJC 318; CoG 15) has obscured an issue which Moltmann's own eschatological conceptuality seems to raise.

Moltmann's discussion of the alternative trend, the 'transposition of eschatology into time', focuses especially on the issue of the so-called 'delay of the parousia', which for Schweitzer and the school of 'consistent eschatology' (consistent, according to Moltmann, only in its thoroughgoing abolition of eschatology [WJC 316]) disproved the eschatological hope of Jesus and the early church. The parousia did not arrive. But for Schweitzer, Weiss and the others the problem was not simply that, as it happened, the expectation proved mistaken. Such an expectation of a transcendent rupturing of the historical process was in any case incredible in view of the modern view of endless and homogeneous time, which they accepted as axiomatically as the nineteenth-century Liberal Protestants whose non-eschatological Jesus they exposed as unhistorical. Moltmann's distinctive observation, however, is that they did not in fact take the transcendence of the eschatology of Jesus and the early Christians seriously enough. They envisaged the parousia in the *temporal* future, allotting it a place in the general flow of time, in which it could be expected sooner or later (WJC 316). Ironically, despite the incredulity with which they viewed the eschatology of Jesus, they attributed to him the same fundamental eschatological error which (in Moltmann's eyes) they committed themselves in retaining the historical progressivism of the nineteenth century. This was the error of placing the eschatological future (whether history's end, in Jesus' case, or history's goal, in their own) on the same time-line as the past and the present.

Oscar Cullmann, whose highly influential[41] *Christ and Time* was written in part to defuse the problem of the 'delay of the parousia' without transposing eschatology into non-temporal terms, as Barth and Bultmann did, incurs fundamentally the same criticism from Moltmann as the 'consistent eschatology' school. He not only assumes linear time, placing the incarnation and the parousia simply at different points along the line. He explicitly argues that such a conception of time was central to the early Christian message[42] (and so cannot be discarded in a demythologized version of the gospel). Therefore he does not successfully meet the problem of the delay of the parousia, sharing with the 'consistent eschatology' school the basic mistake of supposing that the parousia should occur in time, at a date in the calendar. Moreover, by missing the essential point that all that occurs in time must pass away in time, that any future along the same time-line as the present must become past, he robs the parousia of its truly eschatological nature:

[41] For some indication of its influence, see B. Reicke, 'Christ et le temps', in Leuba (ed.), *Temps et Eschatologie*, 68–70.

[42] The 'centre' of the Christian proclamation 'is the Christian conception of time and history' (O. Cullmann, *Christ and Time: The Primitive Christian Conception of Time and History* [tr. F. V. Filson; London: SCM Press, 1951] 32).

The reduction of eschatology to time in the framework of salvation history also really abolishes eschatology altogether, subjecting it to *chronos*, the power of transience. (CoG 13)

Moltmann undoubtedly scores excellent points against Cullmann, far too much of whose thesis has been widely taken over without adequate criticism. Cullmann's assumption that the biblical theologian must set aside all philosophical categories in order to see simply what the New Testament says (e.g. 'If we wish to grasp the Primitive Christian idea of eternity, we must strive above all to think in as unphilosophical a manner as possible'!) [43] is shown to be hermeneutically naive by its result. Cullmann finds in the New Testament precisely the modern notion of time ('a *continuous time process*', [44] 'this simple recti-linear conception of unending time', [45] 'it is thought of as a straight line, not as a circle', [46] 'the symbol of time for Primitive Christianity . . . is the *upward sloping line*'), [47] presumably suppos-ing that this modern notion, to which the biblical one turns out to be so remarkably similar, is simply a common-sense view, unlike, for example, the Greek philosophical view. This at least seems implied in his request to readers to 'put aside completely the question . . . whether a New Testament statement can be an important part of the Christian message if it contradicts this or that philosophical conception of whose correctness we are convinced,' concentrating rather on the question 'what is there which [the New Testament revelation] does not have in common with philosophical or religious systems.' [48] Of course, what he considers really distinctive of the New Testament is the salvation-history which takes place along the continuous line of

---

[43] Cullmann, *Christ and Time*, 62; cf. also 48, 66.

[44] Cullmann, *Christ and Time*, 32: italics original.

[45] Cullmann, *Christ and Time*, 49.

[46] Cullmann, *Christ and Time*, 51. In *Salvation in History* (tr. S. G. Sowers; NTL; London: SCM Press, 1967) 13, he writes: 'Though I still use the figure of the *line* as the general direction for salvation history, it is now important to me to stress that I did not mean a straight line, but a *fluctuating line* which can show wide variation.' The 'straight line', of course, came from a modern conceptuality which in *Christ and Time* Cullmann had not yet seen could not, even in this respect, represent the biblical writers' conceptions.

[47] Cullmann, *Christ and Time*, 51: italics original.

[48] Cullmann, *Christ and Time*, 12.

time, but the latter is indispensable. Cullmann's unreflective attribution to the New Testament writers (who, of course, never speak of a 'line' of time) of the characteristically modern image of time calls, as Moltmann sees, for a more radical critique than James Barr's justified but exaggerated critique of Cullmann's word-study method.[49] Just as the modern concept of time suppresses, as we have noticed, the issue of transience and mortality as intrinsic to the human historical experience of time, so Cullmann's reading of this modern concept into the New Testament writers blinds him to the same issue, despite the centrality of the question of mortality and eternal life to New Testament eschatology. He does not even raise, as an issue surely needing to be asked and discussed, whether the New Testament treatment of transience, death and eternity does not require the notion of a transformation of time. The image of the 'upward, sloping line' surely reflects the immanent historical progress of the modern time myth much better than the radical disjunction implied by resurrection and new creation?

On the other side, however, it has to be said that Moltmann leaves it wholly unclear how he knows that Jesus and the early Christians understood the relation of time and eternity the way he does, rather than the way Cullmann does. What little exegesis he offers tends to be remarkably ignorant and incompetent. For example, he takes Revelation 10:6 to say that at the eschaton 'time shall be no more' (CoG 280),[50] whereas, according to virtually all modern exegetes (followed by most modern translations), the context shows the meaning to be that when the seventh angel blows his trumpet there will be no more time left before the completion of God's purposes. The text makes no reference to the end of time. Moltmann could profitably have learnt this even from Cullmann.[51] The bizarre

[49] J. Barr, *Biblical Words for Time* (SBT; London: SCM Press, 1962); cf. F. Watson, *Text and Truth: Redefining Biblical Theology* (Edinburgh: T. & T. Clark, 1997) 18–23, for a partial defence of Cullmann against Barr's attacks, which constantly move from demonstrating specific methodological errors to claims that the whole enterprise of biblical theology is fatally flawed.

[50] So also K. Barth, *Church Dogmatics* III/2, 624.

[51] Cullmann, *Christ and Time*, 49. Barr, *Biblical Words*, 76 n. 2, criticizes the detail of Cullmann's argument here, but admits the general point.

idea that Revelation 5 (in which the Lamb proves worthy to open the seals on the sealed scroll, in order to unroll and to read it) means that at the eschaton '[t]he unfurled times of history will be rolled up like a scroll' (CoG 294–295) requires an exegesis that no hermeneutic, however pre-modern or post-modern, could conceivably support.[52] The job of explicating the conception of time with which the New Testament writers work was badly done by Cullmann and needs to be done better.[53] It should not proceed in despite of philosophical and theological issues, nor in ignorance of the modern history of concepts of time, as Cullmann did, but nor can theological arguments, still less exegetical fantasy, be a substitute for disciplined exegesis.

Returning to the theological arguments, we must finally press the issue of the delay of the parousia, which features so prominently in Moltmann's discussion of the 'transposition of eschatology into time'. It is, of course, true that if the parousia is supposed to be scheduled, as it were, for a specific date in the calendar time of the future (cf. WJC 158, 321; CoG 13),[54] then its non-arrival at that date is problematic. Moltmann is right that it is not the passage of time which will produce the parousia, as the linear concept of time tends to suggest,[55] but the parousia

[52] A blatant example of demonstrably erroneous exegesis is the following: 'even the end of the world cannot be total annihilation and new creation. It can only be a transformation out of transience into eternity. This is also indicated by the verb used in Rev. 21.5 – not "*Behold, I will create*" (Hebrew *barah*), but "I will *make* (Hebrew *asah*) all things new". The divine "making" is a forming and shaping of that which has been "created"' (CoG 271). Of course, Revelation 21:5 is written in Greek, not Hebrew! The Greek verb it uses (ποιέω) is used actually in the Greek translation of Genesis 1:1 to translate *barah*. Moreover, Revelation 21:5 echoes Isaiah 65:17 ('I create new heavens and a new earth') where the Hebrew verb is *barah*.

[53] A fine study of Old Testament concepts of time, which is aware of Barr's methodological criticisms of Cullmann and avoids the errors he highlights, is DeVries, *Yesterday, Today, and Tomorrow*. See n. 6. It does not seem to be known to systematic theologians.

[54] Cullmann himself (*Christ and Time*, 159) is clear that 'the divine omnipotence is . . . fully preserved, since here [i.e. in the New Testament conception of the parousia] man controls this date neither by his action nor by his knowledge', though he seems to imply that God has already determined the date.

[55] Note that Cullmann can at any rate speak this way: 'it is a "redemptive necessity" for time itself to continue in order to carry the redemptive history to its goal' (*Christ and Time*, 93).

that will end and transform time (WJC 321; CoG 13). However, it is not at all clear that Moltmann has, by this argument, disposed of the problem of the delay of the parousia as such. For Moltmann, the parousia, the eschatological moment, happens both in time and to time (WJC 327). It does bring an end to the process of historical time, while also transforming the whole of the diachronic extent of historical time. The last day is 'more than a day in the calendar' (WJC 327), but in a certain sense it must also be the last date in the calendar, since it will bring all calendrical reckoning of time to an end.[56] This does not mean that the date which will turn out to be the last date in the calendar is preordained and predictable: Moltmann rightly reminds us of God's freedom (CoG 13). Nor does it mean that the prospect of the parousia should be seen in terms of the modern concept of homogeneous time. It does mean that the alleged problem of delay is not solved by insisting that the parousia will not happen in time. Since it ends time, the issue is how the time from the present until the end of time is understood. Rejecting the modern concept of homogeneous time entails not seeing the issue in terms of a purely quantitative notion of sooner or later, but it does not make any notion of sooner or later inappropriate. This can be seen from Moltmann's own insistence on the real futurity of the parousia, in his criticism of Barth and Bultmann, whose view means, he objects, that

> There is then no future end of time . . . But this puts an end to all the real and futurist expectation of the parousia which echoes in the early Christian 'maranatha – come soon!' (WJC 318)

The prayer is that God will soon bring an end to transient temporality, eliminating evil and suffering and death, transforming this temporal creation into the eternal new creation. If this 'soon' has any meaning at all, there has to be a corresponding sense in which God delays, not in mere calendar time, but in the experience of believers who long for the end of transience, death, suffering and evil.

[56] Therefore Moltmann is quite capable of sentences like this: 'before the final end of history there will be a concentration of humanity's both constructive and destructive opportunities' (CoG 201).

The 'solution' to the problem of the delay of the parousia is not to claim that, if we understand time and eternity properly, there is no such problem, as Barth and Cullmann do in their different ways, and as Moltmann in *The Way of Jesus Christ* and *The Coming of God* appears to seek another way of doing. The 'solution' is to recognize that the problem of the delay of the parousia is the form that the theodicy problem takes for Christian eschatological faith, as Moltmann himself recognized in an earlier treatment of the issue (FC 39–40, first published in 1966). For those who suffer the contradiction between God's promise of the new world of righteousness and eternal life and the persistence of this world of evil and transience, it is an agonizing problem that God 'delays' fulfilling his promise. This is the theodicy issue which eschatology must keep open, rather than solving or dismissing as a non-issue. Precisely the problem of eschatological delay lies at the existential heart of eschatological hope.

It is not really possible to envisage eschatological imminence without in some sense also encountering delay. This is why Cullmann can only treat both as belonging to a psychologically understandable error on the part of the first Christians.[57] In respect of imminence at least, Moltmann rightly prefers the messianic thinking of the twentieth-century Jewish theologians and philosophers, especially Rosenzweig. Contrasting redemption with the utopia of historical progressivism, a distant and ever-receding goal which can only be approached by endless movement into the future, Rosenzweig understood redemption as the immediate achievement of everything, and therefore as the violent irruption of the wholly other into the here and now. This transcendent redemption cannot be attained through gradual approximation, but only awaited with 'messianic impatience'. Redemption could always occur at any moment, and in the experience of the anticipation of eternity in the present moment it is felt to be, not distant, but very close at hand. It is Rosenzweig, by contrast with Barth or Cullmann, whom Moltmann finally congratulates on having been 'able to think together eternity and time in such a way that they do not

---

[57] Cullmann, *Christ and Time*, 87–89.

put an end to one another' (CoG 36). The perspective that earns Moltmann's approval here is one that envisages a truly transcendent *future* eternity which remains future while truly entering time in an anticipatory way. The passage Moltmann quotes from Rosenzweig at this point is significantly not one of the favourite quotations he repeats several times in his works, but a passage he had not previously cited:

> Eternity is a future which, without ever ceasing to be future, is yet present. Eternity is a Today, but is aware of being more than Today. (quoted CoG 36)[58]

I.3. Restoration and resurrection

As already explained in chapter I/1 (section 2) the eternity into which creation will be taken at the eschaton is not related to historical time as a future extension of time, but through the recovery and transformation of the whole diachronic extent of this world's time. All times will be gathered into eternity. All that is past will be brought back into an eternal compresence, participating in a creaturely way in the eternity of God (CoG 294–295). In this way the whole creation, in its whole diachronic extent, will be redeemed from transience. In this way, Moltmann's eschatology allows for the double-sided character of transience. On the one hand, the fact that the present creation happens in transient time is essential to the kind of goodness it has. Nothing like it is conceivable without the irreversible flow of time. On the other hand, the continuous loss of what is good in the present as it passes away and the ultimate loss of everything, which transience entails, would make the world deeply tragic were there not the prospect of the recovery in eternity of all that has been lost in transient time.

The eschatological transformation of time is not merely recovery from transience, as though eternity were a completely comprehensive videotape of all history played, as it were, in a

---

[58] Rosenzweig, *The Star of Redemption*, 224. The previous sentence reads: 'Eternity is not a very long time; it is a Tomorrow that could as well be Today.'

single moment. Nor is it the mere preservation of all time in the memory of God. Eternity is not static. Creation, redeemed and healed from all evil and suffering, will live in a new kind of time. This must be a time in which temporal movement does not entail the loss of the before as one moves on into the after. Moltmann suggests we imagine it, by contrast with the irreversible flow of transient time, as a cyclical flow:

> According to ancient ideas aeonic time is conceived as *cyclical*, not as a time-pointer or hand.[59] Irreversible historical time is replaced by reversible time,[60] as a reflection of God's eternity. In the aeonic cycles of time, creaturely life unremittingly regenerates itself from the omnipresent source of life, God. An analogy is provided by the regenerating cycles of nature, and the rhythms of the body, which already sustain life here. The purposeful time of history is fulfilled in the cyclical movements of life's eternal joy in the unceasing praise of the omnipresent God. The preferred images for eternal life are therefore dance and music, as ways of describing what is as yet hardly imaginable in this impaired life. (CoG 295)

However, the cyclical image suggests that nothing new can happen. It is not clear that, in the attempt to conceive a kind of time without transience, we need exclude any kind of novelty. What is required is that the new must be added to the already without replacing it. Nothing is any longer lost, but more may be added.[61] Whether we need such a notion of novelty in eternal time can be better considered in relation to Moltmann's understanding of resurrection.

Corresponding to the general idea that eternity is the eternalization of all history is the notion of the resurrection of persons as the resurrection of persons in the whole diachronic extent of

---

[59] On ideas of cyclical time in antiquity, see R. Sorabji, *Time, Creation and the Continuum: Theories in Antiquity and the Early Middle Ages* (London: Duckworth, 1983) 182–190. He points out that the usual idea was strictly an idea of eternal recurrence of events in time, rather than of time itself as cyclical (184–185). If time itself were cyclical, there would be no recurrence. Perhaps this is what Moltmann intends, but the idea of the endless circular recurrence of identically the same time is not coherent.

[60] But, properly speaking, a cyclical movement does not reverse; it repeats.

[61] The issue could perhaps be put in this way: Is the new creation once and for all, or is there in any sense continuous new creation in eternity?

their lives,[62] the eternalization of the mortal lives they have lived
in time (CoG 71, 84–85).[63] Indeed, Moltmann can treat the
resurrection of the dead[64] as the paradigm case and the key
element in the eschatological transformation of time (CoG 294).
It is in the case of human persons that it is easiest to appreciate
that human lives need healing and completion before they are
fit for eternity. For people to have the whole diachronic extent
of their lives redeemed from transience and simultaneously
present to them would not be truly redemptive if the suffering
and evil of their lives were recovered simply as suffering and
evil (CoG 70). Nor would it be a genuine form of life in eternity
for those who have died before birth or early in life unless there
were also some kind of scope for the completion of otherwise
unlived life after death (COG 117–118). Moltmann therefore sees
the need for 'an ongoing history after death with our lives as we
have lived them' (CoG 116). Only in this way can eternal life be
envisaged as 'the final healing of this life into the completed
wholeness for which it is destined' (CoG 71). We might begin to
see how this healing could be possible through the analogy, in
this life, of the healing of painful or repressed memories.

If nothing new can happen in the eternal time of the new
creation, then the healing and growth of human persons after
death cannot take place in eternity. They would have to occur,
one would think, in the process of the transformation of time
into eternity. Moltmann, however, solves this problem by locat-
ing them in the intermediate state (see chapter I/1 section 4

[62] This does not seem to mean that resurrected persons are simultaneously
what they were at every point in their temporal lives, but that what they are is
the outcome of the totality of their lived experience brought into an integrated
and healed whole. Cf. CoG 76: 'the new quality of the person's totality, as the
outcome of a lived life' (though this refers to the intermediate state). It is
not clear how this idea of the resurrection of one's whole diachronic life
differs from that of the restoration of complete memory of one's whole
diachronic life.

[63] So also K. Barth, *Church Dogmatics* III/2, 624. The use of 1 Corinthians
15:54 in this connexion by both Barth and Moltmann (CoG 70) is unjustified.
In the context of Paul's argument, the reference is not to the diachronic
extent of mortal life but to the body.

[64] That is, we should probably infer, the resurrection of all that has lived,
not just humans.

above) between death and resurrection. This raises significant problems. First, one might ask how, if the intermediate state provides the time needed for healing and transformation, such time will be available for those who die shortly before the parousia or have not died at all when it occurs. Secondly, when does any transformation required in the non-human creation occur? Must an intermediate state be postulated for any creature (or event?) that needs healing or completion of its existence in time? Thirdly, the notion of the intermediate state fits awkwardly with the idea that the eschatological moment in which time is transformed occurs simultaneously with all the times of history (WJC 328). What have to be taken into eternity, on Moltmann's view, are not human lives as they have happened within the whole historical process, but human lives as they have been healed and transformed after death.

The difficulties are such that it might be easier to postulate that (1) since the end of time occurs simultaneously with all time, we do not need to imagine a temporal interval between death and resurrection; and either (2a) that new things can happen in the eternal time of the new creation; or that (2b) transformation occurs in the eschatological moment itself (cf. 1 Cor 15:51–52). As suggested above, option (2a) need not introduce transience into the new creation. Historical time is transient not because new things happen in it but because old things pass away. Can transformation be understood as a process in which new occurrences are added but nothing passes away? The difficulty with (2b) is especially in relation to uncompleted lives, including those barely lived at all. However, this issue is problematic even if the completion is assigned to the inter-mediate state. Even in the intermediate state it is not possible for such persons to have the kind of experiences they would have had in this life.

The problems we have encountered in this section may point to the limits of our language and conceptuality in relation to what transcends our experience. We can say what 'eternal time' is not – it is not transient – more easily than we can say what it is. We can envisage the relation of time and eternity more adequately from time's side of the relationship than from eternity's side.

I.4. Moments of eternity

Historical progressivism, with its homogeneous linear time, sees time as a continuous movement from the past through the present to the future, where the goal of history lies. The present is merely the transition from past to future. Every moment is just a point on the continuous line, and can be related to the utopian goal in the future only via the line that stretches between it and this future goal. As Moltmann suggests in chapter I of *The Coming of God*, the rejection of this whole approach by seminal Christian and Jewish thinkers in the first half of this century, in the wake of the historical catastrophes which made the attribution of meaning to the immanent historical process no longer tolerable, had in common a new sense of the present moment in its qualitative uniqueness. They speak of an experience of the moment unconnected with its immediate before and after, the moment not as a point of transition on a continuous line but as discontinuous, a moment in which, while it lasts, time ends or stands still, an eternal Now (*nunc aeternam*). In this present moment the 'eternal' or the 'eschatological' is experienced immediately, not as a distant prospect along the line of the temporal future.

It is really only in *The Coming of God* that Moltmann attempts to integrate this conception of the moment into his eschatology, though one aspect of this attempt was anticipated in *The Spirit of Life*.[65] We begin with his attempt at a systematic classification of three ways in which eternity is experienced in the present (CoG 290–291):

(1) The present[66] as simultaneity. Following Augustine, Moltmann points out that, owing to memory and expectation, experience of the present in time is always to some degree an experience of the simultaneity of past and future in the present

[65] On the mystical moment in SL, see R. Bauckham, *The Theology of Jürgen Moltmann* (Edinburgh: T. & T. Clark, 1995) 238–242.

[66] It is important not to forget that the nature of the present is a debatable issue: is it experienced as duration and of varying duration, or is it the point in time that has already gone before one can experience it in itself?

(CoG 290).[67] This is 'a *relative eternity,* for simultaneity is one of the attributes of eternity' (CoG 287). This experience of time does not fit the simple modern concept of time as the continuous line, since it experiences the present not as a mere point between past and future, but as a moment into which past and future are to some extent gathered and made present. However, it is not, like the other two experiences, an experience of the present as discontinuous with its immediate past and future. Perhaps this is why Moltmann refers to its experience of simultaneity as 'the *aeonic eternity* of the invisible world of heaven, which is bound up with the time of this visible world of the earth' (CoG 290),[68] rather than as anticipating the aeonic eternity of the new creation. But it is surely, in its own way, also the latter, since in that eternal time all the times of history will be gathered together in simultaneity.

(2) The present as *kairos.*[69] In this experience, certain times are differentiated as times of special significance and opportunity, especially the 'Now' of 'the day of salvation' (2 Cor 6:2; cf. Rom 13:11), in which one hears the call of the Gospel and responds in faith. In this moment the continuity of the flow of time is ruptured and the believer stands in the dawn of the eschatological future. It can therefore be seen as an anticipation of or analogy to the eschatological moment in which time will end and the new future of the resurrection begin (CoG 293–294).

According to Moltmann, it was to this kairological moment that Barth (in his 1922 *Romans,* under the influence of

---

[67] On this 'thick' present, containing memory and expectation, in William James, Josiah Royce, Husserl and James Joyce, see Kern, *The Culture of Time,* 82–86. Note James' image (quoted on p. 83): 'the practically cognized present is no knife-edge, but a saddle-back, with certain breadth of its own on which we sit perched, and from which we look in two directions into time'.

[68] For this aeonic eternity of heaven, see CoG 282–283. On heaven, see GC VII.

[69] The New Testament itself by no means consistently observes a distinction between *chronos* as undifferentiated, chronological time, and *kairos* as qualitatively different time, time as favourable opportunity (Barr, *Biblical Words,* chapter 2). But, since the distinction itself is useful, there is no reason to discontinue the use of this terminology, provided it is not read into New Testament word usage.

Kierkegaard)[70] and Bultmann were (or should have been) referring, when they spoke of the moment without past or future which is 'an atom of eternity' (Kierkegaard and Barth) or the possibility of the eternal moment which slumbers in every moment (Bultmann) (CoG 14, 20, 292–293). They erroneously interpreted this moment which anticipates the eschatological moment within history as itself the eschatological moment which ends history. Moltmann, of course, is concerned here to restore future to their eschatology. It is significant that he finds in this experience not sheer non-temporality, but a discontinuity with transient time which orients the believer to the eschatological *future*. By finding, in this discontinuous, qualitatively unique, moment, anticipation (not presence, or presence only by anticipation) of the transcendent future, he breaks as decisively as Barth and Bultmann with historical progressivism, but without collapsing eschatology into a timeless moment unrelated to time. Here the transcendent future casts its light into the present, rupturing the continuity of time, breaking the power of past and present to prolong themselves into the future, enabling the believer to live out of the radically new possibilities of the promised future of God.

(3) The present as mystical moment. This is the fulfilled moment, the depth-dimension of the present which is experienced when one is wholly present in the present. To this experience of the intensity of life in absolute presentness Moltmann gives the significance-loaded German term *Augenblick* (moment), and also applies the Kierkegaardian notion of 'an atom of eternity' without past or future which Barth had applied to the *kairos* moment. For Moltmann the 'absolute presentness' of this moment makes it a real presence of eternity:

> It is the experience of 'the fulness of time' in the wholeness of the lived life: all time becomes present. In the midst of historical time this is, indeed, only a momentary, a moment-like experience of eternity, but an experience of eternity it is. (CoG 291; cf. 57)

---

[70] See especially S. Kierkegaard, *The Concept of Dread* (tr. W. Lowrie; Princeton: Princeton University Press, 1967) 76–81.

This is the mystical moment which Moltmann had more extensively characterized in *The Spirit of Life* (18, 39–40, 52, 206, 211, 303), where he also understands it as mystical experience of God as the immanent Trinity beyond history (SL 303–306), a dimension surprisingly absent from the account in *The Coming of God*.

The eschatological orientation of this experience lies in its mere momentariness which creates in us a longing for the permanent and complete experience of this kind of fulfilled life. It is because this moment does not tarry that we hope for the truly eschatological moment to which we can say, with Goethe's Faust, 'O tarry a while, thou art so fair' (CoG 291; cf. 116). In *The Coming of God*, unlike *The Spirit of Life*,[71] it is this quotation alone (cf. also CoG 313) which alerts us to the influence of Ernst Bloch on Moltmann's understanding of the fulfilled moment.[72] According to Bloch, '*the "Stay-awhile, you are so fair", spoken to the moment, describes the utopia of Being-There par excellence*'.[73]

> In the goal-content of Faust's wager Goethe thus identified the human-worldly final problem per se; the adequation of the most deeply intending, intensifying, realizing, into the Here and Now (the fulfilled moment) of its content. The moment is the That-enigma of being which itself is hidden in every moment as this moment and which finally wishes to urge itself on to its What-solution or content-solution. 'Stay-awhile, you are so fair', spoken to the moment: here is the *metaphysical guiding panel for full existence and without hinterworld*.[74]

In Bloch's own eschatological mysticism, the 'darkness of the lived moment' already contained in a non-temporal moment

---

[71] See Bauckham, *The Theology of Jürgen Moltmann*, 240–241.

[72] Of course, this quotation, in a German writer, would not in itself need explaining from the influence of another writer. But Moltmann is very close to the particular way Bloch uses this quotation to label a key concept of his.

[73] E. Bloch, *The Principle of Hope* (tr. N. Plaice, S. Plaice and P. Knight; Oxford: Blackwell, 1986) 1015: italics original.

[74] Bloch, *The Principle of Hope*, 1016 (italics original); cf. also especially 1179, and, on the fulfilment of this hope in religious mysticism, 1298–1299, 1303. For the significance of Faust to Bloch, see T. H. West, *Ultimate Hope Without God: The Atheistic Eschatology of Ernst Bloch* (American University Studies 7/97; New York: Peter Lang, 1991) 151–155.

the goal of the whole historical process, 'the utopia of Being-There' to which he attached the Faustian invitation. Though it is with Rosenzweig's messianic redemption, rather than Bloch's completion of history, that Moltmann is more aligned in his latest work, Bloch's remarkable sense of the immediate presence of the goal of history to the present lived moment (something Moltmann scarcely appropriated at all in his earlier work, despite the strong influence of Bloch in it) in its own way breaks, like Rosenzweig and Moltmann, with the temporal continuity of historical progressivism, even of the Marxism of which Bloch was such an idiosyncratic adherent.

This threefold classification has difficulties. It is not clear that they adequately cover all of the kinds of experience to which they belong, nor whether an experience of eternity might combine features of the second and third views (though clearly the first cannot combine with either of the others). It is also striking that Moltmann never mentions negative experiences which have the intensity of those he treats as mystical moments of eternity.[75] Clearly there are such: for example, the experience of being immersed in present pain, without past or future.

When we turn from this classification to the ideas of the moment which Moltmann in chapter I of *The Coming of God*, finds in Jewish thinkers (including Bloch) and the idea of the messianic moment which he crystallizes from them (CoG 45–46) and to which he attaches great importance ('[o]nly that will again make theological eschatology possible'), it is curiously difficult to tell how these ideas relate to the threefold classification we have just considered. The ideas of the moment in these Jewish thinkers are, of course, not identical, though Rosenzweig and Benjamin are quite close. But when Moltmann poses the question whether the moment they describe should be given a mystical or a messianic interpretation, it is hard to tell whether the former is the mystical moment he categorizes as the real presence of eternity in time (category 3 above) or whether, in speaking of a moment that 'leaves nothing more to be desired', by contrast with the messianic moment which 'discloses everything that is to be desired' (CoG 45), he means

---

[75] I owe this point to Michael Partridge.

an interpetation which takes the moment to be the eschatological moment itself, leaving nothing to expect of even the
transcendent future. This is unlikely, because that would align
these Jewish thinkers with Barth and Bultmann, from whom
Moltmann has just forcibly dissociated them (CoG 45–46).

It seems therefore that Moltmann sees the possibility of
interpreting the moment in these Jewish thinkers either in
terms of his second (kairological) category or in terms of his
third (mystical) category. He opts to draw out the former
possibility, without ruling out the latter. There are certainly
elements of Moltmann's mystical moment especially in
Rosenzweig's understanding of the Sabbath and the presence
of eternity in the moment. It might have been better to
explore the coalescence of the mystical and the kairological
in Rosenzweig and Benjamin, rather than posing the two
alternative interpretations.

The messianic interpretation of the moment, which
Moltmann develops in the closing paragraphs of chapter I (CoG
45–46; cf. also 22, 41), is clearly kairological, but not in the
same way as the kairological interpretation he later gives, as we
have seen, to the eternal moment of Kierkegaard, Barth and
Bultmann. It is much more closely related, as we might expect
in this context, to Moltmann's central concern to develop an
eschatology which is truly eschatological, relating the
transcendent future to the historical present in the crisis to
which historicized eschatology has led:

> The messianic interpretation sees 'the moment' that interrupts
> time, and lets us pause in the midst of progress, as the power for
> conversion. At that moment another future becomes perceptible.
> The laws and forces of the past are no longer 'compulsive'. God's
> messianic future wins power over the present. New perspectives
> open up. The deadliness of progress towards the economic,
> ecological, nuclear and genetic catastrophes is recognized; and
> the modern world's lack of future is perceived. The way becomes
> free for alternative developments. I should like to call this the
> redemption of the future from the power of history in the *kairos* of
> conversion. Only that will again make theological eschatology
> possible, for through that, hope as a theological category will be
> redeemed from the ruins of historical reason. (CoG 45–46)

This is a powerful passage, which seems to introduce a key role for this concept of the messianic moment in Moltmann's eschatology which will be comparable with that of the idea of promise in *Theology of Hope*. One would like to know how the moment relates to promise (less prominent in this book than in *Theology of Hope*, but still present), and how it relates to the rhythmicization of time by the Sabbath of which Moltmann writes elsewhere in this book. Returning to this passage from the rest of the book, it is difficult not to be somewhat disappointed that it does not receive significant further development. The idea of the messianic movement is highly suggestive, but remains disappointingly under-developed.

For an eschatology of the truly transcendent future, the understanding of the present moment as in some sense immediately related to eternity is of great significance. In the reaction – to which Moltmann's own early theology of hope considerably contributed – of recent theological eschatology against purely dialectical or existential interpretations of eschatology, the qualitative uniqueness of the present moment and its relation to eternity have been neglected. It is a merit of Moltmann's recent work that he has highlighted once again this uniqueness of the moment and its importance for a properly eschatological eschatology in the contemporary crisis of historicist immanentism. Any development of Moltmann's insights would have to engage, as he does not, with the emerging postmodern culture's own reaction against historical progressivism and with the postmodern tendency to reduce time to the present.[76]

II. The Eschatological Aesthetics of the Moment

The kind of theological reflection on the present moment which Moltmann adumbrates could be assisted by attention to the

[76] Cf., e.g. H. Bertens, *The Idea of the Postmodern: A History* (London: Routledge, 1995) 162–164, 227–229. For an account of the way 'modernity' (meaning here what others call 'late modernity' or 'postmodernity') has transformed the sense of time and increasingly shrunk it to the present, the instantaneous, the immediate, see J. Chesneaux, *Brave Modern World: The Prospects for Survival* (tr. D. Johnstone, K. Bowie and F. Garvie; London: Thames & Hudson, 1992) 16–31, 164–167. H. Nowotny, 'From the future to the

moment in art, since certain kinds of art enable us to indwell the moment which otherwise escapes us. According to John Berger, 'All the languages of art have been developed as an attempt to transform the instantaneous into the permanent'[77] (where 'the instantaneous' is the aesthetic moment in which beauty is recognized in nature). Especially in the light of Moltmann's understanding of the new creation as the taking into eternity of the whole diachronic extent of this creation, gathering in all the times of historical time, preserving and transfiguring them, the artistic 'attempt to transform the instantaneous [or, better, the transient] into the permanent' evinces an implicit anticipation of the new creation. Artistic creation has often been understood by analogy with divine creation (or *vice versa*), but it may be more illuminatingly understood by analogy with God's eschatological act of *new* creation. At least, art that is in any way representational could be seen in this way, since it is not creation *ex nihilo*, but nor is it mere imitation of what is given in the world. It attempts the preservation of the transient, while making something new of it. Or to put the same point in a different way: it mediates what is and what is desirable.[78] Totally abstract modernist art which aims at a creation 'valid solely in its own terms, in the way nature is valid'[79] and so deliberately repudiates any connexions with natural forms is the attempt to rival or to replace God's creation

extended present', in G. Kirsch, P. Nijkampp and K. Zimmermann (eds), *The Formulation of Time Preferences in a Multidisciplinary Perspective: The Consequences for Individual Behaviour and Collective Decision-Making* (Wissenschaftszentrum Berlin Publications; Aldershot: Avebury, 1988) 17–31, argues that, owing to technological developments, 'we are about to abolish the category of the future and to replace it with that of the extended present' (26). This is close to the kind of thinking about 'the end of history' Moltmann discusses in CoG 218–226.

[77] J. Berger, *The White Bird* (ed. L. Spencer; London: Chatto & Windus, 1985) 9.

[78] Cf. Bloch's notion of 'anticipatory illumination' (*Vor-Schein*) in art: J. Zipes, 'Introduction: Toward a Realization of Anticipatory Illumination', in E. Bloch, *The Utopian Function Of Art and Literature* (tr. J. Zipes and F. Mecklenburg; Cambridge, Massachusetts: MIT Press, 1988) xxxiii-xxxvii.

[79] Clement Greenberg, quoted in P. Fuller, *Theoria: Art, and the Absence of Grace* (London: Chatto & Windus, 1988) 207.

ex nihilo, whereas representational art can be the attempt to anticipate God's new creation out of transience. It does not create eternity, since it is itself transient, but it is an image of eternity within transience and gives the experience of the eternal moment in time. In the analogy with God's new creation weight should also be given to the fact that the artist's loving attention to his or her subject is essential to this kind of artistic creation. The attempt 'to transform the instantaneous into the permanent' – or, perhaps better, to give the transient permanence – reflects the value of the transient as perceived in the artist's loving attention to it, just as God so loves his creation as not to wish any transient moment of it to perish. At least, in so far as this divine love includes appreciation of the unique value of the transient moment, some analogy may be seen.

While almost all literature and visual art reflects in some way the transient reality that all that exists in historical time is, there is, more specifically, the possibility of dwelling in the moment itself, as a unique moment of presentness, its significance experienced not as transition from past to future, not in its connexion to what precedes and succeeds it in the temporal sequence, but in itself, in its particularity and uniqueness. This is the moment as it comes to prominence in theological and philosophical thought in the period from the First World War onwards, as Moltmann describes in chapter I of *The Coming of God*. It is remarkable that a parallel consciousness of the present as unique or eternal moment, an indwelling of the transient as unique and as the transient made permanent, appears prominently in literature and art of the same period. It seems that the philosophers and theologians were in this way in touch with a cultural mood that writers and artists also felt and in which the devastating impact of the First World War was one, though not the only, factor. Virginia Woolf was writing her major novels from the First World War until her death in 1941, of which the richest in implicit eschatology is *To the Lighthouse*, published in 1927 (six years after Rosenzweig's *The Star of Redemption*, five years after Barth's second commentary on Romans). Claude Monet, the painter *par excellence* of the transient moment, worked on his series paintings from the 1890s onwards, and pursued his great experiment in eternalizing the transient, the paintings of his water-lily pool, from the beginning of the century until his death in 1926. We shall take Woolf's *To the Lighthouse* and Monet's *Nymphéas* as our examples for an experiment in eschatological aesthetics in the light of Moltmann's treatment of the relation of time and eternity.

These two examples have not been chosen as *representative* of the way art can be understood within an eschatological perspective. Art and literature which do not privilege the discontinuous moment as these examples do could also be understood in eschatological perspective, but in different ways. The importance of these particular – very distinctive – examples is that they offer the possibility of connexion specifically with the key role Moltmann gives to the rediscovery of the discontinuous moment in the eschatological thought of the early twentieth century. Like Rosenzweig, Barth and the others, these aesthetic examples challenge the simple linear model of homogeneous time. In some sense they envisage eternity in the moment.

Just as Moltmann's theology of hope developed as a Christian-theological parallel to Ernst Bloch's philosophy of hope,[80] so the following two sections may be seen as exploratory forays for a Christian–eschatological parallel to the utopian aesthetics that plays such a major role in Bloch's work.[81]

II.1. The lighthouse at the end of the world

A theological reading of Virginia Woolf's *To the Lighthouse* would be a reading 'against the grain', since she explicitly rules out such a reading at two of the crucial moments in the book.[82] (In considering these two expressions of atheism later, we shall find some reason for justifying such a theological reading nevertheless.) But an *eschatological* reading of the novel is one

[80] R. Bauckham, *Moltmann: Messianic Theology in the Making* (Basingstoke: Marshall Pickering, 1987) 7–22.

[81] For a brief account, see V. Geoghegan, *Ernst Bloch* (London: Routledge, 1996) chapter 2.

[82] Yet Woolf herself said that 'the only meanings that are worth anything in a work of art are those that the artist himself knows nothing about' (quoted in H. Lee, *Virginia Woolf* [London: Chatto & Windus, 1996] 472).

that it explicitly invites. It is a novel whose pervasive themes are transience – flux, change, decay, death ('it was all ephemeral as a rainbow' [20])[83] – and eternity – completion, stability, permanence ('this would remain' [97]). Whether by realizing eternity in a moment in which life stands still and remains so for ever, or by reaching a goal at the end of a movement of purposive endeavour, the central characters triumph over transience and find some form of completion or stability. In the final section (III/13) the two parallel enterprises of the third part of the novel reach completion. Mr Ramsay reaches the lighthouse, and Lily Briscoe completes her painting. 'It is finished', she cries aloud when she realizes that the boat must have landed at the lighthouse, and the aged Mr Carmichael, 'looking like an old pagan God', and voicing the same thought as Lily's,

> stood there spreading his hands over all the weakness and suffering of mankind; she thought he was surveying, tolerantly, compassionately, their final destiny. (191)

Rapidly Lily now completes her painting:

> it was finished. Yes, she thought, laying down her brush in extreme fatigue, I have had my vision. (192)

If Mr Ramsay's arrival at the lighthouse is thus associated with the final destiny of mankind, the vision of wholeness which Lily embodies in her completed painting is the artistic vision as eschatological anticipation. It is the representation, within the story, of Woolf's novel itself, conceived as the bringing into eternal coherence of the otherwise transient and fragmentary.

Of the three Parts of the novel, the first, the longest, takes place in a single evening, the third in a single morning. The second, shortest Part, entitled 'Time Passes', covers the passage of ten years. The story – such as it is, for there is little plot in a conventional sense – of the Ramsay family and their friends gathered in a holiday home on a Hebridean island is thus interrupted and resumed after ten years. The First World War

---

[83] Page references in parentheses throughout this section are to V. Woolf, *To the Lighthouse* (London: Grafton Books, 1977).

occurs during this ten-year interval. Although it receives only a brief evocation, its presence in the novel is far from insignificant. In its own way the novel acknowledges the War as an event which ruptured the continuity of history, ended violently a phase of European civilization which had seemed secure for an endless future, and shattered the facile coherence of any vision of life that minimized loss and catastrophe. The interruption constituted in the novel by its second Part, 'Time Passes', reflects on the very small-scale canvas of the novel the wider cultural consciousness of the War as interruption.[84] Just as Moltmann connects the rediscovery of 'the moment' in European theologians and philosophers with the First World War as the beginning of the twentieth-century catastrophes in which nineteenth-century millenarian optimism foundered, so this novel's desire for the moment in which life stands still for ever both springs from and is challenged by the War and what it represents: all that ruptures the continuity of life and brings to nothing its aspirations to fulfilment and permanence. 'Time Passes' depicts the tragic and violent ends of human life (Mrs Ramsay and two of her children die, the War takes place), and also the more gradual but relentless process of decay, as human constructions dissolve into the inhuman processes of nature (the house slowly falls into ruin). In the famous parentheses of this second Part of the novel, far more actually 'happens' than in the first and third Parts, but these happenings feature only as part of an interruption of the real story.[85] It is across the gulf created by this interruption that what is projected in the first

---

[84] Of Woolf's novels in general, Lee, *Virginia Woolf*, 341, remarks: 'The First World War as a catastrophic break, and as the event which shaped the twentieth century, overshadows Virginia Woolf's work.' Woolf was writing the section 'Times Passes' during the General Strike of 1926, which reminded her of the War (Lee, *Virginia Woolf*, 531; E. Bishop, *A Virginia Woolf Chronology* [Basingstoke: Macmillan, 1989] 96–97). It also worth noting that the early part of the War coincided with the periods of insanity she suffered from 1913 to 1915, the worst in her life so far (she attempted suicide in September 1913) (Bishop, *A Virginia Woolf Chronology* , 27–32). Such periods of insanity were the 'interruptions' in her own life history.

[85] Cf. S. Raitt, *Virginia Woolf's To the Lighthouse* (Hemel Hempstead: Harvester Wheatsheaf, 1990) 32: 'The novel is constructed around an interruption.'

Part must be resumed in the third, what is attempted in the first Part completed in the third, the unity achieved in the first Part recovered in the third, and the past experienced as eternal moment in the first Part retrieved as eternal present in the third. It is the interruption which gives the novel an eschatological structure: the life which longs for eternity (Part I) sinks into the nothingness that engulfs all temporal things (Part II) but is raised from the threat of annihilation into eschatological completion (Part III).

To understand the way the novel portrays an eschatological achievement and retrieval beyond transience and death, we must focus on the contrasted figures of Mrs Ramsay and Mr Ramsay. As all readers of the novel easily recognize, the two represent contrasting visions of life, which are in some way reconciled at the very end. From our perspective, we can say that Mrs Ramsay represents the synchronic, Mr Ramsay the diachronic.[86] Mrs Ramsay finds the eternal in the present moment, while Mr Ramsay seeks it as a distant goal to be achieved by purposive movement into the future.

Mrs Ramsay has the quality of intuitive sympathy which bridges the distances between people and creates unity and wholeness. She has the capacity to lose the egotistic consciousness of self and to experience her oneness with things. She is able to remain still in the present moment and to give permanence to its momentary completeness. Lily Briscoe, remembering ten years later one such moment in which Mrs Ramsay had brought the disparate together, creating something 'which survived, after all these years, complete' in Lily's memory, remembers: 'Mrs Ramsay bringing them together; Mrs Ramsay saying "Life stand still here"; Mrs Ramsay making of the moment something permanent' (150–151). This, for Lily, is of the nature of a revelation, one of the little daily illuminations, 'matches struck unexpectedly in the dark', in which eternity appears. It is a revelation of the eternity of the transient, a point at which chaos gives way to coherent shape and flux to stability. What

---

[86] Cf. J. Graham, 'Time in the novels of Virginia Woolf' in C. A. Patrides (ed.), *Aspects of Time* (Manchester: Manchester University Press, 1976) 192: 'Crudely put, Mrs Ramsay equals eternity, Mr Ramsay equals time.'

Mrs Ramsay is thus able to do in life, Lily Briscoe, the painter, attempts in art. Both give wholeness and permanence to the disparate and the transient. The two aspects – uniting the (spatially) disparate and giving permanence to the (temporally) transient – evidently belong very closely, perhaps inseparably together, just as they do in Moltmann's understanding of the eschatologically new creation.

In the first Part of the novel, Mrs Ramsay herself experiences two rather different kinds of still moments. One is solitary and receptive, the other social and creative. In the first, whose description reminds one of Ernst Bloch's notion of 'the darkness of the lived moment', she goes below the surface of life, letting go of egotistical personality, becoming simply herself, 'a wedge-shaped core of darkness', invisible to others, but de-restricted, free to roam below the surface of life, at one with all things. The key themes are the coming together of the disparate and the sense of stability beyond flux, eternity in the moment (60–61).[87] (It should be clear that in Woolf's own usage, as well as our own in this chapter, the 'moment' is not punctiliar, but has duration. Its distinctive character is that it is experienced as pure present, a pause in the movement of temporal succession.)

Mrs Ramsay's capacity for receptive oneness with all things in the still moment is perhaps what enables her more creative capacity to bring people together in a unity of momentary permanence. The instance of this which forms the climax of the first Part of the novel is the dinner party. Here her intuitive sympathies take the form of the social skills of a consummate hostess, putting all her emotional efforts into creating a social whole out of an ill-matched group of family and guests with widely divergent preoccupations. This social achievement becomes a magical moment of unity, symbolized in a visual description:

> Now all the candles were lit, and the faces on both sides of the table were brought nearer by the candle light, and composed, as they had not been in the twilight, into a party round a table, for

---

[87] For this kind of 'moment of being' in Woolf's experience and novels, see J. Schulkind, 'Introduction', in V. Woolf, *Moments of Being* (ed. J. Schulkind; London: Grafton Books, 2nd edn. 1989) 22–28; Lee, *Virginia Woolf*, 106.

the night was now shut off by panes of glass, which, far from giving
any accurate view of the outside world, rippled it so strangely that
here, inside the room, seemed to be order and dry land; there,
outside a reflection in which things wavered and vanished, waterily.
(90–91)

Thus Mrs Ramsay creates a brightly lit island of unity and
permanence in the midst of the dark sea of evanescence and
flux.

This voluble and active social scene Mrs Ramsay experiences
as a still moment of eternity:

> Just now (but this cannot last, she thought, dissociating herself
> from the moment while they were all talking about boots) just
> now she had reached security; she hovered like a hawk suspended;
> like a flag floated in an element of joy which filled every nerve of
> her body fully and sweetly, not noisily, solemnly rather, for it arose,
> she thought, looking at them all eating there, from husband and
> children and friends; all of which rising in this profound stillness
> (she was helping William Bankes to one very small piece more
> and peered into the depths of the earthenware pot) seemed now
> for no special reason to stay there like a smoke, like a fume rising
> upwards, holding them safe together. Nothing need be said;
> nothing could be said. There it was, all round them. It partook,
> she felt, carefully helping Mr Bankes to a specially tender piece, of
> eternity; . . . there is a coherence in things, a stability; something,
> she meant, is immune from change, and shines out (she glanced
> at the window with its ripple of reflected lights) in the face of the
> flowing, the fleeting, the spectral, like a ruby; so that again tonight
> she had the feeling she had had once to-day already, of peace, of
> rest. Of such moments, she thought, the thing is made that remains
> for ever after. This would remain. (97)

Clearly this is not in any strict sense a timeless moment: it
coincides with her serving William Bankes another helping. It
is a moment of stillness that embraces the transient ('It partook,
she felt, carefully helping Mr Bankes to a specially tender piece,
of eternity') such that the transient is suspended and remains
for ever. It partakes of eternity in the sense that in it the present
is experienced as pure present. Mrs Ramsay is not conscious of
the present as the bridge over which one passes from the past
to the future, but as a moment in which life stands still, a

moment valuable solely for its own sake, not for its relationship to past or present.

The moment cannot last, but yet it remains for ever. Precisely in its transience a permanence is found. This paradox is woven into the account of the end of the dinner party. In the words of the poem Mr Ramsay recites (102), which Mrs Ramsay remembers later (109) –

> And all the lives we ever lived and all the lives to be
> Are full of trees and changing leaves –

evokes both stability, in the trees (soon afterwards, Mrs Ramsay 'used the branches of the elm trees outside to help her stabilize her position' [104]), and transience, in the changing leaves.[88] A moment later, the scene is vanishing as she looks; as she moves, it changes; as she leaves the room, it disintegrates; people go their separate ways, for only Mrs Ramsay had brought them together into a unity (103). (Ten years later Lily would reflect that, without Mrs Ramsay, the house was 'a house full of unrelated passions' [139].) The scene she had created 'had become, she knew, giving her last look at it over her shoulder, already the past' (103). But this past is not only the transient present lost as it passes away; it is also, as something accomplished, permanent in the memory. On her way upstairs Mrs Ramsay acquires this sense, not of the stability the moment had in the experience of it as pure present, but of the stability it consequently has in the memory: 'They would, however long they lived . . . come back to this night' (104).

Not unconnected with Mrs Ramsay's ability to bring the eternal in the transient to consciousness and thereby to give the transient permanence in the memory is her awareness of the tragic loss entailed by the relentless passage of time. Unlike her husband, who, notwithstanding his self-dramatizing pose of pessimism, is a determined optimist (58), she knows that her children are happier now than they will ever be again. Of the necessity of their growing up, she feels: 'Nothing made up for the loss' (57). One reason she cannot believe in a Creator is:

---

[88] Later, 'the leaves shaking' are a symbol of transience for Lily (151).

'No happiness lasted: she knew that' (62). She does not know the transient in the manner of the purposive person who marches through time on the way to a goal and experiences the present only as transition. She knows it as the unique moment of value that she would wish preserved. The sense of loss in transience (see also 20) is the obverse of her ability to enter the pure presentness of the present and give it at least the permanence of memory.

What Mrs Ramsay achieves in life, Lily attempts in art. Corresponding to Mrs Ramsay's intuitive sympathy which brings the disparate together into a whole is Lily's particular form of love:

> Directly one looked up and saw them [the Ramsays], what she called 'being in love' flooded them. They became part of that unreal but penetrating and exciting universe which is the world seen through the eyes of love. The sky stuck to them; the birds sang through them. And, what was even more exciting, she felt, too, as she saw Mr Ramsay bearing down and retreating, and Mrs Ramsay sitting with James in the window and the cloud moving and the tree bending, how life, far from being made up of little separate incidents which one lived one by one, became curled and whole like a wave which bore one up with it and threw one down with it, there, with a dash on the beach. (47)

This final image of the wave is a contribution of genius to the imagery of time. Lily experiences the various times not as points spread out along a line or as portions of a line, but as coming together in a single rapid and powerful movement in which she is no sooner caught up than thrown down again. The love which Lily feels in this passage (cf. also 23, 26) is a form of artistic vision in which the world becomes 'unreal' in that it loses its familiarity, acquires extraordinary vividness and depth, and comes together in a unity both temporal and spatial. It is with such a vision of the Ramsays and their house renewed ten years later that Lily embarks on the final and finally successful attempt to paint the scene (177).[89] She reflects that

[89] Note the occurrence of 'unreality' (twice) and 'unreal' in this passage. This 'unreality' keeps recurring in Lily's experience in Part III (cf. 138, 151, 165).

[i]t was some such feeling of completeness perhaps which, ten
years ago, standing almost where she stood now, had made her say
that she must be in love with the place. Love had a thousand shapes.
There might be lovers whose gift it was to choose out the elements
of things and place them together and so, giving them a wholeness
not theirs in life, make of some scene, or meeting of people (all
now gone and separate), one of those globed compacted things
over which thought lingers, and love plays. (178)

Into just such a wholeness, not otherwise theirs in life, Mrs
Ramsay had brought her dinner guests. Into just such a
wholeness Lily attempts to bring the elements in her painting.
Into just such a wholeness Woolf brings the characters and
events of her novel. In all three cases the creation of completeness is also the preservation of the moment in a permanent
form over which thought can linger and love play. In the first
case this is memory, in the others art. (Woolf habitually thought
of her writing by analogy with painting.)[90] Lily herself reflects
on the permanence of art:

. . . nothing stays; all changes; but not words, not paint. Yet it [her
painting] would be hung in the attics, she thought; it would be
rolled up and flung under a sofa; yet even so, even of a picture like
that, it was true. One might say, even of this scrawl, not of that
actual picture, perhaps, but of what it attempted, that it 'remained
for ever', she was going to say . . . (166)

The words 'remained for ever' echo the conclusion of the
description of Mrs Ramsay's experience of an eternal moment
at the dinner party (97). Another parallel between Lily's
painting and Mrs Ramsay's eternal moment appears when Lily
reflects that the painting should be 'feathery and evanescent'
on the surface, but 'clamped together with bolts of iron'
beneath (159). In other words, it depicts precisely the transient,
while holding it firmly in an eternal moment. Similarly, in
Mrs Ramsay's experience, it is the transient itself that stands
still, held motionless by some more fundamental quality of
immutability (97).

In both cases the transient is given a permanence that is real
but also fragile. The permanence of Mrs Ramsay's creation is

---

[90] Lee, *Virginia Woolf,* 220–221.

dependent on memory and can scarcely outlive a generation (104). Lily, at the moment when she finally completes the picture, remembers again that it will be hung in attics and will be destroyed. 'But what did it matter?' (191). The completion of her painting is a kind of defiance of transience, a courageous bid for whatever permanence is possible. This bid, in the final paragraph of the novel, is also Woolf's. Art cannot conquer transience, but it can give eternity a temporarily enduring place in time, a transient image of the new creation.

There is more to the link – one of the most important structures of the novel – between Mrs Ramsay and Lily, between the real life of the one and the other's 'unreal' vision of life. When Lily undertakes her painting, her principal action in Part III of the novel, she is beginning again the picture she had abandoned ten years earlier, and which had been inspired by her love for the place, and especially for Mrs Ramsay, who in the original painting was represented, reading to her small son James in the drawing room window, by a triangular purple shape (52). The problem of the original painting had been that of bringing all its parts into a unity (53). In the intervening ten years Mrs Ramsay has died. Now, as she sits painting again on the lawn, her memories of her pre-War visits and of Mrs Ramsay become more vivid, and the painting is taken forward and brought to completion through a series of revelations – instances of those 'illuminations, matches struck in the dark', which for her are the daily miracles that take the place of any 'great revelation' of the meaning of life (150) – in which both the reality of Mrs Ramsay comes back to her, more and more powerfully and disturbingly, and she becomes a little more like Mrs Ramsay.

At first, before starting the painting, she feels nothing at all (139–140). She begins to recollect Mrs Ramsay when Mr Ramsay stands by her and her blank canvas, seeking, in his egotistic way, the sympathy he needs from women and which he had especially been used to receiving from his wife, but which Lily, in her spinsterish and artistic detachment, had never been able to give. Now, recollecting Mrs Ramsay, she feels she should try. She fails until in her (to the reader) comic admiration for his boots (144) she at least manages to please him. But this initiates

a sympathy for Mr Ramsay which grows as she remembers Mrs
Ramsay and paints, while Mr Ramsay and the two children sail
to the lighthouse. The first revelation is her memory of one of
the occasions when Mrs Ramsay had brought together the
disparate into a unity and made it permanent for her, saying, as
it were, 'Life stand still here!':

> Mrs Ramsay making of the moment something permanent (as in
> another sphere Lily herself tried to make of the moment something
> permanent) – this was of the nature of a revelation. In the midst
> of chaos there was shape; this external passing and flowing (she
> looked at the clouds going and the leaves shaking) was stuck into
> stability. Life stand still here, Mrs Ramsay said. 'Mrs Ramsay! Mrs
> Ramsay!' she repeated. She owed this revelation to her. (151)

This still only 'faint thought' of Mrs Ramsay impels her, 'driven
by the discomfort of the sympathy [for Mr Ramsay] which she
held undischarged' (151), to look out to sea, where the boat
containing Mr Ramsay and his children is beginning its journey
to the lighthouse.

As her memories of Mrs Ramsay flow and she becomes
conscious of the empty steps of the drawing-room, where Mrs
Ramsay had sat in her earlier attempt at the picture, the
previously 'safe' thought of Mrs Ramsay (165) becomes highly
disturbing, arousing a desperate sense of her loss and a painful
cry for her return (165–166). The cry is not entirely unanswered,
because she has a sense of Mrs Ramsay's presence as she begins
painting again (166), and almost immediately turns her
thoughts again to the old man in the boat whose request for
sympathy she had refused (166–167). Her further recollections,
accompanied by her attempts to solve the problem of the
picture, culminate in her vision of Mrs Ramsay:

> 'Mrs Ramsay! Mrs Ramsay!' she cried, feeling the old horror come
> back – to want and want and not to have. Could she inflict that
> still? And then, quietly, as if she refrained, that too became part of
> ordinary experience, was on a level with the chair, with the table.
> Mrs Ramsay – it was part of her perfect goodness to Lily – sat their
> quite simply, in the chair, flicked her needles to and fro, knitted
> her reddish-brown stocking, cast her shadow on the step. There
> she sat. (186)

At once, 'as if she had something she must share', Lily looks out to sea for the boat, and intuits, though she cannot see, that he must have landed at the lighthouse. Now, she feels, '[w]hatever she had wanted to give him, when he left her that morning, she had given him at last' (191). Finally, looking at the steps now empty again, she is able to solve the compositional problem of her picture, adding the single line in the centre which makes it a whole.[91] She has had her vision.

Thus Lily's vision, creating a wholeness in her art that transcends time, comes not only through her artistic vision, which by itself had failed her, but through her acquisition of something of that sympathy by which Mrs Ramsay had created unity and permanence in life. Mrs Ramsay's own permanence in Lily's memory surmounts the ten-year interruption and Mrs Ramsay's death, recreating for Lily the moment of the past she had failed to paint satisfactorily ten years before. It is the moment in which the novel began that becomes an eternal moment in Lily's vision and in Lily's paint. But it does so only as, absorbed into that moment, Lily is able to give Mr Ramsay the sympathy he craved and which Mrs Ramsay had given him in that moment (38–41). The 'unreality' which had so affected Lily throughout the morning (138, 151, 165, 177) turns to the reality of ordinary life as Mrs Ramsay, the creator of unity and permanence in real life, appears again to Lily, so that her painting can reflect this vision of a moment of real life drawn into a unity that remains.

Mrs Ramsay, we have suggested, represents the transcendence of time in synchronicity: she brings the disparate together in an eternal moment that remains. So does Lily in her art. (Of all forms of art, painting can most appropriately depict the synchronic eternity of a transient moment made permanent.) Together their creations transcend – from opposite sides – the ten-year interruption in which death, destruction and decay do their worst ('Time Passes'), but they do not do so on a temporal line that crosses the interruption and continues.

[91] S. Kaehele and H. German, 'To the Lighthouse: symbol and vision', in M. Beja (ed.), Virginia Woolf: To the Lighthouse: A Casebook (London: Macmillan, 1970) 208, take the line to represent Mr Ramsay. Or does it symbolize the lighthouse?

They do so in the creation and in the recovery of a moment that remains for ever.

Mr Ramsay, by contrast, represents the diachronic. As a rationalist, he values truth, however brutal (10, 34), and logical, linear thought. He pictures his own progress in philosophical argument as a daunting and difficult journey from A towards the distant goal, Z. 'He reached Q. Very few people in the whole of England reached Q' (35). Sadly he despairs of ever reaching R, let alone the far distant Z (36–37), but imagines himself, in the attempt, as the lonely explorer, leading an expedition, braving the destructive enmity of nature, dying in heroic failure, but even (in a passage of comic irony) transcending death (36–38). His is the brave and lonely attempt of the intellect to transcend flux and death, and to achieve stability and order. There are resonances here of the style of Cambridge philosophy at the beginning of the twentieth century,[92] but we may also relate Mr Ramsay to the goals of nineteenth-century science in its orientation to progress and immanent eschatology. Even in his failure he must be for ever marching about, moving on, absorbed in himself and his fear of failure and oblivion, not noticing his surroundings ('[h]e did not look at the flowers' [64]). Egotistic, self-dramatizing and tyrannical, in Part I he cuts a ludicrous figure of fun, a parody of the failure of purposive rationality, except when seen through the eyes of his deeply loving and affectionate wife, who protects and assuages.

---

[92] Cf. B. Russell's famous essay, 'A Free Man's Worship' (first published in 1903):

> The life of Man is a long march through the night, surrounded by invisible foes, tortured by weariness and pain, towards a goal that few can hope to reach, and where none may tarry long . . . for Man, condemned to-day to lose his dearest, to-morrow himself to pass through the gates of darkness, it remains only to cherish, ere yet the blow falls, the lofty thoughts that ennoble his little day; . . . proudly defiant of the irresistible forces that tolerate, for a moment, his knowledge and his condemnation, to sustain alone, a weary but unyielding Atlas, the world that his own ideals have fashioned despite the trampling march of unconscious power. (*Mysticism and Logic and Other Essays* [Harmondsworth: Penguin, 1953] 58–59)

Like Mr Ramsay, Russell's 'Man' defies transience in part through self-dramatization.

In Part III, however, he is at least in part redeemed. At the beginning of the novel he had insisted that the trip to the lighthouse on which his son James had set his heart for the following day would not be possible because it would certainly rain. In his determinedly unsentimental pursuit of truth, he trampled on the generous hopes that bound James to his mother, who was always ready to disguise the strictly factual in the interests of kindness and sympathy. Ten years later, following his wife's death, Mr Ramsay is intent, as a kind of ritual in memory of his wife, on finally accomplishing the expedition to the lighthouse, ordering his unwilling children, James and Cam, to accompany him. The boat journey is described in ways that echo his imagined expedition in pursuit of truth in the early part of the book: he is a lonely figure (186; cf. 44) embarked on a dangerous voyage (Cam, finally won round to admire him, as her mother had, sees him as 'leading them on a great expedition where, for all she knew, they would be drowned' [189]), traversing a vast distance, encountering the destructive forces of nature. Continually through the journey he and the boatman talk of shipwreck. The lines of poetry he cannot help speaking ('We perished each alone' [154; cf. 138, 155, 176], 'But I beneath a rougher sea/Was whelmed in deeper gulfs than he' [155]) express his characteristically self-dramatizing bravado and fear of failure.

The voyage is portrayed as diachronic passage from the past to the future. The sense of distance recurs. When they have only travelled a short distance, Cam sees the land they have left as very far away: 'something receding in which one has no longer any part' (155). Later she sees it 'steadily more distant' (169; cf. 170), and 'very distant' (176; cf. 187). From her position on the lawn, looking out to sea, Lily also observes the distance of the boat, eventually out of sight, and reflects on the phenomenon of distance (151, 169, 174, 176–177), but there is a profound difference between Lily's perspective on the distance and Cam's. Lily feels for the occupants of the boat. Her sympathy for Mr Ramsay bridges the distance. At the end she intuits their arrival at the lighthouse. For Cam, however, the distance separates. At the very moment Lily is looking out to sea, searching for the boat, feeling for them, Cam, looking back to the distant shore, thinks, 'They don't feel a thing there' (169). From the perspective of the boat the island becomes distant like a past they are leaving behind, whereas Lily, for whom the same past is increasingly present, reaches in sympathy across the distance.

As they travel, the three people in the boat leave the past behind.[93] When Mr Ramsay requires that they look back at the island, on which their own house was now difficult to pick out,

> Cam could see nothing. She was thinking how all those paths and the lawn, thick and knotted with the lives they had lived there, were gone; were rubbed out; were past; were unreal. (155)

When the boat is becalmed, this journey away from the past is arrested. In James' memories and reflections during this motionless wait, he is engulfed in the rage against his father that dated back to the incident at the beginning of the novel and 'powerless to flick off these grains of misery which settled on his mind one after another' (173). Ostensibly, the calm resembles the eternal moments which Mrs Ramsay and Lily experience: 'Everything in the whole world seemed to stand still' (169). But whereas in their synchronic perspective a still moment partakes of eternity, in the diachronic perspective of the party in the boat the standstill is a delay in the movement away from the past into the future. They are stuck still in the tyranny of the past. Only when the boat moves on can they begin to free themselves of its entail. Then Cam, noticing how the island looks quite different from far away, out at sea, thinks

> as the boat sailed on, how her father's anger about the points of the compass, James's obstinacy about the compact, and her own anguish, all had slipped, all had passed, all had streamed away. What then came next? Where were they going? (174)

By the time they reach the island the determination of James and Cam to maintain the power of the past has left them. Mr Ramsay's praise of his son (189) is both a small step out of his

---

[93] Cf. S. Davies, *Virginia Woolf: To the Lighthouse* (Penguin Critical Studies; London: Penguin, 1989) 116: 'The journey is made to appear . . . like a journey in Time rather than Space.'

self-absorbed egotism and the occasion for his son's change of attitude. The wound inflicted by father on son at the beginning of the novel is finally healed (not, it should be noted, by his hard-headed reasoning, but by a gesture in the direction of Mrs Ramsay's sympathy). Father and children are reconciled as they reach the lighthouse and Mr Ramsay springs onto its rock. Thus the successful diachronic movement in Part III proves redemptive. In its own way, quite different from Mrs Ramsay's and Lily's, it transcends the great interruption. In reaching the lighthouse Mr Ramsay finally achieves the goal which had been projected at the beginning of the novel, when it was the goal uniting James and his mother through her sympathy. A project which failed before the interruption is taken up and successfully completed ten years later, and in so far as it fulfils Mrs Ramsay's wish and brings them closer to her in spirit, the journey to the lighthouse transcends her death. The elderly Mr Ramsay springing youthfully onto the lighthouse rock (191) suggests the achievement of a goal transcending time and death.

There is a kind of reconciliation of the diachronic and the synchronic at the end of the novel. The landing at the lighthouse is synchronized with Lily's completion of the painting.[94] But whereas Lily, with her synchronic sympathy, is aware of their arrival at the lighthouse, they, pursuing their way from past to future, have left her behind and do not think of her. Her perspective includes them, but not theirs her. The two perspectives remain distinct. Lily's holistic vision draws the past into the present, gathers time and space together, overcomes transience and separateness in her art. Mr Ramsay's purposive journey to a goal leaves the past behind in a journey into the future, crossing time and space, but liberates from the evil entail of the past and achieves reconciliation and healing. They are different eschatological visions: escape from transience through the eternalizing of precisely the transient moment and redemption from evil through the attainment of a future goal.

---

[94] Woolf was preoccupied in writing Part III of the novel with the problem of presenting two sequences of events as simultaneous. The representation of simultaneity, at a time when wireless and telephone had made it possible to experience distant events at once, was a feature of literature in the early twentieth century: see Kern, *The Culture of Time*, 67–81.

Both aspects belong to a Christian eschatological vision. But any theistic interpretation of these themes is pointedly rejected by the novel itself.[95] Disbelief in God is expressed just twice in the novel, each time in relation to one of the two eschatological themes, the synchronic and the diachronic. When Mrs Ramsay experiences her solitary still moment, she says, scarcely voluntarily, 'We are in the hands of the Lord', but is instantly annoyed with herself for saying what she did not mean (61). She could not mean it because

> With her mind she had always seized the fact that there is no reason, order, justice: but suffering, death, the poor. There was no treachery too base for the world to commit; she knew that. No happiness lasted; she knew that. (62)

The second occasion of disbelief occurs when the boat reaches the lighthouse. Mr Ramsay

> rose and stood in the bow of the boat, very straight and tall, for all the world, James thought, as if he were saying, 'There is no God.' (190–191)

Redemption does not come to him from God. It is his own achievement.

Evil and transience require redemption: future freed from the tyranny of the past and present preserved from passing into nothing. But there is no transcendent salvation. Nor is there a redemptive teleology in the immanent nature of things. In Part II nature appears as chaotic, indifferent to human projects, just as likely to assist the human destructiveness of the War as to fulfil human dreams of harmony and completeness (125). Yet, just as chaotic and ruinous nature is taking over the house, just at the moment it might have 'pitched downwards to the depths

---

[95] In 'A Sketch of the Past', Woolf writes of

> what I might call a philosophy; at any rate it is a constant idea of mine; that behind the cotton wool [of daily life] is hidden a pattern; that the whole world is a work of art; that we are parts of the work of art. *Hamlet* or a Beethoven quartet is the truth about this vast mass that we call the world. But there is no Shakespeare, there is no Beethoven; certainly and emphatically there is no God; we are the words; we are the music; we are the thing itself. (*Moments of Being*, 81)

of darkness' (129), the house and the human values it represents are rescued. Mrs McNab and Mrs Bast, like comic angels in an apocalyptic vision, work a miracle of eschatological restoration, recreating the house from the very brink of nothingness: 'In addition to the almost complete destruction of the house, we are also shown its equally dramatic renewal.'[96] But Mrs McNab and Mrs Bast are not angels, agents of transcendence. In their comically human effort they represent very human power and will to live, defeating the forces of destruction. Beyond the rupture of continuity, on the far side of history's descent into chaos and destruction, beyond the end of any immanent theodicy, human resilience can triumph and continuity be reconstructed out of discontinuity. The crucial Part II of the novel, like the arrival at the lighthouse, reveals not an eschatology of historical progressivism, but a promethean one nevertheless.

Life goes on, the interruption is transcended, modest and fragile attempts at eternity take place. Mr Ramsay, despite the youthful vigour of his arrival at the lighthouse, will die. Lily's painting will be hung in attics and destroyed. Yet the artistic bid for such permanence as may be possible, the completion which the novel itself achieves, while careful not to overreach itself, aspires to an eschatology that remains unfulfilled outside the picture it paints.[97]

II.2. The eternal lily-pond

Paintings are static. Ostensibly they depict one moment in time. But the temporal nature of the moment varies. Scenes from classical mythology, biblical story or the lives of the saints – the subject-matter of much of Western art – entail, as it were, the whole story to which they belong. The moment depicted is

---

[96] N. Friedman, 'Double Vision in *To the Lighthouse*', in Beja (ed.), *Virginia Woolf: To the Lighthouse*, 153.

[97] Cf. Davies, *Virginia Woolf: To the Lighthouse*, 17: '*To the Lighthouse* successfully records the failure of art to stem the tides of Time. Some of its unique power and truthfulness resides in the fact that it acknowledges its own frailty, a talent akin to walking on the water, or rooting itself like Mr Ramsay in meditation, as a guidepost out to sea.'

inseparable from its temporal context in a narrative, even when the depiction lacks the explicit references to the moment's past and future which are often included in the painting. The experience of viewing such a picture resembles a 'thick' moment of experience, a present of some duration containing memory and expectation, though, unlike any such lived moment, the depicted moment's future is already known to the painter and the spectator. Scenes from well-known stories are not the only pictures with temporal depth. Many human scenes invite viewers to imagine their immediate or even more extended past and the possible futures to which the depicted moment is open. In a wide variety of ways such paintings invest the depicted moment with the narrative quality of much human experience. A portrait can suggest a whole lifetime in its subject's face. An object as simple as a pair of shoes, in Van Gogh's paintings, can occupy human time with imaginable past and future (as Heidegger showed in his use of them as a key example in his theory of art).[98] Landscapes and cityscapes may depict the relatively unchanging aspects of their subjects. The depicted moment acquires temporal extension from the scene's apparent stability. In all such cases the painting encompasses time. Entering the painting's moment the viewer experiences also the past and future of the painting's own time.

Some such temporal extension of the painting's 'moment' into past and/or future is the norm in representational visual art, though the extent to which it occurs varies very widely. Claude Monet's work, however, presents us with a startling exception. In Monet's paintings, especially the series paintings

---

[98] M. Heidegger, *Poetry, Language, Thought* (tr. A. Hofstadter; New York: Harper & Row, 1975) 33–34:

> From the dark opening of the worn insides of the shoes the toilsome tread of the worker stares forth. In the stiffly rugged heaviness of the shoes there is the accumulated tenacity of her slow trudge through the far-spreading and ever-uniform furrows of the field swept by a raw wind ... Under the soles slides the loneliness of the field-path as evening falls ... This equipment is pervaded by uncomplaining anxiety as to the certainty of bread, the wordless joy of having once more withstood want, the trembling before the impending childbed and shivering at the surrounding menace of death.

from 1890 onwards, the moment depicted is the particular
present without past or future. They display a probably unparalleled concentration on the most ephemeral aspects of
nature abstracted from any implications of a temporal succession
in which they belong. Monet's aim was to record the visual
impression of colour and harmony which a scene made on him
in a moment that is unique and evanescent, pictured on the
point of disappearing. In Monet's sight the visible world
fragments into an infinite succession of such moments. In his
own words:

> One must know how to seize the moment of the landscape at the
> appropriate instant, for that moment will never return, and one
> always wonders if the impression one received was the right one.[99]

> For me a landscape does not exist in its own right, since its
> appearance changes at every moment; but its surroundings bring
> it to life – the air and the light, which vary continually . . . For me
> it is only the surrounding atmosphere which gives objects their
> real value.[100]

> One does not paint a landscape, a seascape, a figure. One paints
> an impression of an hour of the day.[101]

One should not read such remarks in a metaphysical way. Monet
was no philosophical thinker, and what little he said about his
work achieves only rather crude articulation of what he did in
his painting. What matters in these quoted statements is the
clear sense that what Monet intended to depict was not the
relatively stable features of nature, but the most transient
features which make each 'moment of the landscape' different
and unique.

Monet's increasing focus on the instantaneous[102] meant
concentration on the fleeting impressions made by light and
atmosphere, rather than on the stable forms of things, which
tend to dissolve in shifting appearances of colour and light. In

---

[99] Quoted in V. Spate, *The Colour of Time: Claude Monet* (London: Thames
& Hudson, 1992) 209, 217.

[100] Quoted in J. House, *Monet: Nature into Art* (New Haven/London: Yale
University Press, 1986) 28–29.

[101] Quoted in Kern, *The Culture of Time*, 21.

[102] On Monet's own use of this term (*l'instantanéité*), see House, *Monet:
Nature into Art*, 220–221.

his series paintings of the 1890s, depicting stacks of wheat in a field, poplar trees in mist, or the façade of Rouen Cathedral, he painted the same subject many times at different times of day and in different weather conditions, each view portraying a distinctive play of colour and light. He intended each series to be seen as a series, but the aim was probably not for the spectator to observe the continuity through the ephemeral changes. The paintings in each series cannot be ranged in a chronological order. The aim is rather that the uniqueness of each moment should be the more apparent when placed for comparison alongside others. The viewer is not drawn into the moment's continuity with previous and succeeding moments, but is invited to pause in the moment itself, in its pure presentness, however ephemeral.

Especially in the twenty paintings of the façade of Rouen Cathedral (1892–1895) the aim of depicting precisely the transience of each moment can be clearly observed. The cathedral as a building with centuries of continuous history, with its religious significance and its place in human memory, is not the subject. The cathedral's façade is treated just as landscapes are in other series ('everything changes, even stone'):[103] 'the more intensely [Monet] focused on changing light, the more the stable reality of the cathedral disintegrated'.[104] Virtually any other paintings of a cathedral would inevitably evoke, through the building's human, historical and religious significance, some sense of temporal succession. In the 'thick' present of the picture the viewer would find a past remembered and, perhaps to a lesser extent, a future expected. In this respect it is extraordinary that Monet succeeds in this series of paintings in abstracting his subject from all such associations which would inevitably give it temporal extension. The building has no past or future because its form is subsumed into the most ephemeral effects of light and atmosphere upon its surface at the moment depicted. This would be all the more the case if the series were viewed, as Monet intended, as a series. Then the sheer difference of each moment depicted would make it the more

---

[103] Monet quoted in Spate, *The Colour of Time*, 231.
[104] Spate, *The Colour of Time*, 231.

obvious that each picture depicts what is unique to itself, that is, what is most transient.

There was a necessary artificiality in Monet's construction of a unique moment of landscape. The painting could not be executed within the moment of perception. Thus, for example, when working on one of the series depicting stacks of wheat in 1890, he would work on as many as ten studies at once, changing canvas as the light changed, returning to a canvas when he perceived conditions to be similar to those in which its subject was first perceived.[105] And, though substantially painted out of doors, *in situ*, the paintings were often reworked in the studio. Much therefore depended on his memory of the original moment. It would seem that a painting began with a moment of illumination, in which Monet experienced an intense awareness of his subject as a distinctive and harmonious whole, but the realization of this momentary awareness in paint required detached observation and analysis.[106] The painting recreates for the viewer the immediacy of the moment.

Monet's own emphasis on the objectivity of the world he observes and records tends to approximate his work to photography (itself less truly instantaneous at this date than later), but in reality the process of realizing the moment in paint was also a process of subjective appropriation and transformation of his subject. Evanescent nature becomes in his work a kind of dream-world[107] of sensuous abundance, tranquillity and harmony, snatched from disappearance into the past and preserved in its very evanescence. In mediating transience and permanence his paintings also mediate the real and the desired. But Monet's transformation of nature has nothing in common with the technological domination and transformation of nature to which it implicitly presents a desired alternative. It is transformation by intensification of

---

[105] Spate, *The Colour of Time*, 207; cf. 255 (in 1904 he was painting the lily-pond on twelve canvasses at once in this manner); M. Hoog, *The Nymphéas of Claude Monet at the Musée de l'Orangerie* (tr. J.-M. Clarke; Paris: Éditions de la Réunion des musées nationaux, 1990) 33.

[106] Spate, *The Colour of Time*, 206, 217.

[107] This term is used by Spate, *The Colour of Time*, 12.

those qualities of nature which appear in the discontinuous moment.

Monet eschews both narrative time and the continuities of nature in favour of pure presentness in the transient 'moment of the landscape'. But, for all his understanding of his art in positivistic scientific terms, it is not the nineteenth-century model of homogeneous time that his work reflects. His fragmentation of time into discontinuous moments is not the dissection of time into quantitative segments that increasingly characterized the economic life of the cities of his day.[108] It is recognition of the qualitative uniqueness of the moment of encounter with nature. It is in reaction against the allied temporal perspectives of capitalism ('time is money') and the belief in progress (time as the long march towards the goal of history). It grasps eternity in the present moment. Monet is certainly modern in that he does not see the relative continuities and stability of the world as the closest this world comes to a changeless eternity beyond it. He does not seek a changeless eternity at furthest remove from transience, but nor does he adopt the typically modern appreciation of change as significant only in its cumulative progress towards a goal. The minute-by-minute transience of nature has no value for either view. In contrast to both Monet seeks in 'the moment of the landscape', in the natural world at its most evanescent, an eternal moment to indwell.

The intense focus on the momentary by depicting the most transient – light, atmosphere, colour – at the expense of stable forms has the effect of excluding all that could distract from this focus. There are virtually no human figures in Monet's work after 1890. Human figures too readily suggest the before and after of narrative time, and, in their almost inevitable attraction of the viewer's eye, are too resistant to the dissolution of stable form. Similarly, the paintings show no interest at all in the countryside as a place of habitation and work, just as those of Rouen cathedral virtually deprive it of human meaning. The series of paintings of stacks of wheat do not in any way invite us to see these as objects with a history, constructed by people

---

[108] *Contra* Spate, *The Colour of Time*, 9.

and with a human use. They are as far as it is possible for representative art to be from any such implications of past or future. In the series of the 1890s all the continuities of human and even non-human life are left aside in the intensity of Monet's focus on the purely momentary.

This is surely closely connected with Virginia Spate's insistence that Monet sees things 'as pure objects of sight, inaccessible to other modes of experience',[109] and that the paintings reflect the detachment with which Monet observed and studied the scene in the process of painting it, cutting himself off from any emotional identification with what he sees.[110] While this may represent a typically modern subjectivity in relation to the object, it is certainly also closely linked with Monet's focus on the momentary. The concentration on a moment without past or future seems to preclude other ways in which paintings draw viewers into their time, permitting only the purely visual appreciation of the beauty of colour and light. In this sense perhaps it is true that the paintings of the 1890s tend to leave the viewer external to the observed moment. Yet, as Spate herself admits, though in rather different terms, after 1903, in the paintings of the lily-pond, Monet did succeed in depicting the transient as a still moment which the viewer not only observes but indwells. We shall attempt at least some understanding of how this occurs below. Finally, when John Berger complains that in depicting the momentary as momentary, Monet's paintings do not preserve experience but evoke the disappearance of transient experience ('in such a way that *you are compelled to recognize that it is not there*'),[111] we must similarly respond that, however true this might be of the paintings of the 1890s, in the later paintings of the lily-pond Monet really does pull off the miracle of giving the evanescent time.

Monet's increasing focus on the transitory features of light and atmosphere culminates in the vast series of *Nymphéas* (water-

---

[109] Spate, *The Colour of Time*, 9.

[110] Spate, *The Colour of Time*, 7, 12.

[111] Berger, 'The eyes of Claude Monet', in *The White Bird*, 189–196 (quotation from p. 194: italics original).

lilies), comprising more than two hundred and fifty paintings. Their subject is the lily-pond which Monet had constructed in his own garden at Giverny, with the intention from the start of painting it.[112] These paintings (like others of his garden) have a kind of double artificiality. Not only did he reconstruct nature in the paintings; he first reconstructed it in reality. By these two layers of artifice he made possible his mature vision of a transformed world. He constructed paradise[113] and then painted it at its most paradisal.

His painting of the *Nymphéas* began in earnest after 1903, when the lily-pond had been extended, and continued until his death in 1926. Many of the paintings were studies for *les Grandes Décorations*, a project he had already conceived in the late 1890s. The idea was for a round room with panels of waterscape, with water-lilies and reflections, around the walls, wholly surrounding the viewer. Maurice Guillemot, visiting Monet in 1897, saw studies he had already done for this: 'the colors are fluid, with marvellous nuances, ephemeral as a dream'.[114] Later Monet thought of the project as his bequest to France, and planned its installation in the Orangerie in the Tuileries, where, in the year following his death, the eight large panels were set up in two rooms. From 1914 onwards – the proximity to the outbreak of war was not, as we shall see, insignificant – he was deeply preoccupied with this project, which was completed not entirely, but substantially as he wished.

In the lily-pool Monet had a subject which admitted more evanescent effects than any he had attempted before. The subject was not really the *nymphéas* themselves, though they appear in almost every picture, but the water with its two dimensions of shimmering surface and reflecting depth. Trees and plants, sky, clouds, sunset – all appear reflected in the pool:

> The water flowers are far from being the whole scene; really, they are just the accompaniment. The essence of the motif is the mirror of water whose appearance changes at every moment because areas

[112] Hoog, *The Nymphéas*, 12.

[113] Both Monet and his visitors referred to his garden as a 'paradise': Hoog, *The Nymphéas*, 10; Spate, *The Colour of Time*, 268.

[114] Quoted in D. Wildenstein, 'Monet's Giverny', in *Monet's Years at Giverny: Beyond Impressionism* (New York: Metropolitan Museum of Art, 1978) 25.

of sky are reflected in it . . . The passing cloud, the freshening
breeze, the seed which is poised and then falls, the wind which
blows and then suddenly drops, the light which dims and then
again brightens – all . . . transform the colour and disturb the planes
of water.[115]

The water-lilies are essential for the viewer's identification of
their context as still water, as well as for giving shape to the
composition, while their floating quality and the ephemerality
of their flowers assist the overall impression of fluidity. But in
some paintings even the water-lilies are as forms barely dis-
tinguishable. The dominant feature of the paintings is the way
they take to the extreme the dissolution of stable form in fugitive
effects, observable to some extent in all Monet's work since 1890.
This is achieved by excluding almost everything in its own form
while portraying it in watery reflections. The water is the medium
in which everything becomes ephemeral, losing its own form in
a flux of light and colour.[116] Monet's late (1920 onwards) series
of paintings of his garden and of the Japanese bridge also tend
much more strongly than the earlier series towards the complete
dissolution of forms into merging expanses of colour, but it is
in the *Nymphéas* that this feature came most truly into its own. It
is the feature that has led critics to see Monet's later work as
moving far in the direction of abstract art.[117] But this interpretation is misleading: what looks like abstraction is in fact
Monet's intense concentration on the most ephemeral aspects
of nature. This is abstraction in the sense that Monet abstracts
these aspects for depiction, and thereby, in a sense, transforms
nature. But nature in his paintings is nature transformed, not

[115] Monet quoted in House, *Monet*, 221; Spate, *The Colour of Time*, 254.

[116] In an 1883 painting of the church at Verney, the whole of the scene on
land is also seen depicted below in its reflection in the river. The distinction
between the objects in their own stable form and the fluidity of their reflection
in the shimmering water is clear. But in some of the paintings of poplars
(1891) and in the series of paintings of morning on the Seine near Giverny
(1897) Monet used reflection in water to dissolve the distinction between
land and water. This happens in some early paintings of the lily-pond, but in
most of the *Nymphéas* the bank of the pool is not pictured at all. Nothing
outside the pool is seen except in reflection.

[117] E.g. Hoog, *The Nymphéas*, chapter 4 and *passim*.

reinvented. The evanescent is what Monet sees in nature with unparalleled intensity.

It was the endless variety of light and atmosphere that made the lily-pool a sufficient universe for a decade of Monet's work. All the colours of creation, all the shades of light, the sky above and the natural objects around, appear reflected in the pool. The reflections not only fill the depths of the pool which the light penetrates, but are also transfigured in the sheen of the water's surface. The world outside the pool is seen, but not in itself, only in its reflection in the pool and thus transformed. Light and water together transform the world into a shimmering harmony of colour, 'ephemeral as a dream' (Maurice Guillemot). At the same time the viewer is drawn into this dreamworld in a way that Monet's earlier paintings had not achieved. Though some of the early *Nymphéas* depict part of the bank surrounding the pool, Monet largely abandoned this in favour of an expanse of water with no limits within the frame of the picture. Thus, in place of conventional 'views' holding a fragment of nature separate and distant from the viewer, the paintings become 'a new multidimensional space',[118] in which viewers have no secure means of positioning themselves at a definite distance from what they see. Only the lilies act as 'perspectival fragments' establishing space around them,[119] but Monet does not always adhere to conventional perspective in depicting the lilies. The effect is to draw the viewer into the painting's own space, an effect all the greater in the two rooms of the Orangerie, where the huge paintings (Monet's 'immense circle of dreams'[120] as a contemporary critic called them) surround the viewer and cannot even each be seen within a single glance.

The space the viewer enters in the *Nymphéas* is one that transcends the limitations of this world's space. In this world's space each object has form and location which distinguish and separate it from others. Reflected in Monet's lily-pond they lose both distinct form and separateness, merging and overlapping.

[118]   Spate, *The Colour of Time*, 258.
[119]   Spate, *The Colour of Time*, 265.
[120]   Louis Gillet quoted in Spate, *The Colour of Time*, 315.

The distinct spheres of sky, earth and water are no longer distinct. They merge. Thus water and light not only transform; they also unite the disparate parts of the world in unity and harmony. This world's space is transcended by a new kind of dream-like space.

According to a Jewish Merkavah text, the Visions of Ezekiel (fourth or fifth century AD?), when the seven heavens were opened in vision to the prophet Ezekiel, he saw them not by looking up into the sky but by looking down into the waters of a river, in which he saw them reflected: 'Ezekiel stood beside the river Chebar gazing into the water and the seven heavens were opened to him so that he saw the Glory of the Holy One, blessed be He, the *ḥayyot* [the 'living creatures'], the ministering angels, the angelic hosts, the seraphim, those of sparkling wings, all attached to the *merkavah* [the chariot-throne of God]. They passed by in heaven while Ezekiel saw them (reflected) in the water'.[121] Similarly, in Monet's *Nymphéas*, we see the world above by looking down. In the waters of his lily-pond we see reflected, not a world beyond this, but this world itself transformed. In both cases a dimension of reality which cannot be seen directly is seen in its reflection. The dream-like unreality of the *Nymphéas* resembles that of a vision. In Ernst Bloch's terms, it is a 'wishful landscape',[122] a waking dream of what the world might be. It is a 'dream-world' not in the sense of an imagined world other than this, created as it were *ex nihilo*, but in the sense of a vision of how the actual world could be were it transformed. It anticipates new creation, in which, according to Moltmann's understanding, the spatial extension of the world will be transcended in the co-presence of all things with all things, just as the temporal extension of this world will be transcended in the co-presence of all times in eternity.

Not only does the space of the *Nymphéas* transcend this world's space; their time transcends this world's time. By drawing us into their own space they also draw us into their own time, the

---

[121] Translation from L. Jacobs, *The Jewish Mystics* (London: Kyle Cathie, 1990) 28–29; cf. I. Gruenwald, *Apocalyptic and Merkavah Mysticism* (AGAJU 14; Leiden: Brill, 1980) 134–135.

[122] Bloch, *The Principle of Hope*, 794–838.

transient moment which expands with looking and seems, like the surface of the water, to go on without end. The static moment of these paintings is not a moment which expands with its own memories of past and expectations of future. It is the moment without past or future but yet expansive, the still moment the pictures enable us to indwell. Here, if anywhere within this world, the evanescent is preserved as evanescent and given time.

It would be easy to see Monet's dream-world as pure escapism. So much is excluded and seemingly ignored. In Virginia Woolf's work, as we have seen, there is brutal and disastrous 'interruption': eternity can be found beyond transience, even in the artistic vision, only in transcending tragedy and death, decay and destruction. Does Monet's vision transcend such interruption or is it a mere retreat into the artificial paradise of his garden? Doesn't the focus on the evanescent not only exclude the relatively permanent, but also ignore the human tragedy and loss which can be depicted only in narrative time? Monet's vision is undoubtedly limited, but we should not condemn it too quickly. Perhaps, noting the contrast between his friends' involvement in the turbulent French politics of the 1890s and Monet's tranquil paintings of the period, we may suspect with Spate that 'he was wrapping the protective screens of his own creation ever more securely around himself'.[123] But, also with Spate, we should notice that the *Nymphéas* come from a period in which his vision was tragically and violently interrupted. His secure world at Giverny was shattered by his wife's death in 1910; his eldest son died in February of 1914; from 1912 he struggled with defective sight and fear of blindness. No sooner had he set to work in earnest on *les Grandes Décorations*, following his son's death in 1914, than the sense that this dream might in truth be realizable was shattered by the outbreak of war.

> Monet's need to create a perfect world existed in intolerable contradiction to facts which he could not shut out now that he was painting in the face of death, not only personal death, but the deaths of untold numbers.[124]

[123] Spate, *The Colour of Time*, 235.
[124] Spate, *The Colour of Time*, 270.

While in one sense, which he admitted, his painting became a way of not thinking of the horrors, in another sense it was a defiance of destruction and evil. And in the post-War years, for those whose world and its ideology of progress had been severely broken, his *Nymphéas*, emerging from the War years, surely offered a defiant and healing alternative, a transcendence of loss in the tranquil moment of eternity.

Whether Monet's paintings explicitly acknowledge the interruption they do objectively transcend depends on the significance of one of the four great panels in the second room of the Orangerie. This, much the smallest of the four, is called 'Reflections of Trees'. The water and the reflections it contains are seen in darkness, which contrasts with the painting opposite ('The Two Willows'), more than twice its size, the largest of the four, and the one most full of light. 'Reflections of Trees' is the first and only time Monet had seriously painted darkness.[125] It is difficult not to see here some reflection of the darkness of the War years and his own near-blindness as he completed the paintings for the Orangerie. Moreover, the darkness of this painting has not been placed, as we might at first suppose, in a natural cycle of light and darkness, which one would follow around the walls of the room. The paintings do *not* constitute 'a *cycle* that has loss built into its very structure',[126] since the two paintings which intervene on each side between the darkness of 'Reflections of Trees' and the bright light of 'The Two Willows' are both paintings of morning ('Clear Morning with Willows' and 'Morning with Willows'). Monet is not finally arranging his discontinuous moments into a natural cyclical continuity. In other words, there is no movement, as in a cycle, which *leads into* the darkness and then out of it. Darkness is 'followed' on both sides by morning, as well as confronted by its luminous opposite. It has been taken, as it were, into the eternity of the *Nymphéas*, *only* as darkness already and for ever succeeded by morning. It is not an interruption incorporated into an endless cycle, but an interruption transcended.

[125] Spate, *The Colour of Time*, 307.
[126] Spate, *The Colour of Time*, 306: my italics.

Monet, as the painter of the most transient, as the painter who turns precisely the most transient moment into a paradise, is at the opposite extreme from any kind of Platonic retreat from the transient to the unchanging. In his work we can experience the eternal value of the most transient moment. We have brought Monet to the aid of the eschatological imagination not, of course, in order to suggest that *only* the most transient has eternal value, but rather in order to demonstrate that *even* the most transient can be such that we wish it to be eternal. In the Orangerie we can learn to envisage the eschatological eternity of the world, not as the abstraction of the unchanging from the flux of becoming, but as the preservation of the transient, the recovery of every moment of value from the past in which it has perished with time.

Monet's own world-view was as frankly atheistic as Virginia Woolf's. In the absence of eschatological transcendence, his paintings rescue a fragment of eternity from time and offer a vision of a world transformed within the aesthetic experience. But viewed in light of the expectation of eschatological transformation, they nourish the anticipatory consciousness and the eschatological imagination. Their gift to us is the intensive experience of the evanescent moment, the temporary but transformative indwelling of its absolute presentness and its potential eternity. Such moments, like the moment on the mountain of the transfiguration for which Peter mistakenly sought permanence, are not yet eternity, but they will not be lost. From them, according to Moltmann, 'we develop a hunger for a wholly and completely unclouded fulness of life, and therefore for the life that is eternal' (CoG 291).[127]

---

[127] I am much indebted to the thoughtful and astute criticisms Michael Partridge made of an earlier draft of this chapter, and for his illuminating suggestions.

꧁꧂

THE BIBLE, THE EXEGETE
AND THE THEOLOGIAN

Response to Richard Bauckham

JÜRGEN MOLTMANN

In this extensive chapter, Richard Bauckham first of all deals with my ideas about time and eternity or, to be more precise, about moment and future, following the introductory chapter of *The Coming of God*, 'Eschatology Today' (3–46). He goes on to discuss the conceptions of the moment in Virginia Woolf and Claude Monet, which he calls 'eschatological aesthetic'. This second part is a completely independent contribution to an eschatological aesthetic still unwritten. I read it with increasing fascination and was very impressed. It seems to me to be the beginning of a more extensive work on what is still largely unexplored territory. In this response, I shall confine myself to the first part of the chapter, which is devoted to my own work.

Because Richard Bauckham is captivated by the concept of moment in that eschatological aesthetic of the 1920s, he is naturally interested above all in my account of the eschatology of the eternal moment in the Christian thinking of dialectical theology and the Jewish thinking of the 1920s. In contrast, he does not enter in detail into my theology of time in *God in Creation* (chapter V: 'The Time of Creation', 104–139) and in *The Coming of God* (chapter IV.3: 'The End of Time in the

Eternity of God', 279–295). Let me therefore repeat once more that for my differentiation between the times – past, present, future – the ontological theory of time put forward by Georg Picht and Carl Friedrich von Weizsäcker is important. Both of them have correlated the modes of time with the modalities of being: past is the realm of reality, future is the realm of possibilities, and present is the interface at which possibilities are realized, neglected, or suppressed. This ontological theory of time differs from every linear view of time in that it does not see future and past as homogeneous (so they cannot be plotted along a single line) but perceives their qualitative difference. In the interdisciplinary discussions of the Forschungsstelle der Evangelischen Kirche in Heidelberg, this led to the development of a 'theory of open systems' of matter and life.[1] A very similar theory of time, though it is not scientifically integrated, can be found in Ernst Bloch's *Principle of Hope* (1959; ET 1986). I have therefore myself never used the concept of time in the abstract sense of Newton or Kant, a fact which has prompted Richard Bauckham to note 4, in which he maintains that the general use of the word 'time' is 'potentially confusing'. According to the theories of time I have mentioned, it is justifiable to take 'future' as the transcendental condition for the possibility of time in general, and to distinguish between that and the phenomenal times of future, present and past time. If, as Kierkegaard and Heidegger have shown, possibility occupies a higher position ontologically than reality, then the future enjoys priority in the modes of time too.

If the temporal modes display no linear homogeneity, then the rhythmical interruptions of the times through recurring festivals, and especially through the Old Testament Jewish sabbath and the New Testament Christian Sunday, have a particular point. With Franz Rosenzweig, I have interpreted the sabbath as a messianic interruption of transitory working time, and the Christian day of resurrection as its eschatological interruption. The divine righteousness and justice which is to

---

[1] E. von Weizsäcker (ed.), *Offene Systeme I. Beiträge zur Zeitstruktur von Information, Entropie und Evolution* (Stuttgart 1974); K. Maurin *et al.* (eds), *Offene Systeme II. Logik und Zeit* (Stuttgart, 1981).

be practised in the sabbath years is, over against the usual legal norms, amnesty justice, the liberating justice which forgives sins and puts things to rights. This points to the expectation of righteousness and justice which is focused on the Messiah. But it also includes a periodically recurring settlement of the injustice that has been perpetrated in society.

I have several times expressed my views about these rectifying 'interruptions' of time, work and property in the context of theological declarations on human rights. The sabbath or Sunday interruptions of working time belong to the inalienable dignity of human beings, and are therefore not at the free disposal of arrangements about flexible working hours. They protect the dignity of men and women against the commercialization of their lives. Human dignity is not absorbed or summed up by any market value or non-value. This is important for the survival of a humane society, and is by no means a conservative insistence on traditional ways of living.

So much to Richard Bauckham's critical comments in his section I.1(3) and in note 29. What he adds (section I.1(5)) about my criticism of the understanding of time in modern times is important, and I should like to draw special attention to it here. There is a new advertisement for the internet: 'The Future is Now!' If that is supposed to be true, then this 'now' has itself no more future. Its future is nothing more than the 'extended presence of what is and what we have'.

But the main problem which Richard Bauckham touches on in this chapter is the relation between exegesis and theology, or – to put it more simply – my use of the Bible. In section I.2 he fires off a whole broadside against me, in defence of a 'disciplined exegesis', which he sees as threatened by my 'exegetical fantasy'. He does so at this point in order to defend Oscar Cullmann against my strictures. This was unnecessary here, because I was not censuring Cullmann as an exegete at all. It was as a systematic theologian of 'salvation history' that I criticized him. But the matter is too important for me to leave it there. My relationship to the Bible and to professional exegesis has been subjected to critical questions by other people too. Because in my next book on 'The Foundations and Methods of Theology' (the working title) I shall go into this question systematically, I shall content myself here with a few explanations.

Richard Bauckham is a New Testament scholar and theologian at St Andrews University. I was a systematic theologian, and that alone, at the university of Tübingen. He is bound to literal exegesis and committed to the colleagues in his particular field. This I neither was nor am, by reason of my own position and field. Taking account of exegetical discipline, I can develop my own theological relationship to the biblical texts; for theology is not a commentary on the biblical writings, and commentaries on the biblical writings are not a substitute for theological reflection. If we take the 'hermeneutical bridge' as model, then the disciplined exegesis tells us what the text meant for the author and the people he was addressing in his own time; but the theological reflection is supposed to say what it means today, if we place it in the context of *our* own time. *The hermeneutical bridge* leads from 'what it meant to what it means today'. That is not simply a problem of translation. Hermeneutics is not restricted to the renovation of ancient historical buildings. Theology has to do with the *theological concern* which the biblical texts are trying to talk about in their own way and in their own time. So as a theologian I begin by reading the texts, then ask what they are saying, and turn to their subject and concern, trying to understand it with my own mental categories, which are the categories of my own time. After that I come back to the biblical text and ask whether it brings out adequately the subject or concern as I have understood it with the help of the text itself. That is to say, I enter into a factual discussion with the text, with its author, its *Sitz im Leben*, its influence in subsequent history, and so on. From this a thematic criticism of the texts emerges which is committed to their concern. In this circle joining the text, its subject and myself I then develop my theological viewpoint. A hearer of the texts becomes a friend of the texts, who discusses with them what they are talking about.

Theology is not subject to the dictation of the texts, or the dictatorship of the exegetes. Questionings as to whether the theology is 'in conformity with Scripture' seem to me to be a remnant left over from the old doctrine of verbal inspiration. The great theological outlines and systems of Augustine,

Aquinas, Calvin, Barth, Tillich and so forth do not see themselves as 'disciplined exegesis'. Calvin wrote disciplined commentaries in addition to his *Institutio*. Barth's *Epistle to the Romans* does not fit into the category of scholarly New Testament commentaries. In Paul Tillich's *Systematic Theology* there is hardly a single biblical quotation. Barth's dialectical doctrine of predestination cannot be found in this form in the Bible, nor can the magnificent structure of his doctrine of reconciliation. Richard Bauckham has taken me to be an exegete, and I am not one. I am a theological partner in dialogue with the texts which I cite, not their exegete. Let me explain the difference, illustrating it from three examples which have provoked Richard Bauckham's criticism.

(1) In note 52 he cites as a 'blatant example of demonstrably erroneous exegesis' my opinion that 'Behold I *make* all things new' (Rev 21:5) means the Hebrew *asa*, to make, to form, but not the Hebrew *bara*, which was later rendered as *creatio ex nihilo*. I am actually aware that Revelation was not written in Hebrew, and also that the Greek *poiein* is used in the Septuagint for both *bara* and *asa*. But logic enjoins understanding the word as I propose, for *bara* is used without any matter being presupposed, whereas *asa* takes place on presupposed matter (cf. Gen 1:1 with Gen 2:2). But Revelation 21:5 presupposes 'all things' as already existent, and that it is these that are then to 'be made new'. The difference between this and Isaiah 65:17 (which he cites) where God does not create heaven and earth *anew*, but will create *a new* heaven and *a new* earth, can surely not have escaped him. For in the eschatological new creation it is not something different which replaces creation; it is *this* creation which will be made new.

(2) I also fail to see the force of the other example which he adduces in order to show my faulty exegesis, Revelation 10:6: 'And time shall be no more.' At this point I have cited Elisabeth Schüssler Fiorenza, although admittedly not Oscar Cullmann; so I am not totally 'ignorant' but only partially so. When Richard Bauckham stresses that the passage means: 'There will be no more time left before the completion of God's purposes', and that this completion means 'the realization and extension of

God's rule over the whole world' (Elisabeth Schüssler Fiorenza),
I am unable to understand why that is not to be the end of
time as *chronos*. In the realm of God's eternal presence, *chronos*
can surely have just as little power as death. Even if the text
has not explicitly formulated that 'end of time' which Richard
Bauckham evidently has in mind, simple logic tells one that
'the end of time has come' once 'there is no more time left'.

(3) Finally, the 'bizarre idea' that the image of a rolled-up
scriptural scroll means 'that at the eschaton the unfurled times
of history will be rolled up like a scroll' is – as can easily be seen,
since no passage is cited – my own adoption and application of
an image for 'the fullness of the times'. The image of the rolled
up (book) scroll is also used in Revelation 6:14 as a comparison
for the disappearing heaven ('like'). 'It requires no exegesis
whatsoever to pick up and use images from Revelation.' It does
not emerge from my text that with this image of the times of
history which in the eschaton will be rolled up like a scroll, I am
making any exegetical claim, 'neither modern nor post-modern
or whatever'. Only a mind fixated on 'disciplined exegesis' can
read – and misunderstand – my theological text in this way.

Nevertheless I am grateful to Richard Bauckham for reading
my theological exposition exegetically too. In doing so he is a
rare example of his discipline. Otherwise exegetes read only
exegetes, and theologians only theologians. For the full
multiplicity of standpoints we need more cross-readings; for after
all both he and I still believe in *the unity of theology* in its diverse
disciplines.

AFTER MOLTMANN

Reflections on the Future of Eschatology

MIROSLAV VOLF

Thinking After

Jürgen Moltmann is fond of saying that, as a young theologian, he felt around Karl Barth much like many of Hegel's younger contemporaries felt in Hegel's towering presence. Is philosophy possible after Hegel? they worried, amazed at the greatness of his intellectual achievement. Is philosophy possible, they meant, as anything but a restatement of the great philosopher's thoughts? Is theology possible after Barth? the young Moltmann worried in the late 1950s. Today, some may wonder whether *eschatology* is possible after Moltmann.

Moltmann found refuge from Barth's commanding presence in the freedom of eschatological thinking. Not that Barth himself shunned eschatology. After all, he was one of the first to take on the challenge posed to theology at the turn of the century by Johannes Weiss' and Albert Schweitzer's rediscovery of the eschatological nature of Jesus' teaching.[1] Eschatology was the heartbeat of Barth's theology.[2] But it was an eschatology

---

[1] A. Schweitzer, *The Quest for the Historical Jesus: A Critical Study of Its Progress from Reimarus to Wrede* (London: Adam & Charles Black, 1910); J. Weiss, *Jesus' Proclamation of the Kingdom of God* (London: SCM Press, 1971).

[2] Cf. the often quoted claim of Karl Barth: 'If Christianity be not altogether thoroughgoing eschatology, there remains in it no relationship whatever with Christ' (*The Epistle to the Romans* [London: Oxford University Press, 1933] 314).

that managed to posit itself, so to speak, only by denying itself. It was an 'eternalized' eschatology, which had much to do with the present (the transcendent 'eternal Moment' in the early Barth) or with the past (the 'hour' of Christ's coming in the later Barth), but little with the future – either the future of God or the future of God's world (CoG 15). In *Theology of Hope*, Moltmann reaffirmed the centrality of eschatology for theology and, more significantly, freed eschatology from the stranglehold of timeless eternity and infused it with new life by returning the future back to eschatology. His achievement was a major one, and his theology began now to tower over the theological landscape.

Built over the past thirty years, his tower was a theology developed around the fundamental category of hope and addressed to the modern culture obsessed with the future. With the publication of *The Coming of God*, Moltmann placed on it a capstone, one which holds the tower together from the top as *Theology of Hope* supports it from the bottom. In that latest volume of his contributions to systematic theology, a theology of hope which sought to stimulate 'the forward direction' of the Christian life was complemented by a masterful and compelling explication of 'the horizons of expectation' and of 'the content of that . . . forward direction' (CoG xii).

Is eschatology after Moltmann possible? The image of the tower is misleading in one important respect. Moltmann's tower managed to stand so imposingly only by *moving*, and doing so in directions that not only corresponded to his journeys deeper into the territory of the Christian tradition but also correlated with the movements of social and cultural landscapes. In a sense, Moltmann himself always thought *after* Moltmann. What Moltmann's own movement demonstrates is that 'eschatology after Moltmann' is possible; his own work over the years is the proof. It also suggests that eschatology after Moltmann will be necessary. But what shape should it take?

I want to propose that eschatology after Moltmann ought to follow the trajectory of his own movement, ought to be 'after' Moltmann in an older sense of that word. Since the relation to modernity is crucial not only in Moltmann's eschatology but in any contemporary eschatology, I will first locate Moltmann in relation to modernity – the early Moltmann close to the centre of modernity's project and the later Moltmann navigating at its edges. By reflecting on the issues of the millennial transition, on the relation between completion and redemption as dominant categories for final salvation, and on the nature of eschatological discourse I will then argue that eschatology needs to be 'after Moltmann' by continuing to press further in the same direction as he was moving.

Location

Here is how Richard Bauckham, whose work on Moltmann has received the most unambiguous endorsement by Moltmann himself,[3] summarizes the intent of the early Moltmann in *Theology of Hope*:

> He [Moltmann] wished to show how the modern experience of history as a process of constant and radical change, in hopeful search of a new future, should not be rejected by the church, as though Christianity stood for reactionary traditionalism, nor ignored by the church, as though Christianity represented a withdrawal from history into purely subjective authenticity. . . . Rather the eschatological orientation of biblical Christian faith towards the future of the world makes it possible, indeed imperative for the church to engage with the possibilities of change in the modern world, promote them against all tendencies to stagnation, and give them eschatological direction towards the future kingdom of God. The Gospel proves relevant and credible today precisely through the eschatological faith that truth lies in the future and proves itself in changing the present in the direction of its future.[4]

The quotation expresses well the three defining features of the early Moltmann's work. First, he considered himself a theologian of modernity; his task was to show that the Christian faith is credible within the plausibilities of modernity whose prime feature is the stress on historical process and hopeful search for a better future. Second, much like modernity itself,

[3] R. Bauckham, *Moltmann: Messianic Theology in the Making* (Basingstoke: Marshall Morgan & Scott, 1987) vii–x.

[4] R. Bauckham, *The Theology of Jürgen Moltmann* (Edinburgh: T. & T. Clark, 1995) 31.

Moltmann was fascinated with 'possibilities', with 'constant and radical change', with a 'movement' toward a goal, with 'the future', and he sought to interpret Christian tradition accordingly. Hope ought to be the central category of Christian theology, he argued, because the orientation toward the future is the defining feature of modernity (TT 88; CoG 192). And inversely, modernity's orientation toward the future, though often expressed in non-Christian and even implicitly or explicitly anti-Christian terms, is a secular form of genuinely Christian hope.[5] Third, though at points there seems to be a parity between the strength of Moltmann's commitments to Christian faith and to modernity, the commitment to the Christian faith is still prior. He is not offering a religious legitimation for the project of modernity, but showing how Christian faith is socially relevant in the context of modernity.

Over the years Moltmann has grown much more ambivalent toward modernity. Though reluctant to side with a still rather diffuse and discordant crowd of 'postmodernists', he has come to recognize some basic – even fatal – flaws of modernity and has made the critique of these flaws central to his own theological project. Instead of primarily celebrating the possibilities opened up with the dawn of modernity, he is now critiquing the pernicious consequences of the possibilities seized, and suggesting ways to avert a possible and even likely catastrophe caused by the inner dynamics of modernity itself. In the trail of its victorious march modernity has left the wreckage of what he calls 'sub-modernity'. Modernity's celebration of freedom reduces human beings to disconnected individuals, naked subjects of will and reason, who are incapable of community. Its economic successes rest on a centuries-long pattern of exploitation both of the peoples and the treasures of the southern hemisphere. Its technological successes have been achieved at the cost of the objectification of nature and of unprecedented damage to the ecosystem, and have resulted in a permanent threat of humanity's extinction. Hence his warnings about the 'modern world's lack of future' (CoG 45)

---

[5] J. Moltmann, 'Probleme der neueren evangelischen Eschatologie', *VF* 11 (1966) 116–117.

unless our contemporaries can rediscover a vital community with one another and with nature.

Against my account of Moltmann's shift from celebrating to critiquing modernity one could argue that in all his critique he still remains within modernity's embrace. A critical voice has become dominant, but this is but one among the plethora of voices which comprise a discordant community of modernity's internal critics whose presence is part and parcel of its very identity. Moltmann has moved to the periphery and from there seeks to reform and thereby stabilize the whole. Arguing along such lines, Arne Rasmusson claims that for Moltmann 'the world critical character of Christianity' is but 'a mediating principle to the critical culture of modernity'.[6]

At one level Rasmusson is right. Far from giving up on modernity, Moltmann wants to help create a better modernity. The overarching goal of his mature political theology is 'the rebirth of modernity out of the Spirit of life'. But how should we interpret the relation to modernity implied in that goal? Clearly, Moltmann's stated primary commitments are not to modernity but to the God of Israel as revealed in Jesus Christ and attested in the Scriptures. Consider how he introduced a lecture devoted mainly to the role of the Christian faith in the context of modernity:

> It is simple, but true, to say that theology has only one, single problem: God. We are theologians for the sake of God; if we are not, then we ought not to call ourselves theologians at all. God is our dignity. God is our agony. God is our hope.[7]

Similarly, in *The Coming of God* 'the different horizons of eternal life, the eternal kingdom and the eternal creation draw together to a single focus: *the cosmic Shekinah of God*' (CoG xiii). So the crucial question in assessing Moltmann's relation to modernity is whether the call for the 'rebirth of modernity' is a universal or a contextual one. Is a 'reborn modernity' what the social

---

[6] A. Rasmusson, *The Church as Polis: From Political Theology to Theological Politics as Exemplified by Jürgen Moltmann and Stanley Hauerwas* (Lund: Lund University Press, 1994) 95.

[7] J. Moltmann, 'Theology in the Project of the Modern World', in *A Passion for God's Reign* (ed. M. Volf; Grand Rapids: Eerdmans, 1998) 1.

world would look like if Moltmann were creating it from scratch? Or is a 'reborn modernity' the shape that the concrete anticipations of the eschatological reign of God should take in the public realm of an unalterably modern world?[8] I believe that the later Moltmann's call for the 'rebirth of modernity' is a contextual one. Moltmann has moved away from the centre of modernity's project towards its edges, and is straining his eye to discern the shape of God's future in order to nudge modernity into closer correspondence to that future. Has he perceived God's future rightly? Has he addressed modernity faithfully? The dispute over these questions is important, but its outcome has little bearing on my main point: that Moltmann's primary commitments are to the reign of God and not to modernity and that the later Moltmann should be located at the edges and not at the centre of modernity's project.

Whatever the later Moltmann's own relation to modernity may be, any notion that modernity more adequately anticipates the reign of God than did premodernity or than a postmodernity may turn out to do must be firmly rejected – a notion that the early Moltmann entertained at least with respect to the 'project' of modernity if not with respect to any of its concrete embodiments. Christian faith has no particular stake in modernity, which, like any of the 'forms of the world' is 'passing' (1 Cor 7:31). To have a particular stake in modernity would be to advocate that peculiarly modern narrow-mindedness that is intelligent enough to place itself within a sequence of epochal shifts but blind enough to consider itself as the pinnacle of historical progress. From the vantage point of God's revelation in Jesus Christ, no such progress is discernible and all such claims appear as sinful and dangerous ideologies. The Christian relation to modernity, as to culture in general and therefore to any other epochal form of social life, can consist neither in

---

[8] I read Moltmann's talk of 'imperfect' modernity – a free rendering of *unvollendet*, which is more literally to be translated as 'incomplete' modernity – in the same way (TT 87). In German public discourse, this is a widespread way of talking about improving the inescapable modernity. In the same volume he also says that 'theology must accept the changed circumstances of the world in order to change these in its turn towards peace, justice, and the life of creation' (94).

principled affirmation nor in principled rejection, but in 'a complex and flexible network of small and large refusals, divergences, subversions, and more or less alternative proposals, surrounded by the acceptance of many cultural givens'.[9] At a meta-level, one may describe such a relation to modernity as 'post-modern', provided one recognizes that it was also practised by the earliest Christian communities, which were very much 'pre-modern'.[10]

One important gain from such a complex relation between Christian faith and culture is freedom from modernity, whether conceived of as ally or foe. For those who like to think of themselves as 'modern', one can term the proximate social goal of such a complex Christian insertion into contemporary societies as the 'rebirth of modernity' (though one may equally well want to subvert their expectations focused on modernity by abandoning the positive appropriation of the term 'modern'). For those who like to think of themselves as 'post-modern', one could describe such a complex Christian insertion into contemporary societies as an attempt to help give birth to healthy postmodernity (though one may equally well decide that appealing to postmodernity will in the end be as counterproductive as were the appeals to modernity over the past two centuries). Such freedom, even playfulness, with respect to modernity is possible because, after all, what matters ultimately is not 'modernity' or 'postmodernity', but the coming of God's Messiah and of God's reign (Rev 22:20; Matt 6:10). Which, from one angle, is what eschatology is all about.

Transition

Talking to a group of his former students just after the publication of *The Coming of God*, Moltmann described the book as *ein bischen apokalyptischer als sonst* ('a bit more apocalyptic than

---

[9] M. Volf, 'When Gospel and Culture Intersect: Notes on the Nature of Christian Difference', in *Pentecostalism in Context: Essays in Honor of William W. Menzies* (eds W. M. and R. P. Menzies; Sheffield: Sheffield Academic Press, 1997) 233.

[10] M. Volf, 'Soft Difference: Theological Reflections on the Relation Between Church and Culture in 1 Peter', *Ex Auditu* 10 (1994) 15–30.

usual') – apocalyptic, that is, in a more colloquial sense of stressing the catastrophic side of 'the end'.[11] In a sense, the move in the direction of apocalypticism was not difficult for Moltmann to make. Until *The Way of Jesus Christ* he was hardly apocalyptic at all! He was a millenarian.

In *The Coming of God* he remains faithful to his more youthful theological self and continues to advocate millenarian eschatology: 'Christian eschatology – eschatology, that is, which is messianic, healing and saving – is millenarian eschatology' (CoG 202). To substantiate the claim, he latches not so much onto the claims of sparse biblical texts about the millennium as onto the function of the millenarian hope.

> Only millenarian eschatology understands the eschaton as the goal of history, as future history, as the consummation and final condition of history. Non-millenarian eschatology can only talk about a rupture of history, which can have no relevance for present ethics. (193)

As an inner worldly goal of history, the millennium serves as 'the most powerful motivation' for the Christian ethic (201).

Moltmann's move is typically modern. Admittedly, it is somewhat at odds with a 'non-utopian strand' of modernity which operates with 'the promise of steady improvement with no foreseeable ending at all'.[12] It fits well, however, with modernity's 'utopian strand' which strives to bring history to a happy ending – more precisely: to a happy new beginning, as the thought of Karl Marx illustrates. A historical future serves both as the motivation for and the criterion of present action. Future possibilities offered to the imagination pull the present toward themselves, and the shape of history's end gives form to human action in its middle.

In *The Coming of God* this modern move is balanced by a non-modern countermove. After the section on the necessity of

---

[11] In *The New Testament and the People of God* (Minneapolis: Fortress, 1992) 280–299, N. T. Wright offers a helpful, more technical discussion of apocalypticism.

[12] C. Lash, *The True and Only Heaven: Progress and Its Critics* (New York: W. W. Norton, 1991) 47.

millenarian eschatology follows a section on the *necessity of apocalyptic eschatology*. Moltmann writes,

> eschatology begins with apocalypticism: there is no beginning of a new world without the end of this old one, there is no kingdom of God without judgment on godlessness, there is no rebirth of the cosmos without 'the birth-pangs of the End-time'.[13] (CoG 227)

Between the *Theology of Hope* and *The Coming of God* the negativities of the history which the promise of God contradicts have grown into a deep rupture at the end of history which God's new creation will mend. The death of Christ is now associated for Moltmann not simply with the negativities of history but with its end (WJC 151–212; CoG 134ff.), just as resurrection was always associated not simply with historical improvements but with the glory of the new creation. 'Eschatology,' he now writes,

> is not a doctrine about history's happy end. . . . No one can assure us that the worst will not happen. According to all the laws of experience: it will. We can only trust that even the end of the world hides a new beginning if we trust the God who calls into being the things that are not, and out of death creates new life. (CoG 234)

Whereas millenarian eschatology directs our gaze to the possibilities of new life (things that are not yet), apocalyptic eschatology underscores the truth that new life can emerge only through death (things that are not). The first encourages 'active hope for the future'; the second gives 'a resisting, enduring expectation, capable of suffering, in a situation in which nothing more can be done to avert disaster' (230).

In *The Coming of God* a modern hope, typical for the 'cultures of progress', which drives a person to transform the world in the light of future possibilities, has been complemented by a non-modern hope, typical of the 'cultures of endurance', which

---

[13] In *Apocalypse Now and Then: A Feminist Guide to the End of the World* (Boston: Beacon, 1996) 18, Catherine Keller objected that Moltmann's eschatology is destructive because Moltmann advocates the final end not only of injustice, but 'of finitude itself'. She fails, I think, to appreciate sufficiently Moltmann's stress on 'the beginning' that is present in 'the end' and on the continuities between the present and the ultimate future contained in Moltmann's vision of redemption *of* history (see CoG 265).

enables a person to face even the tragedies of cosmic pro-portions with an uplifted head (see Luke 21:28).[14] The hope which transforms, I hear Moltmann now saying from the peri-pheries of modernity's project, is truncated without the hope which endures in the face of a reality that cannot be trans-formed; the eschatology of making 'all things new' is deficient without the eschatology of rupture within the things old. Moltmann, the critic of modernity, has grown 'a bit more apocalyptic than usual', and the result has been two hopes and two eschatologies grounded and held together in the narrative of the death and resurrection of Christ as a single complex hope and a single complex eschatology.

Moltmann, the advocate of modernity, however, married this newly-won, complex eschatology to the notion of 'millenarian transition'. By 'transition' he means 'a consummation of historical time *in* history before "the Last Day" and the dawn of the new, eternal creation' (199). The apocalyptic woes form the edge of the transition which faces the present; the transi-tion itself is the future millennium. It can be argued that the millennium (conceived of as transition) is unnecessary in Moltmann's thought. It is unnecessary since he believes that the entrance into 'eternity' does not entail flight from time but a restoration of all of times and that the 'new creation' comes about through the transformation rather than the annihilation of the old. A millenarian fulfilment of history within history is not needed to offset the 'apocalyptic' destruction at the end because Moltmann conceives of 'eternity' as the fulfilment of history. Arguing along such lines, Richard Bauckham insists that the millennium is dispensable in Moltmann's eschatology: all theological functions of the millennium can equally well be fulfilled by the new creation to follow upon the millennium in

---

[14] In Richard Rorty's correspondence with Anindita Balslev, Rorty distinguishes between 'cultures of endurance' and 'cultures of social hope' (A. N. Balslev, *Cultural Otherness: Correspondence with Richard Rorty* [Shimla: Indian Institute of Advanced Study, 1991] 21). I prefer the term 'culture of progress' over 'culture of social hope', because within a culture of endurance there can also be hope that can properly be termed 'social' even if it does not centre 'around suggestions for drastic change in the way things are done' (21).

Moltmann's scheme of things.[15] I want to push Moltmann harder and argue that, understood as transition, the millennium is not only unnecessary but *detrimental.*

'The most difficult problem of millenarian eschatology', writes Moltmann, is how to 'think of a consummation of historical time *in* history' (CoG 199). Moltmann casts the difficulty as a problem of time, and, so far I can tell, never solves it. But why create the difficulty in the first place, especially since other difficulties beset an eschatological millennium interpreted as transition? In addition to the problem of time, 'transition' also creates the problem of historical 'space', so to speak. The consummation of history in history requires, according to Moltmann, that one posits 'eschaton' as the historical goal of history (193). Such a goal presupposes that *the* history is one and that it moves or is pushed toward a single goal, which is a typically modern, teleological notion of history. All such notions entail a conceptual imposition of singleness and unidirectionality upon the actual multiplicity of partly overlapping and partly independent historical spaces with diverging directions and differing tempos of internal development. With such singularization and homogenization of historical spaces as its presupposition, it is not clear how 'eschatological millenarianism' – understood as transition and functioning as motivation for concrete historical action – can avoid slippage into 'historical millenarianism' whose oppressive character Moltmann has sought to expose (157–192). *If* 'eschatological millennium' is *the* goal of *the* history and *if* it lays moral claim on us in the form of a concrete social project, it will share the basic flaw of all historical millenarianisms because it will be inherently oppressive: the one future, declared as divine, will suppress many human histories whose utopian imaginations diverge from it.[16] This flaw becomes all the more apparent as

---

[15] Chapter IV/1 above.

[16] The conditional character of my formulation is intentional. For it could be argued that Moltmann defines eschatological millenarianism in such a way that it can never slip into historical millenarianism for the simple reason that he seeks to avoid the dangers of historical millenarianism by situating the millennium so firmly in the future that it can do no real work in the present – except for fueling critique of the present. Similar reconstructions of

Moltmann construes the distinction between eschatological millenarianism, which he affirms, and historical millenarianism, which he rejects, primarily in terms of time (the one is future and the other asserted as present),[17] rather than in terms of the nature of power (the one defined by self-giving and the other by coercion).[18]

I have just argued that 'transition' is unstable in relation to what it makes a transition *from* – the unredeemed present. From this perspective, 'transition' conceived of as the historical goal of history emerges as a form of unredemption. It can also be argued that 'transition' is unstable in relation to what it makes a transition *to* – God's new creation. If we wanted to redeem the transition, it would have to look very much like the new creation. Moltmann recognizes the need for a breach with the present history if the goal of history is to be reached. At least in *The Trinity and the Kingdom of God* the reality of the eschatological millennium is predicated on the resurrection of the dead (235 n. 45).[19] The life of the resurrection, however, is not history; it is the redemption of history into eternal life (cf. CoG 69). The problem of history cannot be resolved as consummation of history, but requires the creation of 'all things new', implies Moltmann rightly.

Moltmann's thought generally lie behind the objections leveled against him by liberation theologians (R. Alves, *A Theology of Human Hope* [Washington DC: Corpus Books, 1969] 55–68; J. M. Bonino, *Doing Theology in a Revolutionary Situation* [Philadelphia: Fortress, 1975] 139–152; G. Gutiérrez, *A Theology of Liberation: History, Politics, and Salvation* [2nd edn; Maryknoll: Orbis Books, 1988] 216–218). If this reconstruction is accepted, then Moltmann's thought on the eschatological millennium as transition faces the following dilemma: if the millennium is allowed to set foot in history, the dangers of historical millenarianism loom large; if the millennium is maintained as an exclusively future reality, it cannot direct action toward the goal of history.

[17] The basic distinction points to eschatological millenarianism as the hope for a future, this-worldly realization of the kingdom of Christ in history, whereas historical millenarianism is the interpretation of the present historical projects or realities as the realization of the millennial reign of Christ (CoG 146, 192).

[18] R. Bauckham in chapter IV/1 above.

[19] In order to ground the 'transition', in *The Coming of God* Moltmann differentiates between 'the special and messianic "resurrection *from* the dead"' and 'the universal and eschatological "resurrection *of* the dead"' (CoG 195). For exegetical and theological reasons I remain unpersuaded.

How should we conceptualize the creation of all things new in a way which avoids the reemergence of the imposition of singularity and unidirectionality upon multiple histories, but at the same time does not leave multiple histories behind by taking a flight into timeless eternity? Moltmann himself gives us a lead in answering the question. Its full contours will emerge as we discuss the issue of 'completion'.

Completion

The category of *novum* is the dominant figure for the ultimate eschatological state in Moltmann's thought (27–29). He understands *novum*, however, with the help of the category of 'completion', which, though not invoked nearly as frequently, is even more basic to his thought. The category owes its prominence to Moltmann's central concern not simply with the future but with the future of *this* world. The new creation must be linked to the original creation so that the original creation can be understood in the light of the new creation. 'Completion' is designed to do the job; *novum* is adequately conceived only as a form of 'completion'.

What does *novum* as completion mean concretely? For Moltmann, the world never was and is not now what it is meant to be. The creation in the beginning was unfinished, in need of completion in the new creation. If done in line with God's coming reign, transformations of the world in history are anticipations of the eschatological completion of the world. Divine transformation of the world at the end is, so to speak, the completion of completions of the world from which all historical anticipations draw their meaning and power. 'The *creatio ex nihilo*, the creation out of nothing, is *completed* in the eschatological *creatio ex vetere*, the creation out of the old' (265, second italics mine). Even the final eschatological act, the annihilation of 'the temporal possibility for this perversion of the form of the world' (271), does not fall in Moltmann's thought conceptually outside the figure of completion. The same holds true for 'redemption'; he subsumes redemption under the larger category of completion.[20] For instance, justification of the

---

[20] R. Bauckham in chapter I/1 above.

ungodly by grace is not the restoration of a human being to the original state of innocence, but 'a new beginning of his anthropogenesis at his end' (ZS 175). In other words, justification along with other soteriological actions such as glorification completes the creation of human beings.

The category of 'completion' is a typically modern one. It correlates with the modern fascination with change, the future, and linear progress. If change is positive and the future is better than the past or present, then every present experience is an experience of incompletion and human beings will strive to transcend them on the way toward the final completion – a completion understood either as a goal to be reached or as a regulative ideal to be approached asymptotically. A host of modern thinkers in one way or another shared Johann Gottlieb Fichte's notion that the true paradise was not a gift of grace that humanity enjoyed in the distant past, but the promised land to be built by humanity's efforts in the future.[21] In the meantime, however, modernity has lost the belief in its own innocence which allowed it to have such exalted dreams about a completion of history. Especially for Jewish thinkers, the tragedies of the two world wars have exposed history's intransigence before all attempts at its completion. As Moltmann puts it, 'The question about redemption pushed out the question about the utopian goals of historical progress' (CoG 44).

With respect to eschatology, one response to the ruptures in history was closed for Moltmann. It was the temptation to seek refuge in the notion of 'redemption *from* history and time, into the eternity of God' (CoG 44, italics added). The dialectical theologians, notably Karl Barth, took this path after the disillusionments of the First World War.[22] From the outset, however, Moltmann's eschatological thinking developed as an alternative to theirs, mainly because for him, as for the contemporary Jewish thinkers, 'such an "eternal present" of redemption' was inconceivable 'in this "unredeemed world"' (44). Refusing either to exit history or to be ensnared by it, Moltmann proposed

---

[21] J. G. Fichte, *Sämtliche Werke* (Berlin, 1845–1846) 7.342.

[22] Barth, *Epistle to the Romans*, 500.

instead to place eternity in positive relation to temporality rather than in opposition to it. Eternity is not timelessness, but 'fulness of time' (264). The eschaton is neither outside of history in timeless eternity nor is it the last segment of history's linear progression. Both of these options would amount to the abandonment of history to non-redemption, either of all history (as in platonizing forms of Christian eschatology) or of the long stretches of history prior to its goal (as in Marxian eschatology). If God is the faithful creator, however, redemption is thinkable only as redemption *of* history, not as redemption *from* history. Hence Moltmann suggested that we

> link the eschatological category of *novum* with the anamnetic category of repetition in such a way that the beginning is gathered up into the end, and the consummation brings back everything that had ever been before. (265)

Provided we understand 'everything' rather loosely (as 'everything that is redeemable' rather than everything – absolutely), this suggestion is helpful since the resolution of the problem of history it implies does not require a highly problematic postulate of the single goal of the history at the end of history. Put differently, the anamnetic category of repetition repairs in the ultimate eschatological state the damage that, in Moltmann's account, the penultimate eschatological state (transition understood as the historical goal of history) has created, albeit only diachronically and not synchronically. All histories with their own directions and paces of development are not forced into a single history at the end, but will be met, judged, and redeemed where the coming God finds them. Moltmann writes,

> In 'the restoration of all things', all times will return and – transformed and transfigured – will be taken up into the aeon of the new creation. In the eternal creation all the times which in God's creative resolve were fanned out will also be gathered together. The unfurled times of history will be rolled up like a scroll, as Revelation 5 intimates. Only this can be called 'the fulness of the times'. (294–295)

Apart from the philosophical and scientific questions about the nature of time, the key question with respect to this ingenious proposal is whether it will work if pursued within the overarching framework of 'completion'. I want to suggest that it will work only inadequately. To support the suggestion I need to give a sketch of the relation between what I understand under 'completion' and 'redemption' as the two dominant and complementary aspects of eschatological consummation (which is itself often termed 'redemption' [*Erlösung*]). I want to state at the outset that what is at issue here is not the old and still important question of the relation between creation and eschatological consummation; Moltmann rightly wants to understand God's work in the beginning in light of God's work in the end. What is at issue is *the character of the eschatological consummation* itself.

The category of eschatological *completion* rests on the assumption that creation is good but not yet quite an adequate expression of the Creator's purposes. The 'act' of creation in the beginning will be completed by the 'act' of new creation at the end. Traditionally, the category was more or less consistently applied to the *physical* dimension of creation, both human and non-human. It concerned itself above all with the questions of transience and mortality. This aspect of eschatology was formulated as the hope that the creation in which transience reigns will be completed by the new creation in which transience – and all the pain associated with transience – will be no more.

The category of eschatological *redemption* rests on the assumption that creation, though remaining basically good, has been spoiled by humanity's evil ways. The protological creation is an inadequate expression of the Creator's purposes not only on account of its transience; the Creator's purposes have been in part thwarted by human transgression. The category of redemption was consistently applied to the *moral* dimension of creation. This aspect of eschatology was formulated as the hope that the creation which is shot through with injustice, deception, and violence will be redeemed to become a world of justice, truth, and peace – a world of perfect love. Eschatological redemption, though postulated as occurring at the end of history, was seen as applying across historical times and spaces.

Though the categories of completion and redemption have been seen as complementary, the Western tradition has historically given preeminence to the category of redemption. This was in part conditioned by the belief that transience can be traced back to transgression. If, as the Apostle Paul put it, death entered the world on account of sin (see Rom 5:12), liberation from sin would entail liberation from death (Rom 8:19ff.). The Eastern tradition, on the other hand, saw sin not so much as corruption as the fundamental human problem; the Fall was a turning away from life to death, 'from incorruption to corruption'. Correspondingly, *theosis* as the ultimate goal of human life means 'triumph of life over death' and a change of human beings 'from being corruptible to being incorruptible again'. In my terms, the category of completion dominated eschatological thinking.

Partly under the influence of the Eastern tradition and partly on the basis of the claim of natural and social sciences that transience and therefore death is part of the very fabric of our creation, Moltmann, a Western theologian, has advocated completion as the overarching eschatological category. The new creation completes the old, he argues, and it does so primarily by overcoming transience; the resolution of the problem of history is the annihilation of the possibility of corruption through the eternalization of creation (271). Though on account of transgression human beings need to undergo the transforming judgment of God (eschatological judgment conceived in analogy to justification) (250–255), the transgression will be taken care of above all by the overcoming of transience, because – in a reversal of the Pauline account of the matter – the cause of sin is death (91).

Rooting sin in death is highly problematic, however. Nothing suggests that we kill, let alone commit all other sins, only because we cannot endure mortality, as Moltmann argues. It is easy to imagine how imperishable beings could sin, as the tradition has consistently taught.[23] Though the problem of death is resolved through 'eternalization', the problem of sin is not –

[23] Aquinas, for instance, argued that angels are both 'by nature imperishable' and that 'the possibility of failure is inherent' in them as in any other created nature.

neither the problem of the possibility of sin nor the problem of the actuality of sins past. The problem of evil, though exacerbated through transience, is not caused by it.

Hence to propose 'eternalization' as the solution to the problem of sin will not do, as Moltmann is well aware. To 'gather all and everything into the realm of his glory', he argues, God will have to liberate sinners 'from their deadly perdition through transformation into their true, created being' (244, 255). Since sin manifestly does not exist 'because of death' this liberation cannot take place simply through destruction of transience. Hence in the whole section on 'The Restoration of All Things' (235–255), he employs the language of reconciliation, not of completion. The reason is that the transformation of perpetrators, if it is not to be an act of injustice toward victims, requires fundamentally a moral act of forgiveness and redemption.

The talk of 'forgiveness' and 'redemption', however, lies properly outside the conceptual scope of 'completion'. History does not only need to be improved or finished; it is, in fact, so deeply flawed that no amount of completing will remove those flaws. History must be 'repaired'. That the language of completion breaks down can be seen clearly when we consider the need to deal with the *past* if the present is to be healed. The transformation of perpetrators is not possible without redemption of their past; a murderer *is* a murderer because he *has* murdered (though, of course, 'murderer' is not all, not even most, of what a person who has murdered is).[24] He will eternally remain a murderer if his life is only transformed in an act of eschatological 'completion' without his *past* also being redeemed.[25] Moreover, the perpetrator's past cannot be redeemed by itself because it is defined by the victim's relation to the

[24] It is anthropologically and soteriologically crucial to distinguish 'person' from 'work' and not to identify the two, pure and simple. Yet the distinction should not degenerate into separation. A 'work' – in the above case, the fact of having murdered – always qualifies a 'person'. It takes the work of salvation (whose possibility rests on the reality of the distinction between 'person' and 'work') for a human being to be freed from negative qualification by his or her activity.

[25] M. Volf, *Exclusion and Embrace: A Theological Exploration of Identity, Otherness, and Reconciliation* (Nashville: Abingdon, 1996) 131–140.

perpetrator. The only way to reconstitute the perpetrator's past is by reconstituting the victim's relation to the perpetrator, including her past. Here again, the category of completion is not simply inadequate, but inappropriate. What is called for is redemption.

The point I wish to make – and the point with which Moltmann might end up agreeing – is *not* that 'completion' ought to be *replaced* by 'redemption', but that 'redemption' cannot be subsumed under 'completion'. The two stand in a relation of non-reducible complementarity as essential elements of the eschatological consummation. And, arguably, within that complementary *the category of redemption is more crucial* because sin is a more fundamental obstacle to the creation of the new world than transience.[26] Without redemption, the fullness of time in which the past has been preserved will be nothing but the eternalization of this same unredeemed world, and the rolling back of the unfurled times of history into the aeonic 'scroll' of the new creation will be nothing but the eternal repetition of the sins and sufferings of these same unfurled times. With all imaginable completing done, the world will forever remain 'old'. As Paul argues in 2 Corinthians 5, the passing away of the old world and creation of a new world rests on redemption.

Undergirded by the divine act of redemption, the gathering of all history into God's eternal time ('completion') will place

---

[26] Using the terminology of 'consummation' and 'redemption' and employing it to different ends, Kendall Soulen has argued that 'consummation' is the larger circle of God's work in which 'redemption' is situated. God the Consummator – the God whose work consists in 'the providential management of and care for the household of creation,' including the final eschatological reign – 'economizes the human condition in a manner logically antecedent to the crisis of sin and therefore logically antecedent to the economy of redemption' (R. K. Soulen, *The God of Israel and Christian Theology* [Minneapolis: Fortress, 1996] 111). In one respect the argument makes sense: if there is nothing to redeem then redemption is impossible, and if the goal of redemption is not set with creation then redemption is in danger of degenerating into alienation. Hence redemption presupposes creation, preservation, and consummation (in Soulen's sense). But clearly, when it comes to making the creation into a 'world' than which none better can be conceived, redemption is the most fundamental work that needs to be done because sin is the most fundamental problem.

this same history into the realm of innocence that can never be lost. It will be the post-historical realm beyond good and evil in which evil will no longer lurk at the edges of God's creation, but in which human beings will be 'lost' in the goodness, truth, and beauty of God and God's creation. In the eternal joy of this ultimate 'lostness' human beings will have finally found their proper home – a 'world' than which none better can be conceived.

Discourse

The Christian hope, I have just argued, looks toward the redemption of all histories into the eternal divine realm beyond good and evil. This is, ultimately, what Christian eschatology is about. What kind of discourse is appropriate to this kind of hope?

Throughout his career Moltmann has argued that eschatological knowledge is practical rather than pseudo-scientific or speculative knowledge. Eschatology is not 'apocalyptic prediction' which seeks to piece together and explicate God's alleged advance narration of future history, above all of its final stages. Equally, eschatology is not 'a theory about universal history' which seeks to read off the ultimate meaning of history in the mirror of its proleptically known final end. Both of these approaches to eschatology satisfy a certain kind of curiosity, but do not direct and motivate action (though direction and motivation for action can be derived from them). In contrast, Moltmann believes that eschatology is 'a theology for combatants, not onlookers' (CoG 146). He is right, provided we do not construe theoretical knowledge of onlookers and practical knowledge of combatants simply as polar opposites.[27] But what kind of practical knowledge does eschatology offer? I will start answering this question by reflecting on how the future figures within eschatological discourse.

---

[27] In *Theology and Practice: Epistemological Foundation* (Maryknoll: Orbis Books, 1987) 210–213, Clodovis Boff has rightly argued that praxis is always infused with theory and that theory, more specifically theology, is also a kind of practice.

Because it seeks to articulate the hope for the ultimate redemption of all histories, eschatology is a specific kind of discourse about the future. It is not about the future understood either as an imminent or a distant tomorrow. As much as it is about tomorrow, eschatology is also about today and yesterday. Eschatology is fundamentally about *the future of yesterday, today, and tomorrow*; it is about the *future of all times*. (For those who fear that such an understanding of eschatology comes close to substituting the future for timeless eternity, one can say that eschatology is about the future of all those futures which already have and are yet to become the past.) It follows that one of the central features of eschatological discourse is *transtemporality*. Eschatology speaks about the future in such a way so as to speak at the same time about every time and to every time. Transtemporality as a feature of eschatological discourse not only corresponds to the nature of ultimate redemption, but also fits the paradigmatic eschatological discourses in the biblical traditions. The book of Revelation, for instance, talks about Rome of its own time by employing the image of Babylon and conflating texts about Babylon and Tyre from the oracles of the prophets Isaiah, Jeremiah and Ezekiel (Isa 13:1–14; 21:1–10; 23; 47; Jer 25:12–38; 50–51; Ezek 26–28). Though the prophets spoke concretely about Babylon and not Rome, from the perspective of the writer of the Book of Revelation their proclamation *was in fact also* about Rome. So from the perspective of the kind of discourse employed in the Book of Revelation, the prophets' proclamation was also about any of the subsequent systems of economic and political oppression. In talking about the future of Babylon, the prophets and the apostles talk about the future of Babylon *and* about the future of Rome, *and* may be talking about the futures of Buenos Aires, Cairo, Moscow, Tokyo, and Washington – about the future of any 'city which the prophetic cap fits'.[28]

The transtemporal character of eschatological discourse goes hand in hand with its *ethical* character. As a discourse about the future of all times, eschatology passes moral judgments on all

[28] R. Bauckham, *The Theology of the Book of Revelation* (Cambridge: Cambridge University Press, 1993) 153.

times. Eschatology is categorically different from futurology, the prevalent mode of discourse about the future in contemporary societies. Futurology tries to extrapolate about a segment of time to come on the basis of past occurrences and present tendencies. Eschatology, on the other hand, tries to discern the character of all historical times in the light of the future ultimate redemption. Futurology is a mode of descriptive, scientific discourse based on the past and present configuration of things and directed toward the future; eschatology is a mode of evaluative, prophetic discourse based on the future ultimate redemption and directed toward all histories.

The light of the ultimate redemption in which eschatology narrates the future of all times exposes what in our world – in all the intersecting or disjointed histories of our world – will remain, as well as what must pass away if the ultimate redemption is to take place. 'It is only when heaven is wide open that hell too yawns at our feet', wrote Hans Urs von Balthasar.[29] In von Balthasar's terminology, eschatology places all events of history between the ultimate options of 'heaven' and 'hell'. In drawing attention to these sharp contrasts, it reveals what is ultimately at stake in any historical action and decision.

Significantly, eschatology speaks of the ultimate redemption ('heaven') as something accomplished by God. In the parable about the Judgment of the Nations, Jesus speaks about 'the kingdom prepared for you from the foundation of the world' (Matt 25:34). And John of Patmos sees 'the holy city, the new Jerusalem, coming down out of heaven from God' (Rev 21:2). Correspondingly, eschatology also thematizes evil in its extreme ugliness ('hell') within the narrative of its final demise. So, thirdly, though ethical in import, eschatological discourse is fundamentally *soteriological* in character. It calls for discernment and action by narrating God's separation of good from evil and God's overcoming of evil with good. As Moltmann has emphasized, eschatology has to do not with that future which will develop out of the past and present (*futurum*) but with that future which is brought into the world with the eschatological

---

[29] H. U. von Balthasar, *Theo-Drama: Theological Dramatic Theory* (San Francisco: Ignatius Press, 1994) 11.

coming of God (*adventus*) (CoG 25–26) and which consists in
the destruction of death and sin and the establishment of 'new
heavens and a new earth'.

Notice that the basic structure of eschatological discourse –
transtemporality, moral import, and soteriological character –
is the same as the structure of that initial proclamation which
stands at the very foundation of Christian faith. As the Gospel
of Mark records it, Jesus started his ministry by proclaiming the
good news: 'the kingdom of God has come near; repent, and
believe in the good news' (1:15). Just as Jesus announced that
'the kingdom of God has come near' without being brought
near by human beings, so also eschatology speaks of the ultimate redemption as the 'New Jerusalem' that comes down 'from
God' (Rev 21:2). Also, just as Jesus called people to repentance,
so also eschatology places before human beings the ultimate
moral choice between 'Babylon' and the 'New Jerusalem' (Rev
17–21). Finally, just as Jesus' proclamation was addressed to all
hearers indiscriminately (and therefore, by inference, to all
times and all spaces), so also eschatology brings the light of the
ultimate redemption to shine on all times and all places.
Eschatology is at its heart the proclamation of the good news in
the form of reflective narration of the coming ultimate
redemption.

But how can one narrate the ultimate redemption and the
future of our world in the light of it? What vantage point does
one need to take? Here, too, the nature of eschatological
discourse corresponds to the initial proclamation of the
kingdom of God. As Jesus went to the desert before he embarked
upon his public ministry (Mark 1:12–13), so John of Patmos,
the most prominent representative of eschatological thinking
in the Christian scriptures, received his revelation on a deserted
island (Rev 1:9). 'Desert' stands for the absence of ties with
civilization. Only a person no longer fully immersed in the mesh
of social relations with all its complexities and compromises – a
person who has stepped with one foot, so to speak, out of these
relations – is able to see what is ultimately at stake in these
relations. Notice in both cases – in the case of Jesus' original
proclamation and in the case of John's final vision – the interplay
between withdrawal and engagement, between distance and

belonging. 'Desert' precedes Jesus' public ministry (cf. Mark 1:14ff.) as it precedes John's reading of the world events of his time. And inversely, 'desert' follows Jesus' call to public ministry (cf. Mark 1:9–11) just as John's reading of world events in the 'desert' is imaginable only after his having been a part of those same events. 'Desert' is a station-post for combatants, not a haven for onlookers.[30]

Desert, of course, expresses in terms of spatial distance the kind of 'spiritual' distance that is the most important precondition for a genuinely eschatological discourse. Being on a deserted island is the outward code for being 'in the spirit' and therefore 'in heaven' (Rev 1:10). 'Revelation' was possible because John (and thereby his readers with him) was 'taken up into heaven in order to see the world from the heavenly perspective', writes Richard Bauckham correctly.[31] Eschatology presupposes taking the vantage point of the ultimate redemption and therefore exists either in the form of prophetic 'unveiling' or not at all.[32] The prophetic unveiling is, however, nothing but the 'revelation of Jesus Christ' (Rev 1:1) – the explication of the shape of the ultimate redemption as determined by the story of the life, death, and resurrection of Jesus Christ.

Eschatology and Modernity

One way to summarize my conversations with Moltmann on the nature of eschatology is to say that we need to free eschatology from the constraints imposed on it by three beliefs central to the project of modernity.

---

[30] In *Christ in the Wilderness: The Wilderness Theme in the Second Gospel and its Basis in the Biblical Tradition* (Naperville: Alec R. Allenson, 1963) 141, Ulrich Mauser has noted in Jesus' ministry a pattern of ministry and withdrawal – 'returns to the place where his mission properly began – to the desert'.

[31] Bauckham, *The Theology of the Book of Revelation*, 7.

[32] It goes without saying that such a taking of the vantage point of the ultimate redemption is a human activity and therefore shares in human limitations. Moreover, it fundamentally comes about not as a result of human skill but as a result of divine gift – a divine gift in earthen vessels, to borrow terminology from the apostle Paul (2 Cor 4:7).

First, contemporary Christian eschatology should give up the notion that the goal of history lies in history. The imposition of unidirectionality and singularity upon multiple histories that such a goal implies is at odds with the nature of the presence of the Triune God in history. The notion of 'the historical goal of history' should be replaced by the notion of 'the eternal home of histories'.

Second, contemporary Christian eschatology should give up the notion that the problem of history can be resolved by a process of 'completion'. Completion is inadequate because it has no way of dealing with the 'wreckage', to use the metaphor employed by Walter Benjamin, that the progress of history leaves in its trail.[33] The notion of 'completion of history' should be replaced by 'redemption of histories'.

Third, contemporary Christian eschatology should leave attempts to 'narrate the future in the present' or 'think the unity of the past from the perspective of the future' to futurologists or philosophers. The ultimate future not having yet arrived, in the hands of theologians both these endeavours would turn into the kind of guesswork that is more appropriate for onlookers than for combatants and that, if taken as a guide to practice, would oppressively force history into a procrustean bed of theory. Instead, eschatology should take on the prophetic task of explicating the hope for the ultimate redemption and reading and changing the present in light of that hope.

Are these the three pillars of an eschatology *after* Moltmann? Well, it depends. I prefer to think of them as the pillars of an eschatology that, though it may not be *according* to Moltmann, has nevertheless remained *with* Moltmann – by having moved in the direction in which he has been going.[34]

[33] W. Benjamin, *Illuminations: Essays and Reflections* (New York: Schocken, 1968) 257.

[34] I owe thanks to Jill C. Colwell, my research assistant, and Ivica Novakovic for thinking creatively alongside me on the issues explored in this text. Richard Bauckham and the participants at the Pacific Coast Theological Society meeting (30–31 October 1997, Berkeley, California), for which the text was originally prepared, also helped bring some issues into sharper focus.

CAN CHRISTIAN ESCHATOLOGY BECOME POST-MODERN?

Response to Miroslav Volf

JÜRGEN MOLTMANN

Every theology has its particular kairos, its particular context and its particular contemporaries whom it wishes to address. Even if it reaches out to an eschatology, it still cannot get beyond its own place and time. So if coming generations want to find their own kairos, their own context and their own contemporaries, they will inevitably ask, what comes after Schleiermacher, after Barth, after Bultmann, and therefore 'after Moltmann' too. It is true that in pre-modern times this was not the case: many generations in antiquity and in the Middle Ages could live with florilegia culled from the Greek and Latin Fathers of the church. But that is the situation in the modern world, under the pressure of 'progress' and unending 'modernizations'. What next? is a typical modern question – generally an American one. So what comes 'after' the modern? We have it: the post-modern. What comes after the post-modern? We have it: the ultra-modern. Or are these merely further instalments of modernity, which is always out to outstrip itself – a kind of post-ism? If we look at the ever-shorter 'shelf-life' of what is produced, and the speeding-up of time, then the post- and ultra-modern are no more than modernity in new packaging. But if old problems at least become outdated, even if they are not solved, and if new questions emerge, then this cannot be said. Then a new kairos comes into being, and a new world of contemporaries with which theologians are bound to involve themselves.

The *Theology of Hope*, which first appeared in 1964 (ET 1967), had its particular kairos in the new movements which were then being launched in the modern world: democracy in Germany, aggiornamento in the Roman Catholic Church, the ecumenical movement in its flowering, in North America the civil rights movement and in Latin America movements for liberation. But with the *Theology of Hope* I did not intervene in the mainstream of modernity. I involved myself in the conflicts of that time, between the conservative and the progressive syndrome. I never had the feeling that I was 'close to the centre of modernity's project' as Miroslav Volf supposes. I always counted as 'controversial', and sufficiently experienced the controversies at first hand, especially in the disapprobation of Pietists and Communists.

It was only in the United States that the *Theology of Hope* was given a warm welcome. Some people were glad that 'the God-is-dead movement is losing ground to the Theology of Hope', as the New York Times wrote in 1967. At that time I was visiting professor at Duke University, and when I saw that the 'theology of hope' was being used to bolster up the officially optimistic society of the United States, I promised friends that if I were to come back I would talk only about 'the theology of the cross'. This is what I then did in 1972 with my book *The Crucified God*, which appeared in English in 1974. If my relationship to modernity is really to be the starting point for 'eschatology after . . .', then what I said in these two books must be seen as two parts of a whole. With *The Crucified God* I did not enter into the 'future' of the modern world. I was concerned with what goes on in its depths, its underground. Later I used the term 'sub-modernity' to describe the suffering history of the modern world's victims, who have to meet the costs of its progress. Incidentally this second book brought me into closer alignment with those suffering under modernity than did the first. I forged friendships and close links with Jim Cone and his 'black theology', with Gustavo Gutiérrez and Jon Sobrino and their liberation theology, with the theology of peace and ecological theology, and not least with the Korean Minjung theology of Suh Nam Dong and Ahn Byu Mon.

I do not believe that I have 'sailed from the centre to the edges of the modern world'. I have remained – as it seems to me – at the centre of the inner contradictions of that world: the suffering and the hope of 'this present time' were important for me in the shadow of the cross and in the light of Christ's resurrection. Of course one also finds confederates in 'the critical culture of modernity' (to use Arne Rasmussen's phrase). It would indeed be dreadful if one were left alone there. But for 'the criticism of the cross' which is 'outside the gate' I have found no secular confederates, and for many of my secular friends the Christian resurrection hope counted as exorbitant and unattainable. 'The sufferings of this present time' which Paul talks about in Romans 8:18 converge at the bottommost depths of our world, and are neither modern, post-modern nor ultra-modern. They are quite simply unendurable, and a protest against the surface progress of civilization. And as far as the sufferings of the earth are concerned, what is being built up here is not even just the potential for indictment; it is the potential for the end of the world of human beings.

I should like now to go briefly into the three critical points which Miroslav Volf talks about. I have no final answers, but expect that it is on the basis of these questions that the eschatological discussion will be pursued.

(1) Although I believe that I am one of the first 'official' theologians to have taken millenarianism and apocalypticism seriously in eschatology, I feel that I am still a long way from understanding the diverse millenarian movements with which the USA blessed the rest of the world from the middle of the nineteenth century onwards (Mormons, Adventists, Jehovah's Witnesses). My interest was first awakened when in the confessional documents of the Reformation period I found that the Jews were given a single mention, at the point where millenarian expectations were rejected as a 'Jewish dream'. I then looked at the *spes Israelis* more closely, and found it in the

Christian New Testament both in Paul (Rom 9–11) and in the book of Revelation chapter 21. If we are not to brush aside Israel's prophetic and messianic hopes by saying that Christ is their fulfilment and hence their end, at least for Christians, then we must affirm them, and preserve and respect them side by side with the *spes ecclesiae*. But that means taking up the End-time millennium hope and carrying it into the transcendent hope for the new creation of all things. The Reformation critics no doubt grasped this fact: anyone who banishes the millennium from the Christian hope has no further interest in Israel and no positive relationship to the Jews. Because I linked the millennium hope with Israel, I did not, either, sense any wavering between an eschatological millenarianism and a historical millenarianism, as Miroslav Volf fears. For most millenarians, the ending of Israel's *galuth* counts as End-time indicator for the eschatological announcement of the times. I do not share their 'prophetic' interpretation of the Bible – the Bible is more than a divine commentary on world history – but I do see as noteworthy their strivings for a theologically based, positive relationship to the Jews as Jews, and to Israel's hope.

(2) The second point which Miroslav Volf touches on has to do with the relationship between redemption and completion/consummation. It seems to me that there is a semantic confusion here, rather than a theological difference. I have always related the word 'consummation' to creation-in-the-beginning. If God created heaven and earth 'in the beginning', we ask first: in the beginning of what? And then, second, where is the completion, the consummation of this beginning? Theological tradition has always related the word *consummatio* to the created world: *De consummatione mundi* is the title given to the relevant article in seventeenth-century Lutheran and Reformed theology: the old heaven and the old earth are to become a new imperishable heaven and a new indestructible earth. But *consummatio* is also used to designate the conclusion of God's works in the history of the world for the purpose of its salvation. Redemption, on the other hand, is needed by sinners and lost human beings, as well as by the part of creation which has become subject to 'the form of this world' and its godless powers.

What is the relation between redemption and consummation? Redemption embraces such a 'surplus value' of God's grace that its outcome is not a restoration of the old; something new is created. This new thing 'completes' the old in such a way that there can be no new Fall and no new enslavement of creation. In so far redemption serves the consummation and – if we turn it round dialectically – even the Fall serves creation's consummation. 'You meant evil against me, but God meant it for good.' I do not quite understand why Miroslav Volf thinks that completion is 'a typically modern category'. A glance at any biblical lexicon shows that this word is also applied to the works of God. The redemption of the unredeemed world is dependent on God's 'completion' of the works which he began.

(3) Is my eschatology 'modern', so that 'after Moltmann' eschatology has to be 'post-modern'? If post-modern means 'a new concern for differences, for complexity and the plurality of interests, cultures, places, etc.' (which is the way David Harvey describes it), then I would welcome this new sensibility. But it develops on the level of a similar, or the same, social class – among the well-off – and in a locally defined urban environment such as Upper Manhattan or Kensington. It would seem to me obscene to talk about pluralism when some people live in palaces and the rest in slums, one person in a penthouse and the others on the streets. Nor do I believe that diversity, complexity and plurality are in actual fact the marks of present-day society, desirable though this cultural wealth certainly is. The trend towards the globalization of the free market society is reducing the world to uniformity. First China is Coca Cola-ized, then Moscow is Macdonald-ized, and in the end the world everywhere looks just the same as it does in Chicago, London and New York: the same clothes, the same high-rise blocks, the same brand names on what we buy. The cultural multiplicity and diversity of the different peoples which once existed is now processed into folklore, and that is then marketed by the tourist industry.

Of course the reverse side of this globalization permits a growing individualism; but this no longer has any history, for the people who have been turned into individuals become

a-historical, as we can see from post-modern art and films. I see
little reason to follow Miroslav Volf and to pluralize the concept
of history, and then to talk eschatologically about 'an eternal
home of histories' and 'the redemption of histories'. I am more
convinced by Francis Fukuyama's modern 'end of history'. In
the European Community the Euro is on the verge of its introduction as a single currency, and with that the DM, the franc,
the lira, the peseta and the guilder all lose their 'histories'.

If, finally, with 'post-modern' sensibility for the many and
the different, the modern world is reproached with being a
dictatorship of uniformity and a uniform culture, then it would
also be logical to pass over from modern monotheism to post-
modern polytheism, and in becoming post-modern to become
post-Christian too. I cannot see how Miroslav Volf can avoid
this. If he surrenders the unity of history, he must surrender
the unity of eschatology at the same time. It is true that according
to the Johannine Jesus 'in my Father's house are many dwelling
places', but it is the *one* house of the one God for all that. And
this is what he himself very definitely says.

Perhaps I belong to the people whom my friend Johann
Baptist Metz calls 'the last universalists' (see *The Future of Theology*,
1996, 47–51). After that come the 'post-modern pluralists'. But
I believe that for the sake of the one God and his one, coming
kingdom, and his one single righteousness, I have to try to think
universally – to be catholic, in the best sense of the word. This
thinking leads me to a 'public' theology which discerns the
common dangers which affect us all in a world which is
increasingly becoming a single world – discerns them in order
to establish hope in God at the place of nothingness. In the
past there were human histories in the plural. Now humanity is
on the way to the age of a single humanity – already in the
negative sense and, with first tentative steps, in a positive one
too. Now it has a future only in the singular. And that is for the
first time world history in the true sense. The dangers of the
deadly self-threat of the nations are growing, but, as Friedrich
Hölderlin once wrote in Tübingen, 'where there is danger,
deliverance also grows'. And it is this that I should like publicly
to maintain.

Chapter VII

THE LIBERATION OF THE FUTURE AND ITS ANTICIPATIONS IN HISTORY

JÜRGEN MOLTMANN

Eschatology has to do with 'the Last Things' and, as I would argue, with 'the first things' too – the end of the system of this world and the beginning of the new order of all things.[1] The subject of eschatology is the future, and more than the future. Eschatology talks about *God's* future, and this is more than future time. It is the future of time itself – time past, time present, and time to come. In his future, God comes to his creation and, through the power of his righteousness and justice, frees it for his kingdom, and makes it the dwelling place of his glory. In our language, this future in which God comes is described by the word 'advent', and is distinguished from the future time which we call 'future'. Advent is expected – future develops. But the future always develops out of what we expect. What comes to meet us determines what we become.[2]

Christian eschatology assumes that the divine future which we can expect has already begun with the coming of the Messiah

---

[1] J. Moltmann, *The Coming of God.*
[2] J. Moltmann, 'Hope and Planning' in *Hope and Planning.*

Jesus. With the coming of the Messiah, the messianic time already begins, the time in which the coming kingdom with its righteousness and justice exerts its power over the present, and liberates the present from the power of the past. In Christ's death on the cross, this world of injustice and violence reaches its end, for his resurrection from the dead is already the beginning of 'the life of the world to come'. Christian eschatology therefore sees in the end of this world the beginning of the new eternal creation. A saying of Paul's gives us the Christian qualification of time: 'The night (of the world) is far gone, the day (of God) is at hand.' And this leads on to the ethical consequence: 'Let us then cast off the works of darkness and put on the armour of light' (Rom 13:12). In this daybreak we experience the end of the past and the beginning of the future. The nearness – the 'at-handness' – of the kingdom of God has nothing to do with time. It is a category of intimacy, in which we call God 'Abba', dear Father, and know ourselves to be his child and friend. The concept 'neighbour' has nothing to do with space either. It too is a category of intimacy: 'we are very close'; her fate 'touches me closely'.

Christian ethics therefore have this Christian eschatology as their premise, and are the response to it in the context of this world's conditions. In the Old Testament and Judaism we find the same link between God's future and the ethical awakening of the people concerned: 'Keep justice and do righteousness, *for* soon my justice will come and my righteousness be revealed' (Isa 56:1).[3] And – even more unambiguously – at the end of the book of Isaiah (60:1): 'Arise, *become* light, for your light *is coming* and the glory of the Lord is rising upon you.' The announcement of God's coming, the coming of his kingdom, his righteousness and his glory, opens up for the people touched by it not just a new future, but the way into that future too. A new history and a new 'becoming' spring up. So the Christian life and conduct to which Christian ethics are supposed to

---

[3] B. Klappert, 'Auf dem Weg der Gerechtigkeit in Liebe', in '. . . *und hätte die Liebe nicht'. Texte vom Mülheimer Symposium* (ed. Evangelische Kirche im Rheinland, Düsseldorf, 1997) 23–114.

lead are nothing other than practical eschatology and lived hope.[4]

This practised eschatology and this lived hope do not exist in a vacuum. We find them only in the real history in which we live. But here the concept of eschatology is already 'occupied', and hope lies crushed under a mass of illusions and anxieties. So the first act of practical eschatology must be to liberate the future from the blockades and repressions of the modern world, and to free hope from the false promises and threats of modern times. 'The future must be redeemed from the power of history.'[5] It is only then that we can usefully and effectively talk about the possible and necessary anticipations of God's future in the conditions of this world. So we shall look first of all at 'the liberation of the future from the power of history' and then, in a second step, go on to consider 'the anticipations of the future in the potentialities of history'.

I. The Liberation of the Future from the Power of History

The modern world began with the European seizure of power over the peoples of the world and over nature; and ever since these beginnings, it has been possessed by religious and secular millenarianism. This has meant on the one hand expectation of the impending dawn of a golden age, the end of history, and 'the third empire of the Spirit'; while on the other hand it has meant the religious and secular apocalyptic of the impending and menacing end of the world. The feeling, thinking and desiring of modern men and women are dominated by these two eschatological paradigms. Out of the one there has

[4] This has been brought out best and for many people with convincing force by G. Gutiérrez, *Theology of Liberation* (tr. C. Inda and J. Eagleson; Maryknoll, New York: Orbis, 1973, London: SCM Press , 1974; revd edn 1988).

[5] Moltmann, *The Coming of God* (45):

> The messianic interpretation of the experience of the moment that ends and gathers up time is the *redemption of the future* from the power of history. The power of history is exercised by the mighty. They have to extend their victorious present into the future in order to augment and consolidate their power. *Their* future is without an alternative, and devoid of surprises.

developed what we may call here *the conservative syndrome*, and
out of the other what we shall call *the progressive syndrome*. All
the political and ethical decisions of the last 150 years, and of
the present day, have been – and still are – determined by one
or other of these syndromes. What we have termed the Christian
ethic of lived hope must first of all 'free' God's future from
these modern syndromes, so that history is once more thrown
open, and the Christian ethic of hope is again made possible.
We cannot combat the one syndrome in the interests of a
Christian ethic, and in the process fall victim to the other. So
the future must first of all be re-discovered and set free.

I.1. The conservative syndrome

The conservative syndrome in politics and ethics is based on a
particular eschatology which can easily be detected at every turn:
the fear that the world is about to go down in chaos.[6] There is
no escape from this final downfall, for the human being is
'chaotic' by nature and, according to the secularized doctrine
of original sin, 'evil from his youth up'. Left in his natural
condition 'man is wolf to the man', as Vanzetti put it.[7] Because
of this negative anthropology, the conservative syndrome always
and everywhere cries out for 'a strong state' and for repressive
social institutions. Since human beings are chaotic and evil by
nature, they need 'a strong hand' which will keep their natural
drives in check and their wickedness within bounds. This
strong hand is provided by the authoritarian *state* – the country,

---

[6] The theological side of this conservative syndrome has been excellently
described by R. Strunk in his *Politische Ekklesiologie im Zeitalter der Revolution*,
(Munich, 1971). The thesis of the pietistic theologian Gottfried Menken was:
'All revolutions are contrary to the kingdom of God' (102). The influential
church politician and Prussian statesman Julius Friedrich Stahl believed: 'Only
the church can heal the nations from the sickness of revolution' (154). And
for the Hessian Old Lutheran August Vilmar the church's 'torch' 'shone there
ahead of the returning Lord Christ, and here in the face of the Antichrist'
(230).

[7] For Thomas Hobbes, this negative anthropology was already the most
important argument for the powerful 'Leviathan' state. Cf. J. Moltmann,
'Covenant or Leviathan? Political Theology at the Beginning of Modern Times',
in *God for a Secular Society* (tr. M. Kohl; London: SCM Press/Minneapolis:
Fortress, 1999).

'motherland' or 'fatherland', which promises identity and requires sacrifice – by the patriarchally ruled *family*, and by the religion of the absolute *fear of God*. It is only when they are in these strong hands that human beings learn to control themselves, to master their drives, to develop the power of their wills, and to become obediently subservient.

Monotheism, monarchy and monogamy, or – to put it more simply – God, king and family: that is the holy trinity of the conservative syndrome. 'I am the Lord thy God', proclaim the priests: 'Be subject to the powers that be', demand the political rulers. 'I am the master in my own house', claim the fathers. Disobedient and deviant behaviour is judged to be a reversion to chaos and presented as an apocalyptic dissolution of order. The conservative syndrome is of course a male syndrome. If someone has been brought up 'to be a man', he learns as a result to control the impulses and needs of his body, and to suppress the feminine elements in himself. It is only then that he will one day be in a position to dominate the woman. The pathology of the conservative syndrome is at heart a sexual pathology.[8] So domestic 'patriarchs' always go in for men's groups – the boys down at the pub, the army mess, or the club, according to social status.

'One people – one emperor – one God' ran the slogan in Wilhelm II's pre-1914 Germany. 'One people – one Reich – one Führer' cried the Nazis in 1933, and made the Führer their God. In Latin America 'God, family and country' are values in the name of which protesting land workers and the people's priests have been murdered in the past, and are still being murdered today. Marxism and feminism, chaos and the end of the world: these are the spectres which these 'values' are supposed to put to flight.

[8] This is shown by N. Sombart's brilliant account *Die deutschen Männer und ihre Feinde. Carl Schmitt – ein deutsches Schicksal zwischen Männerbund und Matriarchatmythos* (Munich, 1991). The neo-conservatives of the Reagan era in the USA, such as Norman Podhoretz, Michael Novak, Irving Kristol and Peter Berger, in spite of all the differences between them, also seem to be at one in their anti-communism and anti-feminism. See G. Dorrien, *The Neoconservative Mind: Politics, Culture, and the War of Ideologies* (Philadelphia, 1993).

The people who preach 'family values' today (like the promise-keepers in the United States, and the Pope in every country he visits) do not just mean the family. In talking about the family they mean the rights of 'the master in his own house', and the subordination of the woman. The person who today begins by preaching publicly the strengthening of these family values will inevitably want 'a strong state' as well, and will incline to the fundamentalist invocation of divine 'authority'. But a good marriage and a happy family are gifts of grace which are destroyed once they are turned into a law and made an instrument of domination.

The conservative syndrome in both its militant and its peaceable guise developed its reactionary form in France, in the struggle of the feudal lords and the clerics of the Catholic Church against the popular revolution of 1789, with its new trinity of 'liberty, equality and fraternity'. The political antitype of the authoritarian trinity cherished by the reactionaries was atheistic anarchy, with its slogan *ni dieu – ni maître* (or 'neither God nor state')[9] and, along with that, the revolutionary attempt to build a truly human society without a state that relies on brute force – a community of brothers and sisters in free association – that is to say, a democracy of 'the free and the equal'. But in the democratic movements of the nineteenth century and in the emancipation movements of workers, women and slaves, conservative reactionaries only saw springing up the dragon's seed of the apocalyptic 'beast from the abyss', and in the chaos descried the coming end of the world – which meant the end of *their* world. The democratic, popular sovereignty demanded was thought to be only the devilish antitype to the true state sovereignty by the grace of God.[10] The progressive awareness of liberty in the emancipation movements I have mentioned was denigrated as rebellion against God, and an attempt 'to wrench

---

[9] M. Bakunin, *Gott und Staat* (Berlin, 1995).

[10] This is the substance of the famous Stone Lectures on 'Reformation against Revolution' given by the Dutch theologian and statesman Abraham Kuyper in Princeton Theological Seminary in 1900 (*Reformation wider Revolution. Sechs Vorlesungen über Calvinismus* [tr. into German by M. Jaeger: Berlin, 1904]). Kuyper was the leader of the 'anti-revolutionary people's party' in Holland, and the founder of the Free University in Amsterdam.

oneself out of God's hand'; and it was therefore condemned as the primal sin of blasphemy.

For the conservative syndrome, God has always been solely on the side of order and the authorities, for all authorities on earth are supposed to derive from the sovereignty of God. So wherever that God-given order in state, family and society is 'undermined', 'the dams break' and 'the red flood', 'the flood of immorality' (in the form of pornography, abortion and homosexuality), and 'the flood of unrestricted individualism' bring about the downfall of the world. With the French and American revolutions, the alternatives to the conservative syndrome had become real, possible alternatives; and because of that the preservation of 'the old order' was no longer justified on utilitarian grounds alone but apocalyptically too. But with this justification, the alternatives were forced into an End-time friend–foe relationship, irresolvable by discussion or negotiation, but only through Armageddon, the decisive apocalyptic battle. In the ultimate resort the conservative preservation of order reduces itself to dictatorship, preferably a military dictatorship.[11] And this 'ultimate resort' is the political 'state of emergency'. This expedient has always been potentially to hand since the French Revolution, and it is declared at every convenient opportunity to be the essential requirement of the moment.

Which eschatology is cultivated in this conservative syndrome? It is the *eschatology of the katechon*, the delay, the holding back.[12] The political and the moral order 'hold back the end of

[11] This is the fundamental idea of the disputed German constitutional lawyer Carl Schmitt in his book *Die Diktatur. Von den Anfängen des modernen Souveränitätsgedankens bis zum proletarischen Klassenkampf* (Berlin, 1921), with its appendix: 'Die Diktatur des Reichspräsidenten nach Art. 48 der Weimarer Reichsverfassung'. The thesis of his *Politische Theologie* (2nd edn, Berlin, 1934) is: 'That one is sovereign who can declare the state of emergency' – which is simply as much as to say: sovereign is the dictator who proclaims the dictatorship. His argument in favour of dictatorship is a theological one: 'In the face of radical evil, there can only be a dictatorship' (*Politische Theologie*, 83) – as if dictatorship itself were not the 'radically evil' thing in politics!

[12] This apocalyptic eschatology goes back to 2 Thessalonians 2:6–8:

> And you know what is restraining him now so that he may be revealed in his time. For the mystery of lawlessness is already at work; only he who now restrains it will do so until he is out of the way. And then the

the world' and must therefore be preserved under all circumstances and with every expedient. It is characteristic of this negative eschatology that Constantinian Christianity should already have replaced the early Christian prayer 'Maranatha, come Lord Jesus, come soon' (Rev 22:17, 20), and the petition 'May thy kingdom come and this world pass away', by the prayer *pro mora finis* – the petition that the end be delayed. This meant that the justification for the Christian ethic changed too: a life in the community of Christ in accordance with the righteousness and justice of God's future world, was replaced by the backward-looking transfiguration of the existing political and moral order (which was traced back to the dispensations of creation or to natural law) and therefore by the preservation of its present condition in the spirit of love. The alteration of changeable structures in accordance with the kingdom of God which Jesus preached, and with the Sermon on the Mount, was superseded by Christian love in structures that were to remain as they were (see the Augsburg Confession Article XVI).

But because the restraining powers can postpone the end of the world only for a certain time, in the conservative syndrome the end has to be expected, and preparations for the final struggle must be made. This is the dualistic *Armageddon eschatology*.[13] If one day the power of the state can no longer hold back 'the red flood' or the waves of emancipation – then the day of the decisive apocalyptic battle is approaching: 'on to the final battle', as the Communists also sang in their

---

lawless one will be revealed, and the Lord Jesus will slay him with the breath of his mouth and destroy him by the appearance of his future.

All his life Carl Schmitt was fascinated by this 'katechon', and was concerned to uphold it. Cf. H. Meier, *Die Lehre Carl Schmitts. Vier Kapital zur Unterscheidung Politische Theologie und Politische Ethik* (Stuttgart and Weimar, 1994), 243–253. Conservative circles thought that the USA was this katechon when it entered on the Vietnam war, and was afraid that the 'hindrance' would cease to exist when the USA was unable to win this war against 'the red flood'.

[13] This dualistic apocalyptic about the final struggle between Christ and Antichrist can be detected in the biblical writings. But is it Christian, in the christological sense of the word? It seems to reflect Manichaean influence, rather than to be an expression of the hope founded on the raising of the crucified Christ.

'Internationale', though from their opposite viewpoint. This is the appearance of the Antichrist and his annihilation in Christ's parousia (2 Thess 2:6). This is the clash of good and evil, which will be decided through God's intervention on behalf of the good, as the prophecy about the battle in the valley of Armageddon proclaims (Rev 16:16).

This expectation that the end will mean the apocalyptic separation of humanity into the good and the evil inevitably means that all differences and conflicts will already culminate here in history in friend–foe relationships, and in the demand for uncompromising decisions. It is not unifications, compromises and peace treaties which anticipate the end; it is divisions, severances, and decrees. Anyone who postpones the clarifying end through peacemaking, and amelioration of conditions in this world is accounted a heretic – the proponent of an 'inner-worldly eschatology' – or a starry-eyed do-gooder who stands in the way of the power struggles among the proponents of Realpolitik by giving them a bad conscience – whereas their own concern is, of course, not to have a conscience at all, for 'men of action never have a conscience', as Friedrich Nietzsche said of them.

I.2. The progressive syndrome

But it is the progressive syndrome which dominates the world of modern times. The conservative syndrome is merely its reverse side and its sombre companion. In the progressive syndrome too the ruling eschatology is easily detectible. It is the millenarian belief in the progress of humanity and the perfectibility of history. We are already living in 'the third stage' of world history as the millenarian Positivist Auguste Comte described it. This is the End-time stage in which history will be consummated. Now at last what human beings have sought for from the beginning will be reached, and the desire behind all their struggles will be fulfilled. In this stage of humanity's development science and technology will spread unhindered, education and prosperity for all will be attained, morality and humanity will grow; but there will be no further qualitative revolutions in history. The first, religious age gave way to the second age of philosophy, and both will be succeeded by the secular and scientific-technological era which is now beginning. Science will now be the vehicle for demonstrating truth. Because humanity has hitherto experienced history as crisis, conflict and revolution, 'the third age' will be 'the end of history' and the beginning of eternal peace.

With this age, an era without history begins, the *posthistoire*.[14] Warlike military states will be replaced by the joint administration of the economy. Authorities employing force will be replaced by the free world of responsible, educated people, in which 'the free development of each is the condition for the free development of all', as the Communist Manifesto of 1847 proclaimed, with liberal conviction, in the messianic spirit of enlightened humanism.[15] Human beings are by nature good; if they are bad, it is only bad social conditions that have made them so. Human beings are capable of improved development through upbringing and education. According to the apocalyptic idea, in the millennium the Devil will be bound 'for a thousand years', so that goodness can spread unhindered.

This positive anthropology was the foundation for anarchist criticism of the allegedly divinely willed authorities in state, family and nation. These can and will be replaced by 'the free association of free individuals'. The need for 'the state' was justified by the sinful, chaotic nature of human beings. But this no longer applies. It was merely an expression of what Friedrich Engels called 'humanity's fear of itself'. The humanity that has come to itself no longer requires repressive government, or its transcendent justification from above. The state based on power gives way to the state founded on a constitution; the sacred family is replaced by a partnership for shared living; and the exclusive nation is superseded by the multicultural society. With this, the different forms of exclusiveness find an end. The human society which is emerging will build a state without wars between the different countries, and therefore without armies or national

[14] L. Niethammer, *Posthistoire: Has history come to an end?* (tr. P. Cammiller; London and New York: Verso, 1992) is an exposition of the French tradition. Cf. also the earlier study by R. Seidenberg, *Posthistoric Man* (Boston: Beacon Press, 1950).

[15] K. Marx, *Die Frühschriften* (ed. S. Landshut; Stuttgart, 1950) 548.

foreign policies. The foreign policy of the single nation will be replaced world-wide by shared domestic policies. Consequently politics will no longer be ruled by the notorious friend–foe relationship which Carl Schmitt talks about. Once established, the democratic constitutional states already ceased to wage war against one another. So the vision of eternal peace seems within reach. This of course means that previous politics, which worked with the threat of force, will be replaced by the world-wide economy of the multinationals and the trans-national groups. The economic policies of the single state will be dispersed as the economy is deregulated and its responsibility privatized. A globalized economy will ultimately liberate the politically subjected colonial peoples too, and turn their low-wage countries into high-tech locations. The totalization of the economy will put an end to class rule.

A global economy – a global ethic – a global society: that means global peace! This is the golden age, the end of world wars, and hence the end of world history.

In characterizing the progressive syndrome in this way I have deliberately thrown together utterances made in the eighteenth and nineteenth centuries by Comte and Kant, Marx and Adam Smith, and in our own time by Michel Camdessus[16] and Francis Fukuyama.[17] My purpose in so doing is to show that we modern men and women live, feel and think in this syndrome as if it were self-evident, and apparently have no other alternative to hand. Even if the onward march of technology, space travel and genetic engineering no longer asks for the 'faith' required in the nineteenth century, it has nevertheless become the driving force of the system of permanent modernization to such an extent that we hardly notice it. The 'progress' which so fascinated the minds of the ruling western nations in the nineteenth century has long since become a compulsion towards continually accelerated

[16] M. Camdessus is the director of the IWF. His lecture on 'The Market and the Kingdom of God in the Globalization of the World Economy' is critically commented on by F. J. Hinkelammert in *Orientierung* 60, 15 May 1996, 98–102; 31 May 1996, 115–119.

[17] F. Fukuyama, *The End of History and the Last Man* (New York: Free Press/ Toronto: Maxwell Macmillan, 1989).

modernization.[18] The new magic word 'globalization' is merely a more agreeable way of describing what people in the nineteenth century called 'imperialism'. For the total commercialization of life, from the private sphere to the care of the old, we have invented the amiable euphemism 'privatization'. Wicked old capitalism is now called 'the global marketing of everything'. Freedom, we are told, grows with the progressive individualization of human beings, and with the demolition of the particularist communities which restricted their individual liberties.

If, now that the socialism of the eastern bloc has come to an end, there are no longer any alternatives to this global and total system, then an 'end of history' or 'the end of a history' has indeed been reached, and with it a 'brave new world' without any other threatening options. The millenaristic consummation of history is in sight. In 1989 the most recent secular, Right Hegelian millenarian, Francis Fukuyama, of the State Department in Washington, proclaimed 'the end of history';[19] and from these viewpoints he was right. But Karl Marx too must posthumously be called correct; for globalized and totalized capitalism conforms precisely to his scenario, with the sole qualification that there is now no transition to a post-capitalist socialism and communism. On the contrary, it is the transition from socialism to capitalism which is to be 'the end of history'.

Which eschatology is cultivated in this progressive syndrome? The millenarian eschatology that is dominant here has two remarkable characteristics.

(1) The people who know that they are standing at the end of history, or are already in the *posthistoire*, no longer have any future in front of them; instead they live in a present without any temporal end. What they see ahead of them is not an alternative future; it is merely a prolongation of the present – progress in every direction – improvements wherever possible – expansions unbounded – but without any alternative, because

[18] W. Stahel, *Die Beschleunigungsfalle oder der Triumph der Schildkröte* (Stuttgart, 1995).

[19] F. Fukuyama, 'The End of History', in *The National Interest* 16 (1989) 3–18.

'there is no alternative' to our present condition, as every politician and economist never tires of telling us today at every turn. What was once in the era of history 'future' no longer exists in the *posthistoire*.

(2) When the repressive forces in state, society and the family end, 'God' as their transcendent ground and legitimation ceases to be applicable too. In a world without lordship, 'the Lord God' no longer has any place. Everyone must develop their own possibilities, fulfilling themselves in the process (hetero-, homo-, bi- or multisexually). Human autonomy no longer permits theonomy. The more the modern millennium becomes anarchistic – that it, democratic – the more the atheism that is practised simply as a matter of course spreads. It is no longer a militant anti-theism as it was in the nineteenth century. It is merely a theism that has got lost and become superfluous. If every effort for 'fulfilment' is directed towards nothing other than the self, then the self is to all intents and purposes the human being's God and Lord – if that human being has a self, and does not fall into the vacancy of everything possible, like Robert Musil's *Man without Qualities*. This used at one time to be called pantheism or, to be more precise, anthropotheism. But today many people are losing even this ancient over-valuation of the self, and both theism and atheism are being replaced by a cheerful nihilism or a trite complacency about things as they simply happen to be, and by the self's hollow emptiness. We were once promised the fulfilment of historical hopes; but all that remains is the impression of a helpless lack of alternative. The *posthistoire* is as tranquil as it is tedious.

I.3. The liberation of the future

The liberation of the future must lead to a new opening up of history, with its alternative possibilities, to the present. The conservative syndrome blocks every alternative future, because it immediately identifies new possibilities and changes with the dreaded downfall of the world. Because the authoritarian powers of history only 'hold back' the end, they make it impossible for new possibilities to arrive. This conservative *blockade* of the future is matched in the progressive syndrome by the *repression* of all alternative future possibilities through the extension of the present and its prolongation. The end of history which is 'progressively' sought is, as we have seen, always the desired 'end of the future' too.

In order to gain space for innovatory action in history, every Christian eschatology must critically address and challenge both the conservative *blockade* of the future and the progressive *occupation* of the future. Christian eschatology assumes that future issues from God's creative energy, and therefore expects that the historical future of the world will acquire its openness, its potentialities and its alternatives in the coming of God. For this eschatology, the creative expectation of God's coming is founded on creation's openness to the future, on Israel's history of promise, and on the raising of the crucified Christ, together with the outpouring of the creative energies of God's Spirit which is bound up with that raising. For the people affected, these recollections of 'future' neither terminate history nor do they put it out of commission; they throw it open afresh. In these recollections the end is not 'held back'; it is 'at hand', as the New Testament stresses throughout. But because the coming kingdom of God and his righteousness and justice are already near, they can and must already, as far as possible, be 'anticipated' today.

But is the future which is an alternative to the obstructing or extending system of life in the present, and which is actualized in the Jewish and Christian history of promise, really desirable? If we already exist in the final world, or in the best of all possible worlds, an alternative future is unwelcome. But if the contradictions are continually growing, and if the victims of the present system of living are becoming more and more numerous, we are bound to look round for alternatives. The people who control the present system, and the system's beneficiaries, always have only a conservative interest in its preservation, or a progressive interest in its expansion. But the victims can survive solely by virtue of the hope for an alternative future. The victims of the present system are:

(1) Unemployed 'surplus people', whom nobody wants and nobody needs. Automated industries and digitalized communi-

cations no longer merely exploit. They also produce more and more of these surplus people.

(2) Future generations, which will have to pay off the mountains of debt which present generations are heaping up so that they can enjoy their own present existence.

(3) Nature, which is being driven into ecological catastrophe and left 'without form and void'.

(4) This present system itself, which is going to founder on the contradictions it produces, and will annihilate the human race unless history is opened up afresh, and real alternatives emerge which will make this system reformable. Today the modern capitulation of politics before the globalized economy is already destroying the human community and is ruining public finances. An economic system which produces ever greater inequalities between people destroys political democracy.[20] The participatory democracy which was the original goal is then replaced by an apathetic absentee democracy. When men and women are de-politicized from above they respond from below with disinterest in politics. People can withdraw into private life and pursue their own interests without having to fear intervention by the state.

II. Anticipations of God's Future in History

Where can this future of God's be experienced in the midst of human history, so that it can be anticipated and lived by men and women? The answer is simple. It can be experienced wherever this future *happens* in history – wherever, that is, God gives his future of the kingdom *in advance*. According to the Jewish idea, this future of God's occurs *discontinuously* in time on the sabbath, in the sabbath year and in the Year of Jubilee; and will one day be present *continuously* in the messianic time.[21] On the sabbath, God 'interrupts' the purposeful working time

[20] H.-P. Martin and H. Schumann, *Die Globalisierungsfalle. Der Angriff auf Demokratie und Wohlstand* (Hamburg, 1996); cf. also Marion Gräfin Dönhoff, *Zivilisiert den Kapitalismus* (Hamburg, 1996).

[21] Cf. A. Heschel, *The Sabbath Its Meaning for Modern Man* (7th edn, New York, 1981); J. Moltmann, *God in Creation,* chapter XI: The Sabbath: the Feast of Creation, 276–296; E. Spier, *Der Sabbat*, Schriftenreihe Kirche und Judentum (Berlin, 1992).

of human beings and makes this interruption the place of his presence in time. The sabbath is the temporal place of his indwelling (his Shekinah). That is why in the sabbath time the laws of this world are suspended and only the righteousness of God counts. Fleeting time makes people restless; the sabbath gives rest in the happiness of the presence of the Eternal One. Work allows people to exist in their own world; the sabbath rest leads them into God's creation again, and into his pleasure in them themselves. On the sabbath the future redemption of the world is celebrated, for the sabbath rest is already a foretaste of the redeemed world. Consequently in Israel the sabbath has always been especially close to God's expected Messiah. 'The sabbath is a sixtieth of the coming world.'[22] 'If Israel were to keep one single sabbath rightly, the Messiah would immediately come.'[23]

In this way the sabbath festival links Israel's particular experience of God with God's general presence in creation, and with the general hope of redemption for this unredeemed world. The sabbath rest links the experience of God *in* history with the messianic hope in God *for* history. The laws about the sabbath in the Old Testament must therefore be viewed as the special form of the redemptive righteousness of God's kingdom in the midst of history. They become a pattern for the messianic form of the righteousness and justice of the kingdom in the midst of history, the righteousness and justice which Jesus proclaimed in the Sermon on the Mount.

We shall look at the laws about the sabbath with reference to social justice for human beings (II.1), and ecological justice for the earth (II.2). And we shall look at both in their reference to the messianic righteousness and justice of redemption.

II.1. Social justice for human beings

(a) The first thing we notice about the sabbath laws is *the principle of equality*. The sabbath rest, and the presence of God

---

[22] Berachot 57b.

[23] Exodus Rabbah. Cf. here F. Rosenzweig, *Der Stern der Erlösung. Dritter Teil. Erstes Buch* (Heidelberg, 1959) 69 [*The Star of Redemption* (tr. W. W. Hallo; London, 1971]); J. Moltmann, *The Way of Jesus Christ*, 116–136: The Messianic Way of Life.

which can be experienced in it, are given to all equally, and suspend the privileges which otherwise obtain. Men do not rest at the expense of women – parents at the expense of their children – one's own people at the expense of strangers – human beings at the expense of animals. All are meant to come to rest together. Moreover, because the sabbath applies to all equally, all have the same right to rest on that day. The enjoyment of the same divine grace has as its corollary the equal rights of human beings and animals.

The sabbath principle of equality returns in the principle of equality in Christ Jesus. In him 'there is neither Jew nor Greek, there is neither slave nor free, there is neither male nor female; for you are all one in Christ Jesus . . . heirs according to the promise' (Gal 3:28–29). The one same justification of sinners gives the one same right to inherit God's coming kingdom. The seal of this is the one same baptism in the one divine Spirit (Eph 4:4–5). It follows from this community between men and women, Jews and Gentiles, masters and servants that they are equal in their present endowment with the Spirit, and equal in their rights to God's future. Here too the social, religious and sexual privileges of the one, and the corresponding oppressions and belittlements of others, are done away with. A messianic community of 'the free and the equal' is created; and through that community God's future dawns in human history.

The Spirit-filled community of Christ lived this sabbath and messianic equality by setting aside the order of private property: 'The company of those who believed were of one heart and soul, and no one said that any of the things which he possessed was his own, but they had everything in common . . . There was not a needy person among them . . .' (Acts 4:32–35). In a world in which the possessors are becoming ever richer and the have-nots are suffering more and more privation, a community that lives in solidarity like this really is the beginning of a divine future which endures in a world of inequality – a world which will pass away because it has no permanent durability. It has no permanent durability because it is unjust. The Christian religious orders of nuns and monks, and the communities living in radical discipleship of Christ, have always lived this community of possessions.

(*b*) In the sabbath laws, the liberation of prisoners from their enslavement and debtors from the burden of their debts is in the foreground. Because injustices always arise in the course of six years of labour and commerce, in the seventh year the original, divinely promulgated justice is to be restored. The person who has been enslaved because of his debts 'shall go out from you . . . and go back to his own family, and return to the possession of his fathers' (Lev 25:41). Debts are not to be held over for longer than the following six months; after that they must be remitted entirely (Lev 25:14ff.). There must be neither usury nor profiteering (Lev 25:36).

The freeing of prisoners and the remission of debts return again in the messianic works from which we are supposed to recognize Israel's Redeemer. 'To proclaim liberty to the captives and the opening of the prison to those who are bound': that is the charge given to the Messiah who proclaims the time of the messianic sabbath (Isa 61:1). That is why Jesus' first sermon in Nazareth after his endowment with the Spirit (Luke 4:18–19) begins with his reading of this Isaianic prophecy, and his explanation: 'Today this scripture has been fulfilled in your hearing' (Luke 4:21). Remarkably enough, according to Luke, after Jesus has proclaimed 'the acceptable year of the Lord' (that is to say, the messianic sabbath era) he leaves out the Isaianic phrase '. . . and the day of vengeance of our God'. The liberation of prisoners and the remission of debts are also the prophetic proposals for the season of fasting and the 'day acceptable to the Lord' (Isa 58:5). 'Loose those you have unjustly bound, undo the thongs of the yoke, let the oppressed go free. Share your bread with the hungry . . .' (Isa 58:6–8). This is the true worship in the world of everyday. It is only this sabbath and messianic activity which makes 'your righteousness go before you and the glory of the Lord your rear guard' (Isa 58:8). The petition in the Lord's prayer, too, 'Forgive us our trespasses as we forgive those who trespass against us', does not mean moral guilt or religious sins as we generally think; it is talking about remission of debts in the sabbath righteousness of the messianic era which begins with Jesus' coming.

Not least important: the sabbath year is intended for the well-being of Israel's poor, and for the benefit of foreigners in Israel:

'The seventh year you shall let the land rest and lie fallow, that
the poor of your people may eat' (Exod 23:11). 'The sabbath
of the land shall provide food for you, for yourself and for your
male and female servants, and for your hired servant, and for
the sojourner who lives with you, for your cattle also and for
the beasts that are in your land' (Lev 25:6). Here again we find
the principle of equality and the preferential option of the divine
sabbath justice for the poor and the asylum seekers who are
otherwise disadvantaged. Here too we can point to Isaiah 61
and to Luke 4:18ff. This divine sabbath justice is 'the gospel for
the poor', for according to Jesus' promise it is to the poor that
God's coming kingdom belongs.

II.2. Ecological justice for the earth

According to the sabbath laws, God's righteousness and justice
is not confined to human society. It also embraces the
community shared by human beings *and the earth*. Exodus
23:10–11 provides a social reason for the sabbath year: '. . . so
that the poor of your people may eat'. But in Leviticus 25:1–7
we find an ecological justification: 'So that the land may
keep its great sabbath to the Lord.' The sabbath year is not
just a festival for human beings. It is the festival of the whole
creation. In the seventh year *the land* 'celebrates'. That evidently
presupposes a covenant made by God with his land, a covenant
which, when they enter the country God has promised them,
the people must respect by leaving fields and vineyards
uncultivated and unharvested every seventh year. That the
land should rest every seventh year is God's blessing for the
land. It is to lie fallow, so that it can recover from human
exploitation and can restore its fertility. Israel, it is true, rejected
the fertility cults it found in the Canaanite country, but
instead it introduced the fallowing principle of the sabbath year:
'You shall make for yourselves no idols . . . You shall keep my
sabbaths' (Lev 26:1–2). If the people respect the sabbath worship
of the earth they will live in peace and enjoy the blessing of
the land. If they disregard the earth's sabbath, 'I will devastate
the land, so that your enemies who settle in it shall be astonished

at it. And I will scatter you among the nations ... and your land shall be a desolation, and your cities shall be a waste ... Then the land shall rest and enjoy its sabbaths' (Lev 26:32–34). The explanation 2 Chronicles 36:19–21 gives for Israel's Babylonian captivity is that the people had disregarded the sabbath of the earth. The land 'kept sabbath until seventy years were complete'.

Inherent in this sabbath law for the land is the ancient ecological wisdom of the fallowing principle, which agricultural societies have always observed. If the land is the system that sustains life, then the times required for its regeneration must be observed. Once the land is exhausted, the people are forced to emigrate. Only the great world empires have exploited the fertile regions in order to feed their great cities and armies, turning these fruitful lands into deserts through uncontrolled overgrazing and overcropping. If today the expanding human population continues to exploit the earth non-stop by way of monocultures and chemical fertilizers, the deserts will grow, and one day human beings will disappear from the earth, so that God's earth can 'celebrate' its sabbath. The earth will survive. We human beings will not. That is the warning of that Old Testament story about 'the sabbath of the earth'.

The divine justice which the Messiah is to bring will take possession of the land too, and make it fertile, according to Isaiah 32:15–18: 'When the Spirit is poured upon us from on high the wilderness will become a fruitful field and the fruitful field will be deemed a forest. Then justice will dwell in the wilderness, and righteousness abide in the fruitful field. And the fruit of justice will be peace ...'. That reads like a sequel to the Christian community's Pentecost experience, according to which the Spirit of life is 'poured out upon all flesh' – which means not just human life but all the living. But in the New Testament only very little is still said about the sabbath of the earth and its salvation in the messianic time. It is only in 'the new heaven and the new earth' (Rev 21) that the paradisal fertilities will return, when the eternally living God comes to rest in his creation, and everything he has created arrives at its peace in him.

II.3. Guidelines for a Christian ethic

The guidelines for an ethic in the community of Christ follow on the ideas about the messianic righteousness and justice which we find in the prophets and on Israel's laws about the sabbath, and take these ideas up. As we have seen, in both these forerunning concepts, it is no longer a matter of equalizing justice (*iustitia distributiva*). This is the justice that redeems – frees – from misery, brutality and guilt. It is the justifying justice of God (*iustitia iustificans*) which puts things to rights and creates justice. When the biblical traditions talk about 'justice and righteousness', as they do again and again, it is this creative justice of God they mean, the justice which gives human laws their legitimation and at the same time relativizes them.[24] Faithful observance of the established law and the demand for better justice then make of the prevailing human legal system a process that points towards the future. In this process which is aligned towards God's coming and his redeeming righteousness, human institutions are what Wolf-Dieter Marsch calls 'institutions in transition'. This is also true of the Christian ethic itself. It is not a catalogue of eternally valid, unchangeable dispensations given at creation, targeted at the chaos of human caprice, as it were. Nor is it a carte blanche for personal 'decisions of conscience' which no one is permitted to judge. A Christian ethic is an ethic of lived hope and is hence related to the horizon of historical change which is open to the future. It is not an 'ordering' ethic, nor is it a situation ethic. It is an ethic of change, like the Jewish Tikkun ethics. To do what is good means asking about what is better. For this ethic of change we need guidelines instead of laws and regulations. These act as signposts, steadily orientated towards the future, and offer changing responses to the challenges of history. Every *theologia viatorum* demands an *ethica viatorum*.

In the ecumenical discussions of the last thirty years three guidelines of this kind have crystallized out, and point the way towards hope in action:

---

[24] W. Huber, *Gerechtigkeit und Recht. Grundlinien christlicher Rechtsethik* (Stuttgart, 1996); H.-R. Reuter, *Rechtsethik in theologischer Sicht* (Stuttgart, 1996).

(1) The anticipation of God's future

(2) The preferential option for the poor

(3) Correspondence and contradiction in history.

(1) *To live in anticipation* means letting one's own present be determined by the expected future of God's kingdom and his righteousness and justice. In 1968, the General Assembly of the World Council of Churches in Uppsala provided the classic formulation: 'We ask you, trusting in God's renewing power, to join in the anticipation of God's Kingdom, showing now something of the newness which Christ will complete on his day.'[25] The anticipation of the kingdom of God is not yet the kingdom itself, but it is a life which is determined by that hope. It is a historical form of God's kingdom.[26] Here God's righteousness appears in the conditions and potentialities of history, not yet in its own new world. This difference in the anticipation makes the second part of the formulation clear too. There is already a new creation here and now, for there is already here and now a rebirth to a living hope; but it is related to, and differentiated from, the hoped-for new creation of all things which is to come to pass on the day of Christ's coming in the glory of God.

Life and action in *anticipation* of God's future is like life and action in the *Advent* that leads up to Christmas. It is a life in the community of Christ following the guidelines of his Sermon on the Mount. As in the peace movement of 1979–1981, this means that 'peace is possible' in the midst of a time when missiles are being stationed in a mutual threat of universal annihilation.[27] It also means: righteousness that redeems, puts to rights, creates justice and justifies is possible in the midst of a world where evil is 'justly' requited with evil. But to require evil with good is the

---

[25] Cf. N. Goodall (ed.), *The Uppsala Report, 1968* (Geneva: World Council of Churches, 1968).

[26] J. Moltmann, *Creating a Just Future: The Politics of Peace and the Ethics of Creation in a Threatened World* (tr. John Bowden; London and Philadelphia, 1989).

[27] J. Moltmann (ed.), *Friedenstheologie – Befreiungstheologie. Analysen, Berichte, Meditationen* (Munich, 1988); idem, 'Political Theology and the Theology of Liberation' in *God for a Secular Society*.

idea behind a penal law based on resocialization, such as was introduced in Germany by Gustav Radbruch, who appealed to the Sermon on the Mount. Of course in each individual case we have to ask: 'what is objectively possible?' so that we do not chase after unreal dreams. And we have to ask too: what can I, or the community concerned, do subjectively, so as not to come to grief on the tremendous requirements. But even more important is the question: *cui bono?* For whom and in whom is the divine righteousness to be anticipated? And this brings us to the second guideline.

(2) *The preferential option for the poor* goes back to Latin American liberation theology, and found a place in the official documents of the Latin American Bishops' Conferences in Medellin (1968) and Puebla (1979).[28] It has become a component in Catholic social doctrine. This option corresponds (*a*) to the sabbath laws in Israel; (*b*) to the messianic justice of the prophets; (*c*) to Jesus' gospel to the poor; and (*d*) to the judgment of the Son of Man and Universal Judge: 'As you did to one of the least, you did it to me' (Matthew 25). What is new about the option for the poor is that the poor are no longer the object of Christian charity. They are taken seriously as determining subjects among Christ's people (*ochlos*). The church will become the church of the poor for Christ's sake, for in the poor we find Christ's real presence. And society's poor, exploited and humiliated people, who today have been made 'surplus', belong together with the other victims of modern civilization – exploited and despoiled nature, and the coming generations at whose expense present generations are increasingly beginning to live.

The preferential option for the poor is not just an ethical guideline for Christians. It is a daily experience among Christian

---

[28] Cf. *The Church in the Present-Day Transformation of Latin America in the Light of the Council* (2 vols; Medellin: Second General Conference of Latin American Bishops, Colombia, 1968) (official English edition, ed. L. M. Colonnese, Latin American Division of the United States Catholic Conference, Washington, DC); also *Puebla and Beyond* (ed. J. Eagleson and P. Scharper; Maryknoll, NY, 1979). This gives a history of events preceding the conference, a conference report, and the official English translation of the Final Document.

communities which serve as contact addresses or drop-in centres for the long-term unemployed, the homeless and the abandoned. In Christian soup kitchens, shelters and emergency accommodation, and in the agencies and organizations of Christian diaconal service, the victims of the free market economy and its wintry social climate gather together. The more the churches live in the presence of this society's victims, the more they have the right to challenge prophetically the consciences of that society. If they simply restrict themselves to ministering to the poor, they become the accomplices of the ruling society. If they simply confine themselves to prophetic declarations, no one listens. Every declaration on social conditions made by the churches, and every 'report', must be legitimated by the churches' work for this society's victims. But in the name of these victims the unjust conditions in society must be publicly indicted as well. The option for the poor, and criticism of the brutal and violent, anticipate the coming kingdom and the coming judgment, and with that the righteousness of God which will put things to rights.

(3) In every sphere of life there are conditions which are in accord with the awaited kingdom of God as it is present in Jesus' life and teaching, and conditions that are in contradiction to it. The kingdom of God is not indifferent to prices on the world market, because the survival or starvation of millions of children depend on them. That does not mean that juster prices in international trade are already the kingdom of God itself; but, for all that, they correspond to the kingdom more closely than unjust prices. There is no identity between the divine justice of the coming kingdom and the human justice of conditions in our world. Even the best of all the possible worlds open to us is still a human world, and will not become a divine one; for what is divine is not an enhancement of what is human.

But this qualitative difference between divine and human justice is not all. Between the similarity and the difference we find *the historical parables* of the coming kingdom. That is the way Karl Barth defined the relation between divine and human justice in the conflicts and contradictions of the Hitler dictatorship; and in doing so he was picking up the ideas of

Zwingli and Calvin (though not those of Luther and Melanchthon).[29]

Parables, or images, correspond to the thing imaged in different material: 'The kingdom of God *is like* a grain of mustard seed . . .'. In this way the images, for their part, make the other material open to parable and in need of parable. So politics can be a parable – and need to be a parable – for the coming kingdom of God if we use a political vocabulary in talking about that 'kingdom' and its 'citizens'. The same may be said about the economic sector, the lives we live together, and our culture. These 'parables' are correspondences in the sphere of what does not correspond – or simply liberations in this unredeemed world, and acts of human justice on the foundation of the approaching justice of God. 'Do righteousness, *for* my salvation will come' (Isa 56:1).

But whereas the concept of *parable* presupposes that there is an enduring qualitative difference between earth and heaven, the idea of *anticipation*, which we used before, belongs to the difference between history and eschatology. What we ought to do and can do is to correspond to the future of the coming God. And this future 'is at hand' and 'will reveal itself'; and in so far *it thrusts us forward* to do what is right, and towards the actions that correspond to God's future in this present world, which is otherwise in contradiction to that future.

In Christian ethics earthly justice is not just intended to *correspond* to the heavenly justice of God. It should also *prepare the way* for God's coming kingdom.

Christian ethics are eschatological ethics. What we do now for people in need we do filled with the power of hope, and lit by the expectation of God's coming day.

---

[29] See K. Barth, 'The Christian Community and the Civil Community', in *Against the Stream* (ET London: SCM Press, 1954), with the comment in J. Moltmann, *The Crucified God,* chapter VIII: 'Ways towards the Political Liberation of Mankind', 317–338.

INDEX OF NAMES